The Act Book of
St Katherine's Gild, Stamford
1480 - 1534

Edited by Alan Rogers

Published in association with the Stamford Survey Group

Published 2011 by Abramis Academic Publishing

www.abramis.co.uk

ISBN 978 1 84549 509 1

© Stamford Survey Group 2011

Printed and bound in the United Kingdom

Typeset in Garamond 11/16

Abramis is an imprint of arima publishing.

arima publishing
ASK House, Northgate Avenue
Bury St Edmunds, Suffolk IP32 6BB
t: (+44) 01284 700321

www.abramis.co.uk

Contents

Editorial Notes and Abbreviations

All Latin text has been translated (where readings are unusual, the Latin has been given in brackets); all English text is as written with the exception of first personal names which have in most cases been standardised.

Entries in common form have been abbreviated.

Editorial insertions are in square brackets.

Insertions and deletions which exist in the text are in round brackets with the abbreviations *ins* or *del*.

Abbreviations

AASR: Reports and Papers of Associated Archaeological and Architectural Societies
HB: Hall Book, Stamford Town Hall
PRO: Public Record Office
Rogers 2005: Alan Rogers (ed) *William Browne's Town: the Stamford Hall Book 1465-1492* Stamford Survey Group
TNA: The National Archives
Visit. Rut.: *Visitation of Rutland 1681-2* edited by W B Bannerman, 1922, Harleian Society, vol 73

Acknowledgements

We acknowledge the help of the following: Master and Fellows of Gonville and Caius College, Cambridge; Mark Statham, Librarian, Gonville and Caius College, Cambridge; Professor C N L Brooke; Dr Richard Goddard of the University of Nottingham; Dr Ruth Kennedy of Royal Holloway University, London; Dr David Dymond, Cambridge University; Stamford Town Hall, Stamford School, Stamford Museum. Many others have joined the search for St Katherine, and we are grateful to them all.

Members of the Stamford Survey Group compiled the index.
Photographs: Alan Rogers, John Hartley.

Introduction:
The Act Book of St Katherine's Gild, Stamford

This register of the gild of St Katherine, in the parish church of St Paul, Stamford, is an important document for several reasons[1]. First, it records the membership of this gild with meticulous detail over a period of just over fifty years, from 1480 to 1534. Among the members recorded are some of the leading figures of the day such as Lady Margaret Beaufort, countess of Richmond and Derby, mother of Henry VII, from her palace at Collyweston nearby. The gild seems to have attracted many women, and one of its unusual features is that it was apparently in part devoted to the support of the anchoress immured on the north side of St Paul's church and indeed other anchoresses in the town.

But what makes this record particularly important is the fact that the register shows the stages by which a small and humble parish gild changed into a major social and religious institution reaching well beyond the town, in the process changing its nature and functions. In the first years after its refounding in 1480, it experimented with a share system among its limited number of members drawn from the immediate locality, but this did not survive for very long, and the gild began on a long period of growth in membership of a socially elite nature. It is as a changing living gild that this record becomes important.

The document
The document in question consists of the gild book covering the years from 1480 to 1534 with only a small break between 1528 and 1531. It came into the possession of the library of Gonville and Caius College Cambridge by gift of William Moore, fellow of Caius who, although deprived of his fellowship in 1647, subsequently became librarian of the University 1653-9, and on his death in 1659 left "his magnificent collection of manuscripts" to the college[2]. While

---

[1] Gonville and Caius College Manuscript 266/670; described in M R James *Descriptive Catalogue of the Manuscripts in the Library of Gonville and Caius College*, vol. i 1907 pp 321-2
[2] C Brooke 1985 *History of Gonville and Caius College, Cambridge* (1996 edn) pp 132-5; see references cited there. Some lists give the reference number as 670/266 but the college library inform me that the correct call number is 266/670.

its text has been used in a number of studies[3], it is not widely known, and a detailed study of it shows that many of its features have not been recognised as yet.

The book consists of 95 folios of paper approximately 285cms by 400cms. The paper, continental in origin, contains on many folios (but not all) a water mark of scissors together with a symbol looking like a modern capital B[4]. It has been rebound in 1913 using early leather front and back covers. It has been described briefly in several listings of the college's collections[5].

The nature of the book is mixed. It describes itself as 'the Acts of the Gild' (fol 51d). Although it contains some accounts (usually in summary form), it is not an account book, for the 'central' accounts of the gild are missing. It is more in the nature of a minute book of meetings of the gild, providing lists of members and their regular subscriptions, trying to record those present, those in debt to the gild and their payments, and the election of officers. But it would appear that after a time, each year's entry was written up *before* the meeting, copying the previous year's entries while making adjustments (in one or two cases, entries have been copied verbatim and not been altered or deleted); and there are signs that it was read out loud to the gathered members. After that, it was overwritten with notes of payments made and the nature of those payments and other memoranda, some of these entries being made at least two years after the original entry was made. In other words, it was a working document, kept for "administrative convenience"[6].

Although the record starts in 1480, the first four folios were written in 1494. This would indicate that these folios (folios 1-4) were left blank, presumably to write up the gild statutes and other introductory material; but this was not done

---

[3] e.g. M K Jones and M G Underwood 1992 *The King's Mother: Lady Margaret Beaufort Countess of Richmond and Derby* CUP; Ruth Kennedy 2003 *Spalding's Alliterative Katherine Hymn: a guild connection from the south-east Midlands?*, EETS 321 pp 455-482; E A Jones 1999 'A new look into the *Speculum Inclusorum*', in M Glasscoe (ed) 1999 *The Medieval Mystical Tradition, England, Ireland and Wales* Cambridge: Brewer; several biographies such as those of David Cecil, grandfather of lord Burghley, have used it to determine the presumed dates of death.

[4] The water mark appears apparently without any order; for example, it is on folios 6, 7, 12, 13, 16, 18 but not on any of the intermediate folios.

[5] E Bernard, 1647 *Catalogi Librorum manuscriptorum Anglie et Hiberniae*, Oxford; J Smith 1849 *Catalogue of Manuscripts of the Library of Gonville and Caius College, Cambridge*, Cambridge; M R James (see note 1 above); K A R Schmidt 2001 *Index of Middle English Prose Handlist XVII; Manuscripts in the Library of Gonville and Caius College, Cambridge*, Brewer.

[6] V R Bainbridge 1996 *Gilds in the Medieval Countryside: social and religious change in Cambridgeshire c1350-1558* Boydell p 83.

until fourteen years later. What precipitated the filling in of this lacuna is not known. Again, after writing up the possessions of the gild and the names of the known existing members, alive and dead, in 1480, on folios 4d and 5r, the next few pages (5d, 6r and 6d) were also left blank to be filled in later. These were never filled in. The Acts of the gild start on folio 7, again in 1480[7].

The early history of the gild

The late medieval gild of St Katherine in St Paul's parish Stamford was not the richest or most powerful politically of the town's many gilds. That role seems to have been occupied by the combined gild of Corpus Christi and St Mary in the parish church of St Mary at the bridge which had strong links with the town council and provided the town plays[8]. But because of the text which follows, St Katherine's gild is the best documented gild from the town, and we can tell a good deal about its history from this document.

Nothing is known of the origins of the gild. It is not listed in the gild certificates of 1389 or in the 1548 returns[9]. The cult of St Katherine was growing in the late fourteenth and early fifteenth centuries. That there was an altar to St Katherine in the parish church of St Paul is known from about 1409, and it has been suggested that there was a cult of St Katherine in Stamford in the early fifteenth century, with the production there of an alliterative poem to the saint[10]. Surviving copies of wills from late medieval Stamford are very rare indeed, so that only one bequest to the gild during the fifteenth century can be traced; that was by Margaret Browne wife of William Browne Alderman of the gild[11]. There is no other known mention of the gild until this book commences.

---

[7] It is possible that folios 4d and 5r were written up in preparation for the meeting in November 1480 and that folio 7 onwards were written up after that meeting. This would make sense of the gaps.

[8] See J S Hartley and A Rogers 1977 *Religious Foundations of Medieval Stamford* Nottingham: Nottingham University and Stamford Survey Group; Alan Rogers 1973 Late Medieval Stamford: A Study of the Town Council 1465-1492 in A Everitt (ed) 1973 *Perspectives in English Urban History* Macmillan pp 16-38.

[9] PRO C47/38; H F Westlake 1919 *Parish Gilds of Medieval England* SPCK pp 15-16, 30, 34, 177ff; Chantry Certificates i *AASR* vol 37 1923 pp 100-106

[10] B L Deed 1954 *History of Stamford School*, Stamford: Stamford School p 79; Kennedy 2003 op. cit.; see B Millett 1996 *The Ancrene Wisse, The Katherine Group and the Wooing Group: annotated bibliographies* London: Brewer; C Innes-Parker 2002 The 'gender gap' reconsidered: manuscripts and readers in late medieval England, in Studia Anglica Posnaniensia: *International Review of English Studies* vol 38 pp 239-269; R Kennedy 2004 Spalding's Alliterative Katherine Hymn: a guild connection from the south-east Midlands *Viator* 35.

[11] Foster *Wills AASR* vol 41 1935 p205

But that the gild had existed for some time before 1480 when the register commences is clear from its pages. A meeting was held in November 1480 at which the Alderman of the gild, William Browne wool merchant of the Calais Staple and already Alderman (i.e. mayor) of Stamford six times, made a record in a new paper book of all the members of the gild alive and dead. A list of the possessions of the gild was also taken which showed items which had been donated to the gild some time previously. So the gild already had a history, but how far back into the century this history stretched is not known.

The meeting in November 1480 was a stock taking of the gild which seems to have been very run down. Out of the list of 47 family names, only 13 or 14 were 'living' members. A second list[12] is then given of 27 people who would be invited to join the gild. It would seem that a number of these were not present at that meeting, for some of those listed never became members of the gild. William Browne appears to have taken over a dying gild and sought to revive it by more than doubling its 'old' members with twice the number of 'new' members.

The gild statutes

Before the audit of November 1480, the first four folios of the book contain an English summary of the gild ordinances, but these were not written up until 1494[13]. At that time, Latin was still being used for the text of the book; English did not become common until 1510 when William Radclyffe became Alderman (fol 67). But clearly some members felt that they needed an English version of the rules of the gild. 1494-1495 was the last year when Christopher Browne was Alderman, being succeeded in 1495 by Thomas Philipp. Whether the writing of the rules in English was at the instigation of the Alderman is not known but it would have had to have his approval.

The statutes were very simple. The gild was to meet "in the Chapell over the parisshe Churche durre off Seynt Poules" on the eve of St Katherine's day and on the day itself (25 November); the steward of the gild was to enforce attendance. At the meeting on the eve of St Katherine's day, a meal was served

---

[12] After the list of possessions and list of existing members, the register has three empty pages clearly left for some other writing which has not been completed. The list of 'new members' comes after this gap.

[13] It is interesting that the borough Hall Book which was commenced in 1465 also opened with an English summary of the provisions of the borough charter of 1462; see A Rogers 2005 *William Browne's Town: the Stamford Hall Book 1465-1492* Stamford: Stamford Survey Group

and new members were examined and took an oath; they paid an entry fine of 6s 8d in instalments over four years, and an annual *waxshot* of 4d per couple or 2d per single person. A business meeting was held prior to the St Katherine's day meetings, on St Leonard's day (6 November) or the following Sunday in the chapel[14]. The main gild feast (an 'entertainment' organised by two officers of the guild appointed annually) was to be held in the Gild Hall[15] on the Sunday after St Katherine's day, at which the officers were to render their accounts and new officers were to be elected; members were not to refuse to serve as officers of the gild. On the same day, an obit shall be said for all past members of the gild which shall be declared by the "Bellman … goyng aboute the Toun". When any member dies, within thirty days a mass will be said for him or her in St Paul's church and this too shall be announced around the town.

The register records these activities. Each year, new members are admitted, outstanding entry fines are collected, the waxshot payments are recorded from the members, the officers are appointed, a summary of the accounts of the major officers is entered into the book, and a review of the gild stock held by individual members is carried out – although these items do not always appear in the same order. Only the obits are missing.

Admission of new members

The growth of membership of the gild was remarkable and seems to be related to the Alderman of the gild who held office for life (save for Christopher Browne, the only Alderman to resign that office). Between 1480, when William Browne enlarged the live membership from some 13 to 30 members, and 1489 when he died, numbers rose only slowly to 49; under his successor Christopher Browne they rose at approximately the same rate to 59 (1494). Under Thomas Phillips (1495-1508), however, there were increased admissions, including the eminent ladies Margaret Beaufort and Cecily lady Welles the daughter of Edward IV; the numbers reached 110. Under his successor, William Radclyffe, Alderman of the gild from 1510 to c1530, numbers peaked at 120 members and remained over 100 during the whole of his Aldermanry. There is a gap in the

---

[14] In 1480, St Leonard's feast fell on a Monday, the Sunday following was 12 November. The gild then met again on three successive days, on the eve of St Katherine's feast, (Friday 24 November), on the feast itself (25 November) for the religious services, and on the following Sunday (26 November) for the 'entertainment'. No date is given in the register for the meeting recorded for 1480.

[15] There was no gildhall in 1480; one was built in the next few years, before the summary of the statutes was made in 1494.

record from 1528-1531, during which period Radclyffe died and was replaced by Henry Lacey. Numbers were substantially reduced during the gap in the record, down to 66 members – perhaps there was a purge of non-attenders when Lacey took over. Numbers fell slightly to 60 by 1534 when the book ends.

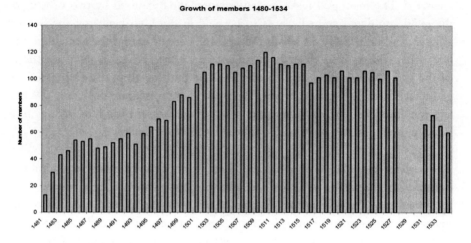

Growth of members 1480-1534

Nature of membership

We can see some signs of change in the nature of membership during this period. During William Browne's Aldermanry (1480-1489), only one woman was admitted in her own right, his sister Alice Bradmedewe, widow of a Coventry merchant. The anchoress was already a member and a few widows appeared in their own names. William Browne proposed Dame Elizabeth Tyssington but she did not join the gild at this time. Four clergy were admitted during this period, all secular priests with local connections like Mr Richard Burton archdeacon of Worcester who was a member of the Tolthorpe family of Rutland by Stamford.

Of the rest, the members appear to be local merchants and tradesmen – and not all of the richer section of society. It is not clear how membership came about, presumably by application and/or invitation. It was not tied to positions in the town government; of the existing 'old' membership of 48 living and dead members, only four were or had been on the town council (which consisted of a First Twelve and a Second Twelve). Of the 27 initial new members, although one was the town Alderman, only two of the rest became councillors subsequently. This pattern continued for some years: three members of the Second Twelve became gild members in 1482, and one councillor, John Nele, resigned (unusually) from the First Twelve in 1482 and was admitted to the gild in 1483; but apart from this, there is no link between the early membership of the gild and the town council[16]. Out of 47 persons who served on the two town councils between 1481 and the death of William Browne in 1489, only 12 became gild members.

Nor was membership closely tied to the parish of St Paul, for few of those appointed to assess and collect the taxes in that parish (who appear to have had residence in that area) were members of the gild. The 1527 tax returns for the parish of St Paul show that at that time, four of the 12 taxpayers were members of the gild and perhaps members of two other families had links to the gild[17]. It was not tied to any occupations: indeed, the early gild membership straddled the rich and poorer members of the community – shoemakers, glovers, labourers, bakers, weavers, candelers, smiths, tailors, mercers, lawyers and at least one doctor. One of the two existing town MPs at this time, Richard Forster, became a new member in 1481 and remained a member until he died in 1494. Both Christopher Browne and David Malpas, admitted as new members in 1481, later became Aldermen and MPs. Apart from Henry Lacey (admitted 1527-31, Alderman of the gild by 1532 and MP 1536) and Maurice Johnson (admitted 1510, MP 1523; son-in-law of Henry Lacey), the other MPs who became members of the gild were admitted after having served as MP – John Thurlby, MP in 1485-92 admitted in 1488, Thomas Edward MP in 1491-2 admitted to the gild in 1494, Thomas Lacey MP 1487 admitted in 1506. The gild was not a path to political achievement. Henry Lacey for example had been the deputy steward of the manor of Stamford (the chief executive officer in the absence of the steward, Sir John Hussey) since 1513 but was not admitted to the gild until 1527-31, although he quickly became its Alderman (before 1531)[18]. Most of those who served the town as Alderman (i.e. mayor) were not members of the gild. Indeed, the gap between the town government and this gild is notable[19] – the life of this gild seems to have been discrete from that of the town government, despite the Alderman of the gild always being a major political figure in the town.

Lacey's appointment suggests that, if there is a link between the gild and any interest group in the town, it would seem to be with the estate of Lady Margaret

---

[16] From comparison between the gild register and the Hall Book. The link seems to have been stronger in the later period.
[17] PRO E179/136/315
[18] S T Bindoff 1982 *The House of Commons 1509-1558* London: History of Parliament i p488
[19] There was a close link between the gild of Corpus Christi and the town council in Stamford.

Beaufort and her successors, at least after the death of William Browne (1489). Christopher Browne, Alderman of the gild from 1489-1495, was a member of her council. Thomas Phillip, the Alderman under whom the gild doubled its membership, may well have been linked with that estate through Sir David Phillip who was a member of the Beaufort council and an official on the estate. William Radclyffe, another Alderman of the gild, was deputy steward to Sir John Hussey the steward, as was his successor Henry Lacey, although Hussey himself did not become a member. St Katherine's gild in St Paul's church thus became linked to a major social and cultural focus in the region.

Changes in membership

Membership began to increase under Christopher Browne and from then on, the gild changed its character. In marked contrast with the William Browne years, regular clergy were now admitted – friars from the Austin and Grey friars, and the prior of St Leonard's priory and his co-monk[20]. But it was under Christopher's successor, Thomas Phillip mercer, that the gild reached the peak of its achievements. A large number of ecclesiastics joined: several of the parish clergy (successive rectors of St Paul; the rectors of St Mary, St George and St Michael, and the vicar of All Saints), as well as neighbouring parish clergy (Stretton, Clipsham, Ryhall, Tallington etc) were enrolled. Successive priors of St Leonard's joined the gild each time there was a change of personnel there. Friars from all the four houses became members, as did clergy from Northampton (Carmelite friars), Leicester (the collegiate church of Leicester) and Fotheringhay, especially successive precentors. In one year (1509), the abbots of Bourne, Crowland and Spalding all enrolled, together with a new prior at St Leonards.

Eminent local citizens such as John Lee mercer, Richard Cannel (MP) mercer of Stamford and mayor of the staple at Boston, David Cecyll (MP), Robert Beaumonde, William Browne's man of business and agent for Browne's Hospital, John Wattes peyntour were enrolled among both the living and the dead members. In 1502, Lady Margaret Beaufort of Collyweston nearby became a member until her death in 1509[21], and associated with her were two of her

---

[20] For much of the fifteenth century, there were only two monks in residence at the priory.

[21] As countess of Richmond and of Derby, she was admitted to the gild in 1502 and remained with it until her death (last recorded in 1508). She paid two instalments of her entry fine, and she is included in all waxshot lists between 1503 and 1508.

Two of her servants were also included in the list – Richard Cotmount domestic servant of the king's mother admitted in 1502 and listed until 1507, and Walter [blank] servant of the king's

servants and two members of her council, William Elmes lawyer and heir to William Browne, and Edmond Browne, a younger son of Christopher Browne who inherited his interests in Stamford. Two years later Cecily lady Welles daughter of Edward IV also enrolled together with an unnamed "servant of the king's mother". William Radclyffe who founded a grammar school in the town of Stamford which came to be located in St Paul's church, became a member of the gild and eventually its Alderman[22]. Country gentry (from Northborough, for example, or from Tallington and Uffington) were among the members.

The pace of admissions declined when William Radclyffe became Alderman in 1510 after the death of Thomas Phillip. A new abbot of Crowland still wished to be a member, as did the wardens or priors of the friaries in the town, the prior of Newstead by Stamford, the precentor of Fotheringhay. The only noble to join at this time was Elizabeth countess of Oxford[23], although Katherine de la Pole lady Grey of Castle Bytham was apparently also a member, although her enrolment cannot be seen[24].

There is a gap in the record from 1527 to 1531 (empty pages were left to be copied up) during which Radclyffe died and was succeeded by Henry Lacey. It is likely this hiatus created an opportunity for the gild to do some spring cleaning,

---

mother admitted 1504 and listed until 1509 when Lady Margaret Beaufort died. Others who were part of her retinue like Christopher Browne (1480 to 1518) and William Elmes (1504; he died in 1504-5) were members of the gild. It may also be significant that Henry Abney servant of 'lord de Ryvers' was admitted in 1504 and was listed up to 1509. The last earl Ryvers died without issue in 1491, *Complete Peerage* xi p25

[22] Deed op cit pp 10-12, 117-8

[23] Elizabeth countess of Oxford 1519-1527 was the daughter and co-heiress of Sir Richard Scrope. She had married William viscount Beaumont of Lincolnshire who died in 1507, after which she married John de Vere earl of Oxford of Hedingham in 1508-9. He died in 1513 leaving her as a long standing (24 years) and rich widow. Called "the old lady Oxford" by Henry VIII during her years at court (she attended the Field of the Cloth of Gold), she chose to be buried with her first husband at Wivenhoe in Essex. Her local connections are not known. She was admitted to the gild in 1520 and paid her entry fine of 6s 8d at that meeting which was unusual; her name appears in every waxshot list until 1527 when there is a gap in the record; it does not appear when the waxshot lists commence again in 1531. She died in 1537, *Complete Peerage*.

[24] There is no sign of the admission of herself or of her husband lord Grey to the gild, but at the November 1494 meeting of the gild, her arrears of entry fine of 6s 8d are recorded (*Dna Katarina Greye wife of the said Lord le Greye owes for her entry vjs viijd*). In November 1495 her entry fine was recorded along with others as '*desperat*' (*My lady Dna Kateryn Grey owes for her entry fine vjs viijd*). In 1496, her name is again in the list but this time it is given as *Dna (M del) Katherine Greye alias the said Dna Katherine (de la ins) Pole owes for entry vjs viijd;* and in the same year she hired the gild's hearse to go to Castle Bytham nearby in Lincolnshire for lord Grey: *Received off my lady Grey for hyryng off the herse to Bytham for my lord Grey and for gratuity ijs vd.*. As Lady Katherine de la Pole, she was included in the waxshot lists for 1496 and 1497, each time without any payment being recorded, and in the entry fine arrears lists for 1497, 1498, and 1499 after which nothing is heard of her.

for when the lists recommence, the numbers of members had been reduced to about 60. In 1532, a number of clergy were admitted – a bishop friar, the new precentor of Fotheringhay, the vicar of All Saints, three other friars from Stamford houses as well as the oldest son of Christopher Browne, Francis Browne of Tolthorpe, a courtier of Henry VIII. And two years later the last entrants were four friars minor from Stamford. The gild had clearly changed its nature since the days of William Browne's refoundation.

Women feature strongly in this gild except in the early years. In 1504, for example, out of 112 members, there were 15 women in their own right, apart from accompanying wives (fols 54-54d). It is however noteworthy that Elizabeth, the daughter of William Browne and widow of John Elmes, did not join the gild; and Elizabeth widow of William Elmes (the son of Elizabeth and John Elmes) remained a member of the gild only from William's death in 1505 to 1509 when she married John Pygot lawyer; Pygot did not join the gild, and so Elizabeth his new wife apparently lost her membership. One feature which is notable is the number of women with the name of Katherine who joined the gild – most of them as wives of members like Thomas Phillip (1480) but some in their own right like Katherine lady Grey (1496; fol 37). At least nine such admissions have been noted.

The gild and the anchoresses of Stamford

One feature of the membership and a key focus of the gild was its relationship with the anchoresses of Stamford. This is not the place for a full account of these religious persons but the link with the gild is clear.

There seem to have been a number of anchorages around Stamford in the later Middle Ages, known widely, if legacies are any guide[25]. But "the anchoress of Stamford" mentioned in some wills[26] refers to the anchorage "abutting on the north wall" of the parish church of St Paul – where the gild had its home – which is known from at least 1382. Ellen Erpingham anchoress of Stamford

---

[25] "hermits and anchorites in or near Stamford" 1383, *Fenland Notes and Queries* 1907-9 vol vii p200; Jones op cit 1999 p142; 1380 will: "to every recluse of Stamford", A W Gibbons 1888 *Early Lincoln Wills* (published in Lincoln as the first of a series of Lincoln Records) p 83
[26] C W Foster (ed) 1912 *Lincoln Wills* Lincoln Record Society (LRS) vol 5 pp17, 102; Historic MSS Commission, *Hastings* i pp 307-8; 102.

had a licence to choose a confessor in 1405, and Emma Tong from Bourne was immured there in 1435[27].

This anchoress had been a member of the gild for some time before 1480; for in the list of possessions of the gild drawn up in the audit of 1480 was

> *"Item a grete maser of Sylver and gilt with a coveryng of the gift of the Ancoryce"* (fol. 4d)

She is not named as such in the list of 'old members' but Margaret Jeralde is named, and as her name does not appear among the waxshot lists which follow, but the title 'the anchoress' does appear, it would seem that Margaret was the anchoress at this time. Dom William Jerald, who was no doubt a relation and who had been rector of St Paul's church from 1458 to 1464[28] and was at that time vicar of Castle Bytham (the residence of lord Grey of Codnor), was on the list of 'new members' in 1480 and joined the gild at this time (fol. 7).

'The anchoress' was regularly included in the waxshot lists. In 1496, 'Dame Agnes Leche anchoress' was admitted to the gild with an entry fine of 6s 8d (which she paid in instalments), presumably on the death of Margaret Jeralde. Agnes Leche came from a family well known in Stamford and Grantham; one Agnes Leche had been a controversial prioress at the nunnery of St Michael, Stamford, in the early fifteenth century, and John Leche goldsmith was churchwarden at St Mary at the bridge and warden of the Hospital of St Thomas at the bridge in the middle of the century.[29] Agnes was clearly regarded with respect: as 'Dame Agnes Leche', her name came second or third in the list of members, and from 1531, her name came first in the list each year. In 1517, the steward of the gild accounted for 10s *"that he hayth ressaved of my lady ankeres"* (fol. 75).

---

[27] M Archer (ed) 1963 *Register of Philip Repingdon*, LRS 57 p 51; Foster 1931 Wills *AASR* 41 p206; Margaret Browne wife of William Browne left a diaper cloth to the gild in 1489, PRO PROB 11.8; see A Rogers, 2008 Some Kinship Wills of the Late Fifteenth Century from Stamford, Rutland and the Surrounding Area, *Rutland Record* 28 pp 279-299

[28] Deed op cit pp 79, 86.

[29] British Library Vesp A24 fol 3d; not St Thomas at the bridge, as in P I King and C N L Brooke (eds) 1954 *Book of William Morton 1448-57* Northants Record Society 16 pp 4-5; for Agnes Leche prioress of the nunnery of St Michael, Stamford, 1413-1429, see VCH *Northants* ii p98; John Leke of Grantham 1420, Lincoln Wills, *AASR* 41 (1) 1931 pp 68-9; John Leche mercer of Stamford in 1373 and 1485, see ROLLR Conant MSS DG11/113, and Lincoln Wills *AASR* 41 (2) 1932 p 198

There was a second anchoress in the town in the later years. In 1504 Dame Margaret White "anchoress at the Nuns" was admitted to the gild as well. From then on, both anchoresses were listed among the members, sometimes with their names and sometimes without. Margaret White, the anchoress at the Nuns, remained a member until the 'gap years' of 1527-1531; Agnes Leche remained a member of the gild until the register closed in 1534.

It may have been the relationship of the gild of St Katherine in the parish church of St Paul with the anchoress in the same church which attracted William Browne. The parish of St Paul had been the parish of the Browne family in the later fourteenth and early fifteenth centuries, although William had moved into the parish of All Saints in the Market where he concentrated much of his attention[30]. But William Browne had a special attachment to the anchoress, for in his relatively short will of 1489, which is noticeably devoid of ecclesiastical legacies, was one which read

> *"Also I bequeith to the ancresse in Staunford aforseid xxs, and x yere after my deceese if eny be there closid, every yere xxs"*[31].

And William possessed an English translation of the *Speculum Inclusorum*, the rule book for the lives of anchorites and anchoresses[32]. We might notice that there was a gild of St Katherine in the parish church of Warmington (Northants) which was the rural parish of his family and of his wife's family[33].

And it may have been this link with the anchoresses which also attracted Margaret Beaufort countess of Richmond and Derby into membership, for she is well known to have had a special attachment to anchoresses, especially the two at Stamford. She is reputed to have visited them, bringing them fruit and wine; she rebuilt the cell adjoining the north wall of the parish church of St Paul, and in her will she made legacies to both anchoresses, including lands to support Margaret White at the Nuns which she entrusted to William Radclyffe (among others), Alderman of the gild[34].

---

[30] Details in forthcoming biography of William Browne of Stamford.

[31] PRO PROB 11/8; see Rogers, Wills

[32] British Library Harl 2372.

[33] 1498: J C Cox 1913 Parish churches of Northants illustrated by wills, *Archaeological Journal* 70 p 425

[34] Jones and Underwood op cit pp 132-3, 169, 239-240

Entry fines

Members were due to pay an entry fine of 6s 8d; only very occasionally was a fee of 3s 4d required of a single man (Thomas Jakson and Robert Saundes, 1511: fol 68). Even "John Thomas by himself" paid 6s 8d (1532; fol 90d). Widows, single women (even the anchoress, 1497, fol 38d) and clergy paid the same. But one of the local clergy was wily: he included his sister in his admission (*"Dom John Forster Rector of the parish church of St George and Elena Owdeby his sister owe vjs viijd which paid and they are quit"*, 1506; fol. 57d). Later in the period, it appears that some women, especially the second or subsequent wives of existing male members such as Agnes the second wife of Christopher Browne (1500), were admitted on payment of 3s 4d, and one was exempted altogether[35]. The only exception I have found to these rules was Margaret [Beaufort] 'Richmunde', who paid the odd sum of 3s 3d on the day of her admission and was stated to owe 16d which she paid subsequently, making a total of 4s 7d instead of the customary 6s 8d.

The rules stated that the members should pay their entry fine in four annual instalments of 20d each. But there was considerable flexibility here. A few paid the full 6s 8d on the day of their admission – William Elmes lawyer (and grandson of William Browne) who was admitted at the same time as Margaret Beaufort (1502), and Elizabeth countess of Oxford (1519; fol. 76d) and

> *"Elyzabeth Wastlen and for the sowles of Rychard Wastelyn and Harre hyr son vjs viijd the qwech ys payd and so sche ys qwytte et quieta est"* (1517, fol 74d)

> *M Richard Burton archdeacon of Worcester vjs viijd which paid and is quit* (fol 16; admitted 1480 but not paid until 1485).

Most members skipped a year or more:
> *John Fissher iijs iiijd. He paid nothing this day* (fol 12)

Some accelerated their payments:
> *M Richard Wermouth paid for ij years iijs iiijd - and owes iijs iiijd* (fol 10).

---

[35] *"Emma wife of Robert Beaumund is admitted into sisterhood. But she paid nothing for her entry because her husband paid in his entry as appears in Acts of the gild of the preceding year 1497 and 13th year of Henry VII",* fol 51d; 1503.

A few gave odd sums instead of the four instalments of 20d as they were able:

> *Fr Thomas Sheppey owes ijs vjd paid xijd and owes xxd* [sic](1534: fol. 94d).

Some were given extra time to pay:

> *William Bryghton by pledge of J Cobbe xxd: he has day until the Nativity of our Lord next.*
> *Dom Richard Purley vjs viijd; he has day to the Purification of BVM [2 February] next* (1496: fol. 37)

Some got others to pay for them:

> *David Cysell iijs iiijd which paid by his wife and is quit* (150: fol. 47).
> *Thomas Edward xxd paid xxd and iiijd for le waxshott by the hand of Andrew Stodard and thus quit* (1498: fol. 40d)

Some never paid. David Malpas esq (one of the town's MPs and an Alderman) is an interesting case study. Nominated by William Browne in 1480, he never paid his entry fine at all; in 1481 it was reduced to 5s:

> *David Malpas owes for his entry of which he will pay nothing this year, but he owes v[s]*[36]

but the next year it reverted in the list to 6s 8d:

> *David Malpas armiger, arrears for several years vjs viijd.*

Some years he paid waxshot (on one occasion paying four years in one go) but most of the time he ran up arrears in waxshot as well:

> *M David Malpas armiger (paid nil but still owes for this day* ins*) iiijd.*

He died in 1497, but his name continued to appear in the lists of overdue entry fines until 1499. There were others whose names appear regularly among the outstanding entry fines – it would seem the gild valued their membership more than they did.

Malpas may be an example of an immigrant into the town using the gild to establish himself[37]; David Cecil may also have done the same, for, admitted to

---

[36] in other words, Malpas is excused payment of his instalment for this year and his debt is reduced to 5s. The quotations are from fols 8d, 14, 14d, 18, 25d

[37] K Farnhill 2001 *Guilds and the Parish Community in late Medieval East Anglia, c1470-1550* York Medieval Press p 33

the freedom of the town in 1492-4, he joined the gild with his wife Agnes in 1497[38], and remained a member until the register closed in 1534.

At times, the accountant despaired of collecting some outstanding entry fines. In 1495, three entries are marked 'desp' and a section is added of 'Desperate debts' which contains another five names, including Katherine lady Grey. Of these eight entry fines which the accountant wished to have written off, three were at 6s 8d, 3 at 3s 4d and one at 1s 8d. But they were not written off: all of these were included in the following year.

The only change in this system of payments was for service to the gild. Successive bailiffs of the gild, Bryghton, Moreton and Stede, were able to trade their admission fee for service as bedell without wages. Hugh Broun friar was excused part of his entry fine:

> *Fr Hugh Broun Augustinian vs of which allowed to him for the celebration of masses in the chapel of St Katherine xxd and thus he owes iijs iiijd* [*nota* marg] (1499: fol. 42d)

Some were recorded as being paid to the steward as if this were not the common practice (fols 74d, 114). One seems to have been paid at least in part to the clerk of the gild:

> *John Sharpe mercer owes for entry vs paid xxd and owes iijs iiijd which paid and is quit* [*sic*] - [*respond per John Goylyn xld* marginalia] (1502: fol. 49d).

The abbot of Crowland was able to pay directly for gilding the statue of St Katherine:

> *The abbott of Corland Dam* [sic] *John Welles ys admytted and must pay vjs viijd the wech ys to the geltyng of sent Kateryn and so he ys qwytte* (1514: fol. 71d)

As time went on, the list of outstanding entry fines lengthened; it clearly became a serious problem. In 1517, only 3 payments were received from 35 outstanding entry fines; in 1518, only 2 out of 38, in 1519, 11 out of 41. The problem did not get any better: in 1532, only 7 paid out of 40. It was clearly taking many years for the full entry fines to be paid. John Broune rector of Casterton was

---

[38] The biography of David Cecil says his wife was Alice daughter of John Dyccons, a glover and Alderman (i.e. mayor) of Stamford, Bindoff 1982 *Commons* p602; this is repeated in D M Loades 2007 *The Cecils: privilege and power behind the throne* (revised 2009) Kew: PRO p 13, and other sources such as S Alford 2008 *Burghley: William Cecil at the court of Elizabeth I* Yale. But the gild book records her name as Agnes. For full biography of David Cecil, see Alan Rogers (forthcoming) *Parliamentary representation of Stamford, 1467-1509*

admitted in 1526 and finally settled his entry fine eight years later, and John Harres and Margaret were admitted in 1525 but again settled their entry fine only in 1534.

The waxshott

Waxshot was the annual payment members made towards the maintenance of the lights in the chapel of St Katherine, either 4d for membership of husband and wife, or 2d for single membership. Thus the annual list of names under the rubric of 'waxshott' is the roll of the membership; it can be assumed that, in most cases, when a name ceases to be given, the member has died. In a very few cases is a note appended *'mort'* (fol 18d: 1486). Sometimes the name of the widow is inserted without comment: *"Alice formerly the wife of John Pykerell ijd"* (1487: fol 20d).
    "John Sharpe (deceased inserted*) wife of iiijd"* (1502: fol 50)

There is no waxshot list in 1480; and in 1481, there is only a list of those who did not pay waxshot (all of them 'new' members in the 1480 lists). Thereafter each year all the members are listed whether they are present or not. Very rarely is there any indication:

> *"Dom John Rydell co-monk of St Leonards paid nothing for this day because he is abroad (quia exivit de patria)"* (1493: fol 32).

Sometimes *nil* is given beside an entry, and again rarely someone else pays up for the absent member:
    "William Sutton by John Yedson ijs quit" (1496: fol 38)

The list normally includes a note of the sum due. Usually (but not always) there is an indication that these sums were paid:

> *"David Malpas armiger for the same owes for iiij years which he paid and is quit".*
> *"Dom William Jerald arrears for ij years paid this day viijd"* (1488: fol.22).

The names are normally in the same order. Several of the lists are annotated with marks but it is impossible to tell what these once meant.

From 1499, the lists begin to omit some of the sums due in substantial numbers: 21 out of 88, almost a quarter. This tendency grew, though some years most of the figures are included. In 1509, the list has no sums against anyone – and the following year sums are omitted against 59 names out of 120 (fol 67). From 1513, no sums are recorded at all – just a long list of names is provided each year.

The list of 1527 – the last before the break – is marked with different symbols. It is possible that this was the list which was used to reduce the membership of the gild from over 100 down to the 60s during the gap years; but careful comparison of the symbols with the names of the members who survived into the 1530s shows that these symbols do not seem to relate to such activity. However, 15 new members were admitted during these gap years.

There is one aspect of the waxshot which is a matter of some interest. The sums collected would have resulted in a large collection of small coinage. In Browne's Hospital stands a fifteenth century 'almsbox', a container which could have been used by a gild to collect these small sums. During the years covered by this register, there was at times a severe shortage of coinage. It may be that the sum collected by the gild from waxshott was distributed among the local shop keepers as small change, in much the same way as many beggars share their small change takings with local stores. The finding in 1866 in St George's churchyard, Stamford, of a hoard of just under 3000 groats and half groats dating from the 1470s is a reminder that behind these lists of names under the rubric *waxshott* stands a container with a large number of small coins which the officers of the gild would need to dispose of profitably each year[39].

Officers

Each year the officers of the gild are named.

It is of course extremely unlikely that contested elections were held; almost certainly the procedure was the same as with most voluntary bodies today, a mixture of self-promotion and reluctance, relief that others have taken on the tasks, and some willingness to retain a post. Motives will vary from person to person and over time.

---

[39] See F. A. Walters, The Stamford find and supplementary notes on the coinage of Henry VI, *Numismatic Chronicle* vol. 11 (1911), pp. 153-175; J. D. A. Thompson 1956 *Inventory of British Coin Hoards 600-1500* London p 128. See B Kumin 1996 *Shaping of a Community: the rise and reformation of the English parish c1400-1560* Aldershot pp82-83.

Alderman: The Alderman was the chief executive. He managed the gild; all the other officers were his officers. He controlled the admission of new members and the gild accounts.

The office of Alderman was held, with one exception, for life. When William Browne wool merchant became Alderman of the gild we do not know – it could have been some years before 1480. On his death in 1489, he was succeeded by his nephew, Christopher Browne wool merchant who however resigned after five years. But Christopher was the resigning sort; he left the town council; he said he was too busy to serve as Alderman (i.e. mayor) of the borough of Stamford except by deputy. He was an ambitious courtier, a member of the council of Lady Margaret Beaufort and was known at the king's court. But interestingly he did not get Lady Margaret to join the gild – that happened eight years after he resigned. He would only be willing to hold the office of Alderman of the gild so long as it did not involve him in too much activity which took him away from higher priorities.

Thomas Phillip his successor was a mercer and town councillor. He was one of the 'new' members enlisted with his wife Katherine by William Browne in 1480 to save the gild. He held the office for 14 years. Under his administration, the gild grew to its greatest size and changed its character. When he died in 1509, there was clearly some crisis, for Nicholas Trygge the clerk of the gild was chosen as Alderman for one year only, to be succeeded by William Radclyffe merchant in 1510. Radclyffe had been admitted with his wife Elizabeth in 1502, at the same time as Lady Margaret Beaufort. He is notable in having endowed the Stamford free grammar school in association with the gild of Corpus Christi. He was also deputy steward in the town of Stamford to Sir John Hussey. He died sometime between 1527 and 1531, when there is a gap in the record; he was replaced by Henry Lacey gentleman, also deputy steward to Sir John Hussey and another prominent merchant and councillor in the town. A butcher, he had been admitted to the gild (as Henry Lay) with his wife Alice as long ago as 1505. It is true of this gild as of others that "those men with the highest office in the gilds also held high office outside"[40].

Steward: the 'steward of the lands' held office for many years, sometimes dying in office. He collected the rents of the gild property and paid for most of the gild activities except the feast.

---

[40] Bainbridge op cit p 133

Henry Cok stainer, a close friend of William Browne, was steward when the gild was refounded in 1480 but he was replaced immediately[41]. John Hikson or Yetson (an 'old' member) held the post from 1481 until his death in 1499, being replaced by Andrew Stottard, a fishmonger. Stottard had been admitted to the gild with his wife in 1484 and had served as procurator of the feast in 1488-1490. His period of office ran until 1510 when he died. Thomas Couper baker held the office for one year 1510-11 and then John (a) Lee mercer was appointed under William Radclyffe from 1511 to 1516. Lee had been a member of the gild since 1496 but had never served as procurator of the feast. He remained a member of the gild until at least 1534. Robert Martyndale mercer was steward from 1516 to 1519 when he died. He had been admitted with his wife in 1505. Maurice Johnson was steward from 1519 until sometime between 1527-1531, the 'gap years'. He too had been admitted in 1505, and procurator for the feast in 1513-1515. Relieved of his post sometime between 1527 and 1531, he remained a member of the gild until at least 1534. In 1531, when the record resumes, the steward was named as Robert Sandwath. He is I think the Robert Saundes admitted without partner for an entry fee of only 3s 4d in 1511, appears as Sandwayth first in 1514 and ran the feast from 1517 to 1519 and again in 1531. He was steward when this account book closed in 1534. All the stewards had been members of the gild for at least ten years before coming to this office. But not all had served in the other gild office of steward of the feast.

Procurators/stewards of the feast - also called 'garners' or 'providers of the entertainment': Two men were chosen for this office, one in the senior position and the other junior; the junior became senior in the following year. There were only three exceptions to this rule during the 54 years of the gild register. In 1492, the senior procurator continued for a third year instead of the junior procurator; in 1508 Thomas Couper (who also stood in for one year as steward of the lands) became senior procurator instead of William Hynkeley who had died; and again in 1534, Thomas Fresschewater stood in for the previous year's junior procurator William Hude.

It is possible that this was a position that no-one wanted, for the procurators put up the money and claimed it from the gild at the end of the year. Very few persons served as procurator on more than the one occasion until the 1520s. William Templer (who was also bailiff for the gild) served twice between 1480 and 1485. A William Clerk served in 1489-1491 and in 1500-1502; John Shilton

---

[41] His desire to stand down as steward in 1480 may indeed have precipitated the steps taken to refound the gild.

(a tenant in one of the gild properties in the town) served 1496-98 and 1504-6, William Jackson 1505-7 and he or another William Jackson served in 1523-5, and then 1525-6. John Fenton served as procurator 1524-5 and again 1526-7. In the 1520s, it may have been hard to find anyone to take the office. The accounts for these years suggest some dislocation of the office. Until 1511, both procurators accounted for their office; from 1511, only the senior procurator so accounted.

Bailiff/bedell: This was a paid office, at 2s p.a. rising in stages to 2s 6d p.a.. William Templer (a labourer) served from 1480 to 1485, and from 1491 to at least 1495, perhaps 1497 (as both bedell and cook for the gild; he remained as cook for the gild until at least 1502). He last appears in the gild record in 1506. He combined this with procurator of the feast in 1480-2 and in 1483-85. William Fawkes was bailiff from 1485 to 1491, William Richardson/Bryghton from 1498 until at least 1502, Thomas Morton for one year (1504-5). Bryghton was allowed to set part of his entry fine against his wages as bedell. In 1505, Robert Stede and his wife were admitted to the gild and in the same year, he was appointed bailiff; his entry fine instalments of 1s 8d and his waxshot payments were to be taken in lieu of wages. He was bailiff from 1505 to at least 1527, perhaps 1530. When the accounts resume, William Halyday (admitted 1525 with his wife) was bailiff as well as steward of the feast, and he was succeeded by William Dubdyke from 1532 until the end of the account book.

Other officers can be seen occasionally. The gild chaplain is rarely named but in 1499 was friar Hugh Broun of the Austin friary who was allowed 1s 8d off his entry fine for the celebration of masses in the chapel of St Katherine. Richard Bedwyn was supervisor of the gildhall in 1500-1. John Goylyn was clerk in 1491 at 1s 8d p.a. (fol 28d), and Nicholas Trygge, a notary public, was clerk to the gild from at least 1504 to at least 1509 when he became stand-in Alderman for one year. He earned 2s a year for his position as clerk.

Two of the officers died during their period of office: John Yetson steward in 1499 and Andrew Stottard steward 1510. In each case, their widow rendered the accounts and paid any sums remaining in the hands of these officers.

The accounts

A summary of the accounts is included in most years. These are summaries only, and there are some gaps and a number of uncertain entries, so that all we can gain is an impressionistic picture of the accounts. Three accounts are listed regularly, the Alderman's account (also the treasury/exchequer of the gild), the steward of the lands, and the steward(s) of the feast. One fragmentary account from the bedell is also included[42].

The *Alderman* held the gild treasury (exchequer). This accounts for the occasions when the accountant reported in their own voice:

> "*wherof I hade in my hands sens the laste accompte xxs viijd and so ys owyng to me yett vs iiijd and xxs that I delyvered to the steward and so ys owyng to me yet xxvs iiijd*" (1520: fol 78)[43].

There were some times when the Alderman held his own surpluses or took the outstanding sums from the exchequer as 'stock' (see below) but these were rare. Only once did this amount to substantial sums: Thomas Phillip in his early years as Alderman held £1; then, in successive years, he held surpluses of £3/18/8, then £5/18/8, and finally £7/18/8, before accounting for payments of £8/18/8 from these sums and claiming from the exchequer the overdue sum of £1 – but this did not happen again.

The receipts came from the entry fines and waxshot (what was called *pecunia numerata*), and from the surpluses (if any) from the steward and the feast. The Alderman had the power to order some of these payments to go direct to the other officers. Only in one year (1531) do we get a full summary: waxshot 7s 8d; the feast/dinner 4s 6d; entry fine instalments 9s.4d; rents (substantially reduced by now) 15s – total receipts 36s 6d. This was well down from the period of greatest income.

This account paid out the cost of the feast to the procurators; it also paid any outstanding sums from the steward's account. It normally paid the stipends of the gild staff (chaplain or priest, bedell, clerk, cook), but again the Alderman could transfer these to some of the other accounts, mostly the steward. Repairs to the gildhall and the chapel were also covered occasionally although these mostly were paid by the steward. One payment was made in relief to a poor woman (13s 4d).

In most years, the 'remnant' (the surplus on the year's account) or part of it was given to the steward as an advance against his costs for the coming year; it

---

[42] 1482: he overspent and drew 6s 6d from the exchequer, fol 10d.
[43] See also fols 79, 82.

formed the first charge on his account in the following year[44]. If the summaries are accurate, the remnant varied widely – from 16d in 1481 to £8 13.4 in 1485. From about 1513, the remnant was considerably smaller, always less than one pound sterling, and for the years 1520 to 1527, each year except one recorded a loss on the total account. It is clear the gild was in financial difficulties: the wages of the bedell and the chaplain were often in arrears and were cut back as were the special and general obits.

The steward's accounts are fragmentary. During the years of William Browne's Aldermanry, the accounts are very brief and unrevealing – and were clearly rendered separately. They become fuller from 1491 when it seems that the Alderman (Christopher Browne) showed some inconsistency in his accounts. Thereafter they are fuller and clearer, but again are still brief summaries.

The main source of the receipts came from the 'remnant' of the Alderman's account (the exchequer or treasury) received as an 'advance' on the next year's account; but such an advance ceased from 1519 (apart from one year in 1532). At times, the Alderman authorised direct payments of rents, of stock instalments (see below), and entry fines, sometimes for specified payments, especially the wages of the gild chaplain (1490-1). From 1505, it would seem that he was responsible for collecting the rents (his title was at times 'steward of the lands'); from the appointment of Maurice Johnson as steward, his only income was from the rents of the gild property, and on these he received allowance for 'decays' (failure of rents for various reasons). His accounts were almost always very small.

The steward paid for obits, both individual and the general obit, and the wax lights. He also paid for any repairs to the gildhall, the gild property and the chapel. After the 'gap' years (1527-1532), it would seem that the steward's account and that of the procurators of the feast were either merged or became confused; indeed, Robert Sandwayth was both one of the procurators and the steward of the lands.

From the start in 1481 to about 1500, there was an overspend in most years, the deficit being drawn from the exchequer; from 1500 to about 1518 there was in almost every year an underspend, the surplus being returned to the exchequer

---

[44] In the case of Nicholas Trygge (notary public), the caretaker Alderman who received the 'remnant' of £2, this was regarded as 'stock' and carried forward for several years – see below.

or carried over. In the later years, the accounts appear to be confused and are probably incomplete.

The procurators (or stewards) of the feast had simpler summaries. They spent money on the "morrow speech", the dinner and the entertainment (1510: "the fest, the morrow speech and the dener") and claimed it from the exchequer at the end of the year. Expenditure on the feast diminished regularly from about 1505: despite the fact that the number of members was increasing, the spending *per capita* on the feast fell in the 1520s to about one third of what it had been in the 1480s.

What we can see from these summary accounts is a gild with an expanding membership up to a peak in 1511, maintaining its membership through the 1520s but significantly reduced in the early years of the 1530s; but its finances became substantially reduced from about 1510 and it seems to have got into financial problems by the end of the period.

The gild property

One main problem was the 'decay' of rents. At the time of the re-launch of the gild in 1480, it possessed two properties, one on Claymont (now Broad Street) and the other described as a cottage "against Star Lane end" (1515: fol 73). In 1480, the tenement on Claymont was said to have paid a rent of 9s and the "tenement in the parish of St Paul" (the Star Lane property) yielded 15s. But the accounts never showed this; only 12s rent was received from the Star Lane property until 1499; no rent was received from the Claymont property which clearly was undergoing extensive alterations to convert what seems to have been a private dwelling into what was later called 'the gildhall' or 'St Katherine's Howse' or 'the Hall'[45]. The gildhall was clearly ready by the time of the revised statutes in 1494. From 1505, the rents of both properties can be seen as 18s for the gildhall[46] and 6s 8d for "Whipp's cottage"[47]. The cottage was increased to 7s pa in 1507 but then reduced again to 6s 8d in 1509; the gildhall was reduced to 13s 4d in 1509 and to 12s in 1511 and these sums remained until 1520 when the total rents were reduced to 18s and again in 1531 to 15s (the

---

[45] See Farnhill op cit p 79 for other examples of this.
[46] Tenanted by John Gibson in 1505 (Alexander Gibson was a gild member in 1505); by John Selby (a gild member) in 1509
[47] Tenanted by John Shilton (gild member and provider of the feast at the time) from 1497 to at least 1506, by Elizabeth Rogers as sub-tenant to William Radclyffe Alderman of the gild in 1509, by Herde in 1511

gildhall only being 10s of this sum). But every year from 1506, these 'official' rents were subject to 'decays' – either vacancies or arrears or reduced rents. In some years (e.g. 1507) nothing was received at all. And both properties incurred considerable costs in terms of repairs.

Wages and obits

The charges for the chaplain of the gild can be seen on occasion. At first, the charge was variable, presumably according to the duties performed – (1488, £1 1s 4d; 1490 £1; 1491 15s; 1518 19s 8d) but from 1520, it was at a standard rate of £1 6s p.a. During the 'gap years', the stipend was reduced to 8s 8d pa. Obits were paid for at 5d per obit and the general obit at 7d; in the 1530s each obit was reduced to 4d per obit[48]. The clerk was paid 1s 8d pa in 1491, 2s in 1506 but in the 1530s, he was paid by his work on the books only a few pence. The cook received 2s p.a. in the 1490s but only 10d in 1514; the bedell received 2s p.a. in the 1490s, 2s 6d in 1506, 2s 4d in the 1520s and only 6d in the 1530s. The 'gap years' saw a strong retrenchment in the gild costs.

In summary, the refounded gild had a stable working balance during the Aldermanry of William Browne while engaging in rebuilding its gildhall; there was some confusion in the accounts during the brief (and it seems inattentive) Aldermanry of Christopher Browne. Thomas Phillip expanded the gild substantially and at first the accounts were healthy, allowing a considerable sum to be spent on the entertainment; but after a time, the costs increased while the income reduced. By the early 1520s, the gild was in difficulties which were attended to during the 'gap' years of 1527 to 1531. The last recorded years are too few and too ill recorded to see how healthy the reduced guild was in the early 1530s.

Religious life

Unfortunately we can see very little of the religious life of the gild. There was a chapel of St Katherine in the parish church of St Paul with its own chaplain, in which lights were continually maintained. There was an image of St Katherine which was re-gilt during this period. The gild met on the eve of St Katherine's feast for a service as well as on the feast day itself. There would have been a procession. From time to time during the year obits would have been held for

---

[48] According to other records, these charges were very low: the minimum stipend for a gild priest was over £5 and a mass was normally 4s, according to Farnhill op cit pp 73-4.

members deceased: we know that in the year 1533-4, the obits of Fr Thorpe, Fr Depynge, John Ley, Joan Trigge, the wife of Edward Broune, William Nettlame, the wife of Robert Wallett and Thomas Wyllams were held, and that members of the gild were required to attend these services.

The stock

There is one last financial element to be discussed, the gild stock. Some gilds, like some parishes[49], had a 'stock' – possessions which allowed the gild to make small amounts of money towards its costs. Loans of money and of gild possessions were of course common[50]. At the re-launch in 1480, the possessions of the gild were listed – furniture, cloths and plate which had been donated to or bought by the gild in previous years: such as

> *Item halfe a doseyn of Spones of Silver marked with St Katerynes whele*
> *Item a broche at the geffte off William Povy*
> *Item a towell off dyaper vij yerds with blewe rewez [tassles?] and the ende off the gyfft off dam Agnes Broun*
> *Item bought of newe to the same gilde a longe fourme of xii fote of lenght and ther remaynyng* (fol. 4d)

But the gild had more than these. Some time before 1480, a sum of £10 had been distributed between the existing members, and each of them was due to pay yearly a sum (an "increment") amounting to 7½ per cent of the stock they held. How long this process had been in operation is not known but certainly for more than one year, since two of the 'old members' had two such sums against their names, presumably received in successive handouts. Each advance was supported by a pledge, which gives them the appearance of a loan; but the sums were all small and standard (£1 or 13s4d or 6s 8d) and all the 'old' members of the gild except the anchoress held one. William Browne himself held 13s 4d and Agnes Browne his sister-in-law held £1. Two of these members, John Basse (a cloth merchant who exported through Lynn) and John Capron chaplain, held such sums but paid no increment, and in 1483 both sought permission to repay the stock in annual instalments of 1s 8d[51].

---

[49] For parish stock ('stores'), see E Duffy 2001 *Voices of Morebath: Reformation and rebellion in an English village* Yale pp 81-2
[50] See for example Farnhill op cit pp 4 , 64
[51] Basse paid 1s 8d in 1485, but Capron seems to have paid back nothing.

The distribution of the gild surplus funds among some of the members in return for some kind of increment was common among gilds; the Kings Lynn gild of St Giles clearly distributed a good deal of its surplus among some of its members in return for such "good will" payments, and these sums were on occasion transferred from member to member[52]. But in this case, the standard increment at 7½ percent[53] and the fact that all members of the gild including William Browne and his sister-in-law Agnes Browne held such small sums make it look like each member having a share in the gild. In the next year, new stock amounting to only £1 6s 8d was distributed to four of the 'new members' at the same rate of increment. One new stock was distributed in 1484, six in 1485. By 1486, the system was beginning to crumble: the steward of the lands had a surplus on his account of £1 9s which was counted to him as 'stock' but no surety was taken and no increment paid. By then, no less than ten of the members found themselves unable to pay their increment. Several began to repay the capital sum held in instalments either to the exchequer of the gild or to some of the officers – 10s (and other sums unspecified) to the stipend of the gild chaplain, 1s 8d p.a. to the wages of the bedell. Time was given to some to pay and at least one had some part remitted:

> *"William Templer [the bailiff] who has by pledge of Henry Cok and John Palmer xls, of which he paid increment iijs and of the stock by the hands of the said John Palmer xxs which remains in the exchequer and thus is quit. And because Henry Cok the other pledge is deceased, therefore the Alderman and brethren of special grace have given to the same William Templer permission to pay the said residue of xxs on his oath taken in person before the Alderman as follows – namely to pay to the steward ijs vjd of this sum in each quarter of the year until the residue of the sum of xxs is fully paid and thus the said Henry Cok the abovementioned pledge shall similarly be quit of this".*

> *"Robert Yerdley has xxvjs viijd of which paid xxs and the residue is pardoned and quit"*

Agnes Browne paid her increment and the capital in 1484, William Browne in 1485. The system held together until the death of William Browne (1489), but almost immediately it broke down completely. No new stock was issued for two years; and from 1491 the payment of increments by all holders of stock was replaced by the payment by only some holders of the stock of what were called

---

[52] Kings Lynn Archives G1/43 ff 10,17 : "the four nobles in Stephen Mudford's hands shall be put into William Potter's hands and the Alderman is to take sureties"; "received of JD of gilde catell remaynyng in his hands 10s; item of his gode wyll geven to the gilde 12d"; the 'good will' money normally amounted to 1d in the shilling.

[53] The normal rate of interest on loans seems to have been 10%; see B Nelson 1969 *Idea of Usury* University of Chicago Press; Farnhill op cit p67.

gratuities (*ex devocione*), the equivalent of the Kings Lynn 'gode wyll' money. When new stock was issued (in units of 1s 8d, 6s 8d, 13s 4d and £1), no increment was required. The last gratuities were paid in 1497. Thereafter the initial sums only were recorded year by year and as they were paid off slowly, so the entries reduced. John Fissher (1486) and John Thurleby (1492) were still holding their stock in 1523 (Fissher) and 1527 (Thurlby).

It is not clear what exactly is going on when William Browne, sometime before 1480, set up this system of all members including himself holding sums of money in return for a standard annual payment amounting to 7½ per cent of the sum. The sums are too small and too regular and apply to all members of the gild at the start for this to be a simple system of money lending at times of necessity. It probably reflects a policy which has been noted elsewhere of the gild investing money rather than hoarding it[54]. But the later sums held may have been matters of convenience for the gild members. The system broke down after the death of William Browne; first the increments became gratuities, and then they vanished altogether, so the sums held were free of any charge to the gild. Some were treated as advances against the wages of officers, especially the bedell; others may have been called in by the officers as needed.

Conclusion

The register of St Katherine's gild in Stamford 1480-1534 is a substantial record of the gild over these fifty or so years. It shows a small parish gild linked to the anchoress in the church of St Paul, already in existence for some years but having become almost moribund with only some 13 or 14 living members, being refounded in 1480. For nine years, it was run tightly by William Browne its Alderman as a relatively small local gild. Under Christopher Browne his successor, the gild seems to have been less well managed (there was some confusion over the accounts). Under Thomas Phillip, it changed its character from a local, largely lay, gild to a larger social gild drawing its members from elites and ecclesiastics outside the town and more than doubling in size. Under his successor William Radclyffe, the gild had to face economic conditions which made finances difficult, and some time between 1527 and 1531, the gild was again reorganised with a reduction in its members to about two thirds and the finances streamlined by merging the feast stewards with the steward of the gild. Further study will no doubt reveal nuances to this overall picture.

---

[54] Farnhill op cit p 166

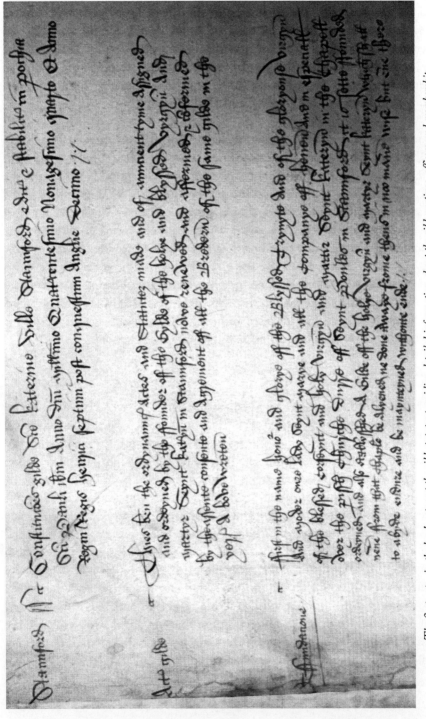

The first entry in the book sets out the gild statutes providing detailed information about the gild meetings, officers and membership.

Text of St Katherine's Gild Book

Gonville and Caius College, Cambridge, MS 266/670

fol 1 blank

fol 1d

Staunford

[1] Constitutions of the gild of St Katherine of the town of Stamford set and established in the parish of St Paul there in the year of Our Lord 1494 and the 10th year of the reign of king Henry VII [55]
(*Constituciones gilde sancte Katerine Ville Staunford edit et stabilit in parochia Sancti Pauli ibidem Anno domini millimo Quartogentesimo Nonagesimo quarto et Anno Regni Regis Henrici septimi post conquestum Anglie decimo*).

Acts of the Gild
Thies ben the ordynaunces Actes and Statutes made and of auncient tyme assigned and ordeyned by the Founder off the Gylde of the holye and blyssed Vyrgyn and martyr Seynt Kateryn in Staunford nowe renewed and affermed and confermed by the assente consente and Agrement off all the Bredern of the same gilde in the yer above wreten

Foundation
[2] ffirst in the name honour and glorye off the Blyssed Trynyte And of the gloryouse virgyn and moder oure lady Seynt marye and all the Companye off heven And in especiall of the blessed Corseynt and holy Virgyn and martir Seynt Kateryn in the Chapell over the parissh Churche durre off Seynt Poules in Staunford it is sette Founded ordeyned and also stablysshed a Gilde off the holye Virgyn and martyr Seynt Kateryn which shall never From that Chaple be alyened ne done awaye frome thens in noo manere wise but evere there to abyde endure and be maynteyned withoute ende

---

[55] The first four pages were written in 1494

29

Divine?[56] Service

[3] Item it is ordeyned and assigned and also inacted that the Alderman of the seid Gilde shalbe at Seynt Katerynis Chapell aforeseid with all his Bredern on Seynt Katerynis Even [24 November] att Evensong and on the daie [25 November] at mateyns masse and later Evensonge holye togedre And that noo man then be absent withoute a resonable and sufficiaunt excuse uppon payn of every Broder absente a pound (*li.*) of Wax to be paied to the Gilde And that the Stuarde off the gilde for the tyme beyng shall truly countrolle them that ben absente And at the next tyme off assemble to presente the names offtheym and everych of theym so absente uppon the same peyne

Admission of brothers and sisters

[4] Item it is ordeyned that whan the seid First evenson is doon The Alderman and his Bredern shall assemble in their halle and dryncke and there have a curteys Comunycacion for the weele off the seid Gilde And then shalbe called forth all tho that shalbe admytted Bredern or Sustern off the Gilde And the Alderman shall examyn theym in this wise, Syr or Syrs be ye willyng to be Bredern among us in this Gilde and will desire and axe it in the worshipp off Allmyghty god oure blissed lady Seynt Marye and of the holy Virgyn and martyr Seynt Kateryn in whoos name this Gilde is Founded and in the wey off Charyte. And by their owne wille they shall answer ye or naye. Then the Alderman shall commaunde the Clerke to gyff this (ow *del*) othe to them in Forme and maner folowyng

Taking oath

[4] This here ye Alderman I shall trewe man be to god almyghty to oure lady Seynt Mary and to that holye virgyn and martir Seynt Kateryn in whos honoure and worshipp this Gilde is founded and shalbe obedyent to the Alderman of this Gilde and to his Successoures and come to hym and to his Bredern whan I have warnyng and not absente myselffe withoute cause resonable. I shalbe redy of scott and lotte and all my duties truly pay and doo the ordynaunces constitucions and rules with the councell off the same gilde kepe obeye and performe and to my power maynteyne to my lyvys ende so helpe me god and holydome and by this boke. And then kys the Boke and be lovynglye receyved with all the Bredern. And then drynke aboute and affter that departe for that nyght.

---

[56] text torn

fol 2

Gild meeting (De maneloquio)

[5] Item it is ordeyned and stablisshed for ever that every yere on Seynt Leonardes
daye [6 November] or ells the Sonday next affter The Alderman and his Bredern
shall assemble and mete in the Chapell off Seynt Kateryn at oon affter noone
And there have thir morowe speche And provyde and ordeyn for the worshypp
profite and all thyngs necessarye at that tyme for the welfare off the same gilde
at which tyme noo broder shalbe absente withoute a lawffull excuse uppon
payne of j li off wax

General feast (De generali convivio) / payments for the feast (soluciones pro prandis)[57]

[6] Also it is ordeyned that uppon the Sonday next affter Seynt Katerynis day
most commenly to be hadde The seid Alderman and his Bredern and Susters
shall come to their Gilde Halle togedr When the more [morning?] Belle att
Powles chirche is knelled and theer dyne togedr and take such as shall be then
provyded by the stuarde of the gilde for the tyme beyng. Att the which dyner a
man and his wyff shall pay iiijd and every other sengle person both preste man
and woman shall pay ijd and what parson be absente From the seid dyner
withoute a reasonable excuse shall paie half a pound (*di li*) of wax and for his
dyner besyde yff he hadde lawffull warnyng to be ther

Rendering account

Also it is ordeyned that anon affter the dyner is doon every olde officer shall come
inne before the Alderman and the Clerke and there make a dewe accompte afore
theym all presente every Officer of such as perteyneth to his office and noon
Officer absente hymself uppon payn of j li wax to be paide withoute pardon

Not refusing office (pro Officium non relinquendum)

Also it is ordeyned that noo Broder of this Gilde shall refuse at any tyme any
office perttyning to the seid Gilde whan he is chosen therto uppon the Fest daye
which is the election day uppon payn off j li wax

Admission of brethren / waxshote[3]

Also it is ordeyned that noo man ne person shalbe admitted unto this Gilde but if
a bee founde of goode name and fame of good conversacion and honeste in his
demeanour and of goode rule and shall paie for his entre in to the gilde vjs viijd
to be paied in iiij yers affter the First yere every yere xxd and every yere affter

---

[57] both headings are in margins against these items

the First yere to paye for the mayntenyng off the wax and lights iiijd a man and his wyff and every soole person preeste and other ijd

General obit

Also it is ordeyned that the same daye Whan the generall Feste is holden at affternoone in the seid Chirch off Seynt Poules shalbe doon and said a *placebo* and *dirige* for all the Sowles off the Bredern and Susters that ben paste in this Gilde and therto rynge iij peeles with Masse of Requiem on the next morowe with as many peeles att the which masse the Alderman off the gilde or his depute shall offre ijd And at the seid dirige the Stuarde off the Gilde shall see that they that seye the seid dirige shal have brede chese and dryncke and the ryngers also and he shall gyff the Clerke for his Ryngyng ijd And the Bellman for goyng aboute the Toun jd and brede chese and drynke

fol 2d

Special obit

Also it is ordeyned that when any Broder or Suster of this gilde is decessed oute of this worlde then withyn the xxx dayes off that Broder or Suster in the Chirch off Seynt Poules the steward of this gilde shall doo Rynge for hym and do to sey a placebo and dirige with a masse on the morowe of Requiem as the common use is, att the which masse the Alderman of the gilde or his depute shall offre ijd for the same soule And to the Clerke for Ryngyng ijd and to the Belman for goyng aboute the Town jd The seid diryge to be holden on the Fryday an it may be and the masse on the morowe. All this to be doon on the Coste and charge of the seid Gylde

[fol 3, 3d and 4 blank]

fol 4d

Anno dni millimo cccc^{mo} lxxx^{mo}
The stock and jewels (Staur' et Jocalia) of the gild of St Katherine virgin and martyr of the town or borough of Stamford in the said year appear below (patent inferius)
In primis j towell of warke
Item vj towelles playn
Item ij bordeclothes[58] playn
Item ij bordcloth of wark

---

[58] tablecloth

Item another bordecloth of wark of litill value

Item ij chargeoures of pewter

Item a basyn and a lavour

Item iiij pottes and a panne of Brasse

[59]Item iiij pleyn bordeclothes

Item a grete maser of Sylver and gilt with a coveryng of the gift of the Ancoryce[60]

Item another masour of silver and gilt and lesse[61]

Item another masour of coper and gilt

Item halfe a doseyn of Spones of Silver marked with St Katerynes whele

Item a morter of Stone

Item an hallyng[62] steyned boght of William Article[63]

Item a Coffer to put in stuffe

Item bought of newe to the same gilde a longe fourme of xii fote of lenght and ther remaynyng

Item another longe fourme of xij fote length

Item a folden Table

Lands and tenements of the same gild

First, one tenement in Staunford situated on Cleymount[64] rendering ixs p.a.

Item one tenement in Staunford in the parish of St Paul[65] in the same town rendering xvs p.a.

[66]Item a broche at the geffte off William Povy[67]

Item a bordclothe of dyape warke ell brode vj yerds and a half (*di*) long

Item a towell off dyaper vij yerds with blewe rewez [tassles?] and the ende off the gyfft off dam Agnes Broun[68]

Item ij peyr trestells

---

[59] this item runs on the previous item

[60] for the anchoress, see Introduction; it is very likely she is Margaret Jeralde; that she is already a member can be seen from fol 10d

[61] meaning obscure: perhaps 'damaged'?

[62] ?a hanging in the hall?

[63] John Article was a taxer in the parish of St Paul 1468 and William Article was a member of the Second Twelve 1469-72, Stamford Borough records, Town Hall, Hall Book (HB); his occupation is unknown but he may possibly be the same as William Marchaunt on the Second Twelve 1465-68. He was a member of the gild in 1480

[64] Broad Street

[65] in Star lane; see below fol. 73

[66] in another informal hand, clearly later

[67] mason; of parish of St George: HB

[68] wife of John Broune brother of William Broune; she was still alive at this time and a member of the gild.

fol 5

Anno dni millimo cccc^{mo} octuagesimo

[69]*Names of the brethren of the gild of St Katherine virgin and martyr of the town or borough of Staunford in the said year appear below*

William Broune marchaunt

John Broune[70]

William Hikeham

Henry Cok

John Dakk

William Hawkes

Robert Yerdley

Laurence Gregory

John Yetson

William Fawkes

John Capron

Margaret Jeralde

Thomas Moreton

John Basse

William Godfrey

William Templer

Joan Ley

William Storeton

Laurence Mylton

John Clerk

Dom John Lyndesey

Dom Henry Clement

Dom John Brampton

William Dakk

Henry Sherp

John Muston

---

[69] The names of several of these 'old' members do not appear again and they may already have been dead in 1480 (like John Broune; see below); other 'old' members appear to have included Joan Clopton and Dom Robert Parnell (see fol 10d)

[70] I suspect that this refers to John Broune the father of William Broune who died in 1442. There is a JB glasier in Stamford at this time but it is unlikely to be this man. If this identification is correct, then this is a list of all the members of the gild, alive and dead. William Artikell had ceased to be a member of the Second Twelve by 1476. The name of John Broune the brother of William Browne, who died in 1476, and Agnes John Browne's wife (who was still living and a member of the gild) also occur on this page in a second column. The name of John Broune does not occur again but Agnes Broune continued as a member.

Robert Jerald
William Ravenell
Robert Straker
John atte Yates
John Plumber
William Artikell
John Parker
Richard Blogwyn
John Murdok
Geoffrey Warner
Thomas Carver
John Paknam
John Skevyngton
Richard Goldesworth
Robert Loryng
William Hebbes
Thomas Broune
Richard Bugden

John Broune[71] Agnes his wife
Richard Sapcote miles and Joan his wife
John Hill
Richard Forster[72] and Margaret his wife

fol 5d, 6 and 6d blank

fol 7
Anno dni m[mo] cccc[mo] lxxx[mo]

Acts of the gild of St Katherine virgin and martyr of the town of Staunford anno domini millimo cccc[mo] octuagesimo

---

[71] The addition of these four names in a separate column on the page is odd. For one thing, these are the only names which give the names of their wives; it is certainly not a list of new entrants. However, it is almost certain that the John B in this second column list is the brother of William Broune whose widow Agnes remained a member of the gild until she died in or about 1484 (fol 15). These four names have a marker beside them but they are in the same hand.

[72] this item represents the admission of a new member, for Forster paid his entry fines from 1481; see fol 8d; he was a royal servant and deputy butler of Boston; admitted to freedom of Stamford in this year, although he had already been MP for the town on several occasions since 1467. There was another Richard Forster ropemaker who was admitted to the freedom of the borough in 1479 but this gild member is almost certainly the MP and not the ropemaker.

Brethren newly admitted

sworn

George Chapman[73] with Elizabeth his wife

Christopher Broune[74]

William Wareyn[75]

Nicholas Vicary[76]

David Malpas

Robert Johnson

John Pykerell

Adam Arnold

John Honne

John Fissher

Thomas Croxton

M Richard Wermouth

John Billesby

Dom John Bothebrok Rector of Market Overton

Thomas Dynnyell

Robert Broune[77]

not sworn

M Richard Burton archdeacon of Worcester[78]

William Sutton[79]

Robert Parsons

Dna Elizabeth Tissington

Thomas Wheteley

William Smyth of Dodyngton

Henry Thorney

M Robert Grymston

Richard Armeston

---

[73] He heads the list as he is the Alderman of the borough in this year; see Rogers 2005

[74] the nephew of William Broune and son and heir of John Broune

[75] of Oakham draper or wool merchant; husband of Agnes daughter of John Broune brother of William Broune

[76] Steward of the the manor of Collyweston where Lord Cromwell had lived and built a house and later Margaret Beaufort mother of Henry VII lived; VCH *Northants* ii 553

[77] almost certainly the weaver and taxer in Stamford

[78] Archdeacon of Worcester; he succeeded John Burton in July 1479, resigned in 1483; Le Neve IV: 63; his inclusion in the gild members may indicate he is a member of the family of Burton of Tolthorpe by Stamford with which the Browne family had strong connections.

[79] William Sutton, leader of the Second Twelve, had died apparently in 1476, according to the Hall Book. There is however a later William Sutton in the gild.

sworn

[7] Dom William Jerald vicar of Castill Bitham

Dom Richard Dowce chaplain

fol 7d

Anno Domini 1480[80]

Stock (Catalla) of the same gild issued (deliberat') in the said year

Robert Yerdeley has xxs by pledge of Lawrence Gregory and he paid for
increment this year xviijd and it was reissued (*reliberantur*)[81] as before

John Dak has xiijs iiijd by pledge of William Hawkes; increment xijd; reissued

William Fawkes has vjs viijd by pledge of William Hebbes; increment vjd

William Hawkes has xxs by pledge of John Dak; increment xviijd

William Godfrey has xxs by pledge of William Templer; increment xviijd

William Templer has xxs by pledge of William Godfrey; increment xviijd

William Hebbes has vjs viijd by pledge of William Fawkes; increment vjd

John Hikson has xiijs iiijd by pledge of Henry Cok; increment xijd

Dna Agnes Broune has xxs by pledge of William Broune; increment xviijd

Arrears[82] owed to this day by John Basse xiijs iiijd

Arrears owed up to this day by dom John Capron chaplain vjs viijd

William Broune has xiijs iiijd by pledge of Henry Cok; increment xijd

Henry Cok has xiijs iiijd by pledge of William Broune; increment xijd

The said Robert Yerdeley has vjs viijd[83] by pledge of William Godfrey

William Godfrey has vjs viijd by pledge of Robert Yerdeley

fol 8

Anno domini 1480[84]

Election of Alderman and other officers

[8] The same day and year the community of this gild elected into the office of
Alderman for the coming year William Broune.

Item into the office of steward for the same year Henry Cok

---

[80] this unusually is written in Arabic numerals

[81] the fact that all these names come from the 'old members' and the use of the word '*reliberantur*'
suggest that this process of handing out stock to gild members had been in existence prior to the
refounding in 1480.

[82] This entry may indicate that these two persons were in arrears for increment from previous
years

[83] this and the next entry are almost certainly new issues of stock.

[84] in Arabic numerals

Item providers (*preordinatores*) of the feast Robert Yerdley and William [blank[85]]
Item into the office of bedell William Templer.

fol 8d

Anno dni 1481[86]

Acts of the gild of St Katherine virgin and martyr of the town of Staunford anno domini m^mo cccc^mo lxxxj^mo

Brethren newly admitted
John Been[87] with [blank] his wife is admitted into the fraternity and sworn; will
pay (sol[88]) for his entry fee [blank]

Entry payments (Ingress' solut')
[89]Richard Forster paid for his entry fee for this day (*ad hunc diem*) xxd
George Chapman paid for the same xxd
Christopher Broune xxd
William Wareyn xxd
Nicholas Vicary xxd
M Richard Wermouth xxd
John Billesby xxd
John Honne xxd
John Fissher xxd
Robert Johnson xxd
William Sutton xxd
Thomas Denyell xxd

Entry fines not paid
David Malpas owes for his entry of which he will pay nothing this year, but he
owes v[s][90]
+Thomas Croxton for the same[91]

---

85 almost certainly Templer
86 in Arabic numerals
87 see fol 10
88 it is not always clear whether the word 'sol' stands for 'paid' or 'will pay'. In this case, it means 'will pay' the usual entry fine of vjs viijd; the next year, on fol 12, he pays xxd and owes vs.
89 see above note 18
90 in other words, Malpas is excused payment this year and his debt is reduced to 5s. All these names are on the B list, so presumably all those on the A list had either fully paid their entry fee or were excused it.

Dom John Bothebrok Rector of Market Overton
Robert Broune
M Richard Burton
John Pykerell
Robert Parsons
Dna Elizabeth Tissington
Thomas Wheteley
William Smyth
+Henry Thorney
M Robert Grymston
+Richard Armeston
Dom William Jerald
+Dom Richard Dowce
Adam Arnold

folio 9

Anno dni m^{mo} cccc^{mo} lxxxj^{mo}

Stock of this gild the said year
Robert Yerdley[92] has xxs by pledge of Laurence Gregory; paid increment xviijd
and redelivered by by pledge of as before
John Dak has xiijs iiijd by pledge of William Hawkes; increment xijd ; stock
remains as before
William Fawkes vjs viijd by pledge of William Hebbes; increment vjd, redelivered
as before
William Hawkes has xxs by pledge of John Dak; increment xviijd, stock before
William Godfrey xxs by pledge of William Templer; increment xviijd, stock before
William Templer xxs by pledge of William Godfrey; increment xviijd, stock as
before
William Hebbes vjs viijd by pledge of William Fawkes; increment vjd, stock as
before
John Hikson xiijs iiijd by pledge of Henry Cok; increment xijd, stock as before
Dna Agnes Broune xxs by pledge of William Broune; increment xviijd, stock as
before
William Broune xiijs iiijd by pledge of Henry Cok; increment xijd; stock as before
Henry Cok xiijs iiijd by pledge of William Broune; increment xijd; stock as before

---

[91] no sums are listed apart from the first entry.
[92] all these names are on the 'old' members' list

Abovementioned Robert Yerdley has another vjs viijd by pledge of William Godfrey; paid increment vjd, stock remains as before

The same William Godfrey has another vjs viijd by pledge of Robert Yerdley; paid increment vjd, stock remains as before

Stock of the gild arrears and owed this year
John Basse xiijs iiijd which he owes and nothing to pay for this[93]
Dom John Capron vjs viijd which he owes and nothing to pay for this

Stock newly [given]
John Honne has newly by pledge of William Godfrey xiijs iiijd
William Godfrey by pledge of John Honne vjs viijd
Thomas Denyell by pledge of John Hikson iijs iiijd
John Been[94] by pledge of Robert Yerdley iijs iiijd

fol 9d

AD 1481[95]

Waxshote arrears this year[96]
John Pykerell owes for le waxshote this year iiijd
Adam Arnold iiijd
Dom John Bothebrok iiijd
M Richard Burton iiijd
Robert Parsons iiijd
Dna Elizabeth Tussington iiijd
Thomas Wheteley iiijd
William Smyth iiijd
Henry Thorney iiijd
M Robert Grymston iiijd
Richard Armeston iiijd
Dom William Jeralde vicar of Castilbitham iiijd

---

[93] this may mean he and his fellow stock holder are excused increment this year or for all time; they continued to be charged for the stock sum but did not pay any increment, see below fol 11 etc. Basse had permission to pay the capital by instalments.

[94] Been was admitted at this gild meeting; he is the only person among the new entrants to receive stock. All the outstanding stock are in the hands of 'old' members and all the new grants of stock go to 'old' members except for Been. No-one from the new members obtains stock.

[95] in Arabic numerals

[96] all these names come from the 'new' members; these thirteen were presumably absent or otherwise did not pay their first waxshot.

Dom Richard Dowce iiijd

[9] The same day and year remains in hands of William Broune Alderman xvjd

[10] Election of officers
Same day and year the commons of the same gild elected as Alderman for the
coming year William Broune as before
steward John Hikson newly for this year
William Templer and John Honne 'garners[97]' for this year
And William Templer bedell for the same year

Fol 10

**Staunford: Acts of the gild of St Katherine virgin Anno Domini millimo
ccccmo lxxxijdo**

Entry fines
Richard Forster paid for his entry up to this day xxd And he owes iijs iiijd
George Chapman paid nothing for this day – and he owes vs
Christopher Broune for this day iijs iiijd – owes iijs iiijd
William Wareyn iijs iiijd – owes iijs iiijd
Nicholas Vicary for the same [blank]
M Richard Wermouth paid for ij years iijs iiijd - and owes iijs iiijd
John Billesby for the same [blank]
John Honne paid xxd - owes iijs iiijd
John Fissher paid for this day xxd - owes iijs iiijd
Robert Johnson paid for this day xxd - owes iijs iiijd
William Sutton paid for this day for ij years iijs iiijd - and owes iijs iiijd
Thomas Danyell paid for this day xxd - and owes iijs iiijd
David Malpas for the same
Dom John Bothbroke Rector of Market Overton paid for ij years iijs iiijd. And
owes iijs iiijd
Robert Broune for the same
M Richard Burton [blank]
John Pykerell paid for ij years iijs iiijd - and owes iijs iiijd
(M Robert Grymston *del*)
Robert Parsons for the same

---

[97] the term is for garrison provisioners

Brethren newly admitted

[8] M Robert Grymston admitted into the fraternity of the gild and will pay for his entry vjs viijd

Dom Edward Hoton vicar of Ryall admitted vjs viijd

Thomas Philip and Katherine his wife vjs viijd

M Thomas Hikeham vjs viijd

John Stede and Anabel vjs viijd

John Wykes and Alice vjs viijd

Geoffrey Hampton and Agnes vjs viijd

Robert Goldsmyth and Margaret vjs viijd

John Moreys and Elizabeth vjs viijd

John Gebon and Margaret vjs viijd

Richard Hert vjs viijd

The said John Been[98] and Joan vjs viijd

fol 10d

Waxshote in above year

William Broune paid this day for lights iiijd

Christopher Broune for the same iiijd

David Malpas iiijd

Dom William Jerald iiijd

George Chapman iiijd

Henry Cok iiijd

John Yetson iiijd

William Hawkes iiijd

Dom Robert Parnell[99] ijd

Dna anachorita[100] ijd

John Fissher iiijd

Robert Broune wever iiijd

Thomas Danyell iiijd

William Templer iiijd

Joan Clopton[101] ijd

John Honne iiijd

---

[98] Been is recorded as newly admitted in 1481 with his (unnamed) wife, see fol 8d

[99] not in either 'old' or 'new' members

[100] The anchoress has not been mentioned in any previous list; it would seem that she is Margaret Jeralde since her name is missing from this list. See introduction

[101] her name is not included among the 'old' members or the 'new' members unless she is the Joan Ley mentioned among the 'old' members having remarried.

William Godfrey iiijd
M Richard Wermouth ijd
Robert Johnson iiijd
John Been iiijd
William Faux iiijd
Robert Yerdley ijd
William Hebbes iiijd
John Billesby iiijd
Dom John Bothbroke Rector of Market Overton ijd
Relict of John Pykerell ijd
Nicholas Vicary iiijd
William Hikeham ijd
William Wareyn iiijd
William Sutton iiijd

Summa [blank]

The same day and year William Templer bidell by his account made in the feast of St Katherine virgin [25 November], all things reckoned, the same William exceeded vjs vjd which were assigned to him from the rents of principal tenements [*prin^lis ten't*]; and quit

fol 11

Stock of the said gild this year
Robert Yerdley has xxs by pledge of Laurence Gregory; nothing paid
John Dak has xiijs iiijd by pledge of William Hawkes; paid increment xijd ; stock remains with him as before
William Fawkes vjs viijd by pledge of William Hebbes; increment vjd; stock as before
William Hawkes has xxs by pledge of John Dak; increment xviijd; stock as before
William Godfrey xxs by pledge of William Templer; increment xviijd; stock as before
William Templer xxs by pledge of William Godfrey; increment xviijd; stock as before
William Hebbes vjs viijd by pledge of William Fawkes; increment vjd; stock as before
John Hikson xiijs iiijd by pledge of Henry Cok; increment xijd; stock as before
Dna Agnes Broune xxs by pledge of William Broune

William Broune xiijs iiijd by pledge of Henry Cok; paid increment xijd; And stock in exchequer. (And newly delivered to same William as before *ins*)

Henry Cok xiijs iiijd by pledge of William Broune; paid increment xijd; And stock remains in exchequer. (And newly delivered to same Henry as before *ins*)

Abovementioned Robert Yerdley has another vjs viijd by pledge of William Godfrey; paid increment vjd; stock as before

William Godfrey has another vjs viijd by pledge of Robert Yerdley; increment vjd; stock as before

John Honne xiijs iiijd by pledge of William Godfrey; increment xijd; stock as before

William Godfrey has vjs viijd by pledge of John Honne; increment vjd; stock as before

Thomas Danyell iijs iiijd by pledge of John Hikson; increment iijd; stock as before

John Been iijs iiijd by pledge of Robert Yerdley; increment iijd; stock as before

[102]John Basse xiijs iiijd which he owes and John paid nothing of this etc

Dom John Capron vjs viijd and John paid nothing of this etc

The same day and year remains clear in hands of John Hikson steward on his account viijs ijd

fol 11d

[*line through whole page*]

This is cancelled here because it is more conveniently in the following year[103].

Account of the steward

The day and year below (*infrascript*) John Yetson steward of the gild accounted for all the issues of his office; of which, all accounts and allowances included, the same steward for this day is in surplus vjs iijd which he received in the exchequer on this account. And he was discharged (*recessum est*) quit.

Account of the providers for the feast.

The same day and year John Honne and William Templer providers for the feast accounted for the expenses incurred by them as appears by a bill of particulars shown up to this time on his [sic] account xxxvijs which were received in the exchequer. And quit.

---

[102] this and the next line have been squeezed in
[103] on folio 13d

The same day and year there remains in the hands of John Yetson steward   vjs viijd

fol 12

Staunford: Acts of the gild of St Katherine virgin there Anno Domini millimo cccc^{mo} lxxxiij°

Entries of brethren (confratr')
Richard Forster paid for his entry up to this day xxd. And he owes xxd
George Chapman paid nothing for this day – thus he owes as before vs
Christopher Broune nothing for this day – owes as before iijs iiijd
William Wareyn nothing – owes as before iijs iiijd
Nicholas Vicary nothing – thus owes as before vs
M Richard Wermouth paid to this day xxd. And owes xxd
John Billesby nothing to this day – thus owes as before vs
John Honne paid for this day xxd. And owes xxd
John Fissher nothing for this day. Thus owes iijs iiijd
Robert Johnson paid for this day xxd. And owes xxd
William Sutton paid xxd And owes xxd
Thomas Denyell paid nothing for this day. Thus owes iijs iiijd
David Malpas nothing. Thus owes as before vjs viijd
Dom John Bothbroke paid xxd. And owes xxd
M Richard Burton archdeacon of Worcester nothing for this day. Thus owes vjs viijd
John Pykerell paid nothing this day. Thus owes iijs iiijd
Robert Parsons nothing for this day. This owes as before vjs viijd
M Robert Grymston xxd. And owes vs
Dom Edward Hoton vicar of Ryall xxd. And owes vs
Thomas Philip nothing for this day. Thus owes vjs viijd
M Thomas Hikeham nothing. Thus owes vjs viijd
John Stede paid nothing. Thus owes as before vjs viijd
John Wykes paid xxd. And owes vs
Geoffrey Hampton nothing. Thus owes vjs viijd
Robert Goldsmyth nothing. Thus owes vjs viijd
John Moreys xxd. And owes vs
John Gebon xxd. And owes vs
Richard Hert xxd. And owes vs
John Been xxd. And owes vs.

Brethren newly admitted

John Nele[104] and Agnes his wife were admitted into the fraternity etc and they will
   pay for their entry vjs viijd

John Palmer and Margery his wife vjs viijd

Thomas Clopton and Joan his wife vjs viijd

Nicholas Parker and Agnes his wife vjs viijd

Robert Broune[105] wever and Alice his wife were admitted; paid for this day xxd
   and owes vs.

fol 12d

Anno dni millimo cccc° lxxxiij°

Waxshote

William Broune paid for the maintenance of the lights this year iiijd

Christopher Broune for the same iiijd

David Malpas armiger iiijd

Dom William Jerald iiijd for two years

Elizabeth relict of George Chapman ijd

Henry Cok iiijd

John Yetson iiijd

William Hawkes iiijd

Dom Robert Parnell ijd

Dna anchoress (*anachorita*) ijd

John Fisher iiijd

Robert Broune wever iiijd

Thomas Danyell iiijd

William Templer iiijd

Joan Clopton ijd

John Honne iiijd

William Godfrey iiijd

M Richard Wermouth ijd

Robert Johnson iiijd

John Been iiijd

---

[104] This would seem to be the John Nele junior barbour admitted to the freedom of the town in
1480; a John Nele councillor left the First Twelve in 1481 according to the Hall Book. The gild
member however was called 'John Nele senior' in the register from 1484 but there is no sign of
another JN being admitted to the gild. This John Nele senior is recorded in the gild until 1491.
[105] this is odd; Robert Broune is among the list of new members in 1480 and as RB wever paid
waxshot in 1482

William Faux iiijd

Robert Yerdley ijd

William (Hawkes *del*) (Hebbes *ins*) iiijd

John Billesby iiijd

Dom John Bothbroke Rector of Market Overton ijd

M Richard Burton archdeacon of Worcester ijd

Alice relict of John Pykerell ijd

Nicholas Vicary iiijd

William Hikeham ijd

William Wareyn iiijd

William Sutton iiijd

M Robert Grymston ijd

Dom Edward Hoton ijd

Thomas Philip iiijd

M Thomas Hikeham ijd

John Stede iiijd

John Wykes iiijd

Geoffrey Hampton iiijd

Robert Goldsmyth iiijd

John Moreys iiijd

John Gebon iiijd

Richard Hert iiijd

John Been iiijd

fol 13

Stock of the said gild in the above year

Robert Yerdley has xxs by pledge of Laurence Gregory which he paid with increment; and it was redelivered as before

The said Robert has another [*als*] vjs viijd by pledge of William Godfrey which he paid with increment; redelivered as before

John Dak has xiijs iiijd by pledge of William Hawkes; paid with increment etc; redelivered as before

William Fawkes vjs viijd by pledge of William Hebbes; paid increment

William Hawkes has xxs by pledge of John Dak; paid increment by by pledge of as before

William Godfrey xxs by pledge of William Templer; increment by by pledge of as before

The same William Godfrey vjs viijd by pledge of Robert Yerdley; increment, by pledge of as before

The same William Godfrey vjs viijd by pledge of John Honne; increment, by pledge of as before

William Templer xxs by pledge of William Godfrey; increment, by pledge of as before

William Hebbes vjs viijd by pledge of William Fawkes; increment, by pledge of as before

John Yetson xiijs iiijd by pledge of Henry Cok; increment, by pledge of as before

Dna Agnes Broune widow xxs by pledge of William Broune; increment, by pledge of as before

William Broune xiijs iiijd by pledge of Henry Cok; increment, by pledge of as before

Henry Cok xiijs iiijd by pledge of William Broune; increment

John Honne xiijs iiijd by pledge of William Godfrey; increment

Thomas Danyell iijs iiijd by pledge of John Yetson; paid in similar fashion with increment, by pledge of as before

John Been iijs iiijd by pledge of Robert Yerdley; increment, by pledge of as before

John Basse xiijs iiijd; and John paid nothing of this etc; and the said John sought permission to pay the said stock namely annually xxd until it was paid off (*petet iudicias ad sol catall predict etc videlicet annuatim xxd quousque persoluit etc*)

Dom John Capron vjs viijd and John paid nothing of this etc – *persoluit*[106]

fol 13d

Accounts of the steward

On 28th July[107] of the year above [1483], John Yetson the steward of the gild accounted for the issues of his office for the past year, and all things reckoned, the said steward has a surplus and exceeds vjs iiijd which he received in the exchequer. And he was discharged quit.

Account of the providers for the feast

The same day and year John Honne and William Templer providers for the feast accounted for certain expenses incurred by them during the past year, as appears by bills of certain particulars on their account then and shown there, xxxvijs which they received in the exchequer, and were discharged quit.

---

[106] this almost certainly means that Capron had the same permission as Basse

[107] this is a very early date for an accounting year which ran from 25 November 1482 to 25 November 1483.

Remains in the hands of John Yetson steward vjs viijd

There remains in the exchequer this day and year vjs viijd which were delivered then and there by the alderman and confraters to John Yetson steward on his account for which he will render account elsewhere.

fol 14

Staunford Acts of the gild of St Katherine virgin in the second year of the reign of King Richard III and anno dni millimo cccc° lxxxiiij°

Entry fines

Richard Forster owes for his entry for this day xxd which he paid this year. And quit

Elizabeth Chapman owes vs of which she paid this day iijs iiijd and she owes xxd

Christopher Broune iijs iiijd which he paid this day and thus quit

William Wareyn iijs iiijd which paid this day and thus quit

Nicholas Vicary vs of which he paid this day xxdid [sic]. And owes iijs iiijd

M Richard Wermouth xxd which paid this day and is quit of this

John Billesby vs of which paid this day (xxd *del*) (iijs iiijd *ins*) And thus owes (iijs iiijd *del*) xxd

John Honne xxd (nil this day [illeg] *del*) which he paid and thus quit

John Fissher iijs iiijd He paid nothing this day.

Robert Johnson xxd which paid And thus quit

William Sutton xxd which paid and thus quit

Thomas Denyell iijs iiijd of which he paid this day xxd And owes xxd

David Malpas armiger for the same vjs viijd

Dom John Bothbroke xxd which paid this day and thus quit

M Richard Burton archdeacon of Worcester owes for the same vjs viijd

Alice formerly relict [sic] of John Pykerell iijs iiijd which paid this day and thus quit

(Richard Parsons vjs viijd *del*)

M Robert Grymston vs paid xxd owes iijs iiijd

Dom Edward Hoton vs paid xxd – owes iijs iiijd

Thomas Philip vjs viijd paid iijs iiijd - owes iijs iiijd

M Thomas Hikeham vjs viijd paid xxd owes vs

John Wykes vs paid xxd owes iijs iiijd

Geoffrey Hampston vjs viijd paid iijs iiijd owes iijs iiijd

John Moreys vs paid xxd owes iijs iiijd

John Gebon vs. John paid nothing (*persol'*)

Richard Hert vs paid xxd owes iijs iiijd

John Been' vs paid xxd owes iijs iiijd
Dom William Jerald paid for the same for ij years iijs iiijd – owes (xiijs iiijd *del*) xxd
John Stede paid xxd for one year – owes vs
John Nele sen paid this day xxd and owes vs
John Palmer paid xxd and owes vs
Thomas Clopton paid xxd and owes vs
Nicholas Parker paid xxd and owes vs
Robert Broune wever paid xxd and owes (vs *del*) iijs iiijd

Brethren newly admitted
Dom Robert Taillour Rector of Great Casterton was admitted into the fraternity
    of this gild and he will pay for his entry iiij years [according to] custom vjs viijd
Richard Chambre and Alice his wife admitted will pay vjs viijd
Andrew Stotard and Joan his wife vjs viijd
John Whippe and Matilda his wife vjs viijd
Alice Bradmedewe[108] widow for the same admission will pay vjs viijd

fol 14d

Anno dni millimo cccc° lxxxiiij°

Waxshote
William Broune merchaunt paid for the maintenance of the lights this year iiijd
Christopher Broune for the same iiijd
David Malpas armiger for the same owes for iiij years which he paid and is quit
Dom William Jerald ijd
Elizabeth Chapman widow ijd
Henry Cok iiijd
John Yetson iiijd
William Hawkes iiijd
Dom Robert Parnell ijd
Dna anchoress ijd
John Fisher iiijd
Robert Broune wever iiijd
Thomas Denyell iiijd
William Templer iiijd
Joan Clopton widow ijd
John Honne iiijd

---

[108] William Broune's sister; see her brass

William Godfrey iiijd
M Richard Wermouth ijd
Robert Johnson iiijd
John Been' iiijd
William Faux iiijd
Robert Yerdley iiijd
William Hebbes ijd
John Billesby iiijd
Dom John Bothbroke Rector of Market Overton ijd
M Richard Burton archdeacon of Worcester [blank]
Alice formerly wife of John Pykerell ijd
Nicholas Vicary iiijd
William Hikeham ijd
William Wareyn iiijd
William Sutton iiijd
M Robert Grymston ijd
Dom Edward Hoton vicar of Ryall ijd
Thomas Philip iiijd
M Thomas Hikeham ijd
John Wykes ijd
Geoffrey Hampton iiijd
Robert Goldsmyth iiijd
John Moreys iiijd
John Gebon iiijd
Richard Hert ijd
(John Been for the same *del*) Richard Forster for the same iiijd
John Nele sen iiijd
John Palmer iiijd
Thomas Clopton iiijd
Nicholas Parker iiijd

fol 15

Stock of this gild in the said year
Robert Yerdley has xxs by pledge of Laurence Gregory
The said Robert has another vjs viiijd by pledge of William Godfrey
John Dak has xiijs iiijd by pledge of William Hawkes; paid with increment xijd
  etc; redelivered by by pledge of as before
William Fawkes vjs viiijd by pledge of William Hebbes

William Hawkes has xxs by pledge of John Dak; paid increment xviijd; redelivered as before

William Godfrey xxs by pledge of William Templer

The same William Godfrey vjs viijd by pledge of Robert Yerdley

The same William Godfrey vjs viijd by pledge of John Honne

William Templer xxs by pledge of William Godfrey; increment xviijd; redelivered

William Hebbes vjs viijd by pledge of William Fawkes of which he paid for increment vjd; redelivered

John Yetson xiijs iiijd by pledge of Henry Cok; increment xijd; redelivered

Dna Agnes Broune widow xxs by pledge of William Broune which she paid with increment xviijd and remains in the exchequer and thus she is quit

William Broune xiijs iiijd by pledge of Henry Cok; increment xijd; redelivered by by pledge of

Henry Cok xiijs iiijd by pledge of William Broune; increment xijd; redelivered

John Honne xiijs iiijd by pledge of William Godfrey; increment xijd; redelivered

Thomas Denyell iijs iiijd by pledge of John Yetson; increment iijd; redelivered

John Been' iijs iiijd by pledge of Robert Yerdley

John Basse xiijs iiijd; and permission was granted to him to pay annually xxd or such greater sum until fully paid (*persoluit*) etc

Dom John Capron has vjs viijd

fol 15d

Account of providers for the feast

Monday vigil of St Andrew Apostle [29 November] anno domini millimo cccc° lxxxiiij° John Honne and William Templer accounted for certain expenses of the feast made by them in the past year namely in the time of this account as appears by bills of such particulars (parcellas) shown at this time xxviijs xd which they received in the exchequer – and quit

The same day and year John Yetson *steward of the gild* accounted for the issues of his office for the past year accounting for all accounts etc; was discharged quit

Remainder. The same day and year there remains in the exchequer iij li ixs xd

Stock newly delivered

Of which there was delivered to John Moreys by pledge of John Yetson in stock (*catalla*) vjs viijd

Remainder

And thus there remains in the exchequer lxiijs ijd in the hands of John Yetson on his account

Election of officers

[11] The same day and year William Broune was elected into the office of Alderman for the coming year as before

Item John Yetson into the office of steward as before

Item William Templer and Thomas Denyell providers for the feast

And William Templer into the office of bedell as before

fol 16

Staunford: Acts of the gild of St Katherine virgin and martyr there the first year of the reign of king Henry VII and anno domini millimo cccc⁰ lxxxv^to

Entry fines

Elizabeth Chapman owes for her entry this day xxd which she paid and is quit

Nicholas Vicars owes for same iijs iiijd

John Billesby xxd which paid and is quit

John Fisher iijs iiijd paid xxd and owes xxd

Thomas Dynyell xxd which he paid this day and is quit

David Malpas armiger owes for same vjs viijd – he paid nothing this day

M Richard Burton archdeacon of Worcester vjs viijd which paid and is quit

M Robert Grymston iijs iiijd paid this day xxd and owes xxd

Dom Edward Hoton iijs iiijd

Thomas Philipp iijs iiijd paid xxd and owes xxd

M Thomas Hikeham vs paid this day (xxd *del*) (iijs iiijd *ins*) and owes (iijs iiijd *del*) xxd

John Wiks iijs iiijd

Geoffrey Hampton iijs iiijd paid xxd and owes xxd

John Mores iijs iiijd

John Gebon vs

Richard Harte iijs iiijd paid xxd and owes xxd

John Been' iijs iiijd

Dom William Jerald xxd

John Stede vs paid xxd and owes iijs iiijd

John Nele sen vs paid xxd and owes iijs iiijd

John Palmer vs paid xxd and owes iijs iiijd

Thomas Clopton vs paid xxd and owes iijs iiijd

Nicholas Parker vs paid (xxd and owes *del*) (nil *ins*)

Rob Broune wever iijs iiijd paid xxd and owes xxd

Dom Robert Taylour vjs viijd this day paid xxd and owes vs

Richard Chambre vjs viijd this day paid xxd and owes vs

Andrew Stodard vjs viijd paid this day xxd and owes vs

John Whippe vjs viijd this day paid xxd and owes vs

Alice Bradmedewe widow vjs viijd she paid this day xxd and owes vs

Admission of new brethren

Thomas Stable and Agnes his wife were admitted into the fraternity of this gild and he will pay for his entry for four years as by custom vjs viijd

John Washingburgh and Alice his wife in similar fashion admitted, will pay vjs viijd

(Robert *ins*) Margaret Skynner (and Margaret his wife *ins*)[109] will pay for the same vjs viijd

fol 16d

anno dni millimo cccc^mo lxxxv^to

Waxshote

William Broune marchaunte paid for the maintenance of the lights this year iiijd

Christopher Broune paid iiijd

David Malpas armiger iiijd

Dom William Jerald ijd

Elizabeth Chapman ijd

Henry Cock iiijd

John Yetson iiijd

William Hawkes iiijd

Dom Robert Pernell ijd

Dna anchoress ijd

John Fisher iiijd

Robert Broune wever iiijd

Thomas Dynyell iiijd

William Templer iiijd

Joan Clopton widow ijd

John Honne iiijd

William Godfrey iiijd

---

[109] Robert Skynner had died in 1481, Hall Book p 88; in 1485, Margaret his widow now registered him as a member of the gild. The entry was first written as Margaret Skynner and later amended to read Robert Skynner and Margaret his wife.

M Richard Warmouth ijd
Robert Johnson iiijd
John Been' (ijd *del*) nil
William Faux ijd
Robert Yerdley iiijd
William Hebbes ijd
John Billesbye iiijd
Dom John Bothbroke Rector of Market Overton ijd
M Richard Burton archdeacon of Worcester ijd
Alice formerly wife of John Pikerell ijd
Nicholas Vicars iiijd
William Hikeham ijd
William Waryn iiijd
William Sutton iiijd
M Robert Grymston ijd
Dom Edward Hoton vicar of Ryall ijd
Thomas Philipp iiijd
M Thomas Hikeham ijd
John Wiks iiijd
Geoffrey Hampton iiijd
Robert Goldsmyth iiijd
John Moreys iiijd
John Gebon iiijd
Richard Harte ijd
Richard Forster iiijd
John Nele senior iiijd
John Palmer iiijd
Thomas Clopton iiijd
Nicholas Parker iiijd
John Stede iiijd
Dom Robert Tailyour iiijd
Richard Chambre iiijd
Andrew Stodard iiijd
John Whippe iiijd
Alice Bradmedewe widow ijd
John Basse ijd
John Dacke iiijd

fol 17

Stock of the said gild the above year

Robert Yerdley has xxs by pledge of Laurence Gregory – paid for increment xviijd and stock remains as before

The said Robert has another vjs viijd by pledge of William Godfrey – paid increment vjd and stock remains as before

John Dak has xiijs iiijd by pledge of William Hawkes; which paid with increment xijd and redelivered as before

William Fawkes vjs viijd by pledge of William Hebbes of which he paid increment vjd and stock remains by by pledge of as before

William Hawkes has xxs by pledge of John Dak which he paid with increment xviijd and redelivered as before

William Godfrey xxs by pledge of William Templer which said William Templer found by pledge of John Hickson to pay the said xxs for three years next following, each year vjs viijd without increment

The same William Godfrey vjs viijd by pledge of Robert Yerdley

The same William Godfrey vjs viijd by pledge of John Honne

William Templer has xxs by pledge of William Godfrey which paid with increment and it remains in the exchequer. Quit

William Hebbes vjs viijd by pledge of William Fawkes; paid increment vjd; redelivered by by pledge of as before

John Yetson has (vjs viijd *del*) (xiijs iiijd *ins*) by pledge of Henry Cock which paid with increment xijd. And remains in exchequer. Quit

William Broune has xiijs iiijd by pledge of Henry Cok which paid with increment xijd and quit; and remains in exchequer.

Henry Cock has xiijs iiijd by pledge of William Broune which paid with increment xijd. And quit; and remains in exchequer.

John Honne has xiijs iiijd by pledge of William Godfrey

Thomas Dynnyell has iijs iiijd by pledge of John Yetson; paid increment iijd. And redelivered as before

John Been iijs iiijd by pledge of Robert Yerdley; paid for increment ijd and owes for increment jd

John Basse xiijs iiijd; and permission was granted to him to pay annually xxd and he paid xxd this year. And owes xjs viijd

Dom John Capron has vjs viijd

John Moreys has vjs viijd by pledge of John Hickson which paid and is quit

John Yetson steward had on his last account lxiijs ijd which he paid with increment and remains in exchequer. And thus he is quit

fol 17d

Account of providers for the feast

Sunday 26 November 1485 (*anno domini m^mo cccc^mo lxxxv^o*), William Templer and Thomas Dynyell [providers] for the feast accounted for certain expenses incurred by them for the past year, namely in the time of this account as appears by a bill of such particulars shown at this time xxixs iijd ob which they received in the exchequer. And quit

Account of the steward

The same day and year John Yetson steward of the gild accounted for the issues of his office for the last year all accounts and allowances included there iijs vijd which he received in the exchequer and was discharged quit

Remainder

The same day and year there remains in the exchequer viij li xiijs iiijd

Stock newly delivered

Of which delivered to William Templer by pledge of Henry Cok and John Palmer xls

Item delivered to Henry Cock by pledge of John Yetson xls

Item delivered to Andrew Stoderd nil

Item delivered to John Yetson by pledge of Henry Cock xls

Item delivered to John Fisher by pledge of John Yetson xiijs iiijd

Item delivered to John Stede then Alderman of the town by pledge of Henry Cock xls

Election of officers

[12] The same day and year William Broune was elected Alderman for the coming year as before

Item John Yetson steward as before

Item Thomas Dynyell and John Fisher providers for the feast

Item William Fawks[110] bedell as before

---

[110] It would seem that the phrase 'as before' (*ut prius*) in this case is an error, for William Templer was bedell before this election, fol 15.

fol 18

Staunford: Acts of the gild of St Katherine virgin and martyr anno domini millimo cccc° lxxxvj° and second year of the reign of king Henry VII

[no heading: Entry fines]

Nicholas Vicars owes for his entry fine to this day iijs iiijd

John Fissher owes for the same xxd which he paid this day and thus he is quit

David Malpas armiger vjs viijd

M Robert Grymston xxd which paid and is quit of this

Dom Edward Hoton vicar of Ryall owes iijs iiijd

Thomas Philip owes xxd which paid and is quit of this

M Thomas Hikeham xxd which paid, and is quit of this

John Wykes iijs iiijd

Geoffrey Hampton xxd which paid for this day and is quit

John (Wykes owes for the same *del*) Moreys owes for the same iijs iiijd

John Gebon vs

Richard Hert xxd which paid for this day and is quit

John Been' iijs iiijd (*ins in another hand* paid entry iijd)

Dom William Jerald xxd

John Stede iijs iiijd of which paid xxd and owes xxd

John Nele sen iijs iiijd of which paid xxd and owes xxd

John Palmer iijs iiijd of which paid xxd and owes xxd

Thomas Clopton iijs iiijd of which paid xxd and owes xxd

Nicholas Parker owes for the same vs of which he paid iijs iiijd and he owes xxd

Robert Broune wever owes xxd which paid etc and is quit

Dom Robert Tailour vs

Andrew Stotard vs paid xxd and owes iijs iiijd

John Whip owes vs paid xxd and owes iijs iiijd

Alice Bradmedewe widow vs paid xxd and owes iijs iiijd

Thomas Stable vjs viijd of which paid xxd and owes for this day vs

John Wasshingburgh vjs viijd paid xxd and h owes vs

Margaret Skynner widow vjs viijd of which paid xxd and owes vs

Brethren newly admitted

The same day and year Humfrey Coton and Agnes his wife were admitted into the confraternity of this gild and sworn; they will pay for this entry vjs viijd

Item Thomas Pernell and Joan his wife admitted; will pay etc vjs viijd

Item William Clerk and Margaret his wife similarly admitted; will pay vjs viijd

Election of officers

[13] The same day and year the commons elected into the office of Alderman William Broune as before.

Item into the office of steward John Yetson as before

Item into the office of providers of the entertainment (*conviv*) John Fissher as before and John Palmer new (*de novo*)

fol 18d

Waxshot anno dni millimo cccc^mo lxxxvj^o

William Broune merchant of the Calais Staple paid for the maintenance of the wax and lights this year iiijd

David Malpas armiger iiijd

Dom William Jerald ijd

Elizabeth Chapman ijd

Henry Cokk iiijd

John Yetson iiijd

William Hawkes iiijd

Dom Robert Parnell ijd

Dna anchoress ijd

John Fissher iiijd

Robert Broune wever iiijd

Thomas Dynyell iiijd

William Templer iiijd

Joan Clopton widow ijd

John Honne iiijd

William Godfrey baker iiijd

M Richard Wermouth ijd

Robert Johnson iiijd

John Been' iiijd

William Fawkes ijd

Robert Yerdley iiijd

William Hebbes iiijd

John Billesby iiijd

Dom John Bothbroke Rector of Market Overton ijd

M Richard Burton archdeacon of Worcester ijd

Alice formerly wife of John Pykerell ijd

Nicholas Vicars iiijd

William Hikeham ijd

William Wareyn iiijd

William Sutton iiijd

M Robert Grymston ijd

Dom Edward Hoton vicar of Ryall ijd

Thomas Philip iiijd

M Thomas Hikeham ijd

John Wykes ijd

Geoffrey Hampton iiijd

Robert Goldsmyth (mort *ins*) iiijd

John Moreys iiijd

John Gebon iiijd

Richard Hert (mort *ins*) iiijd

Richard Forster iiijd

John Nele senior iiijd

John Palmer iiijd

fol 19

John Stede paid maintenance of wax iiijd

Thomas Clopton iiijd

Nicholas Parker ijd

Dom Robert Tailour

Richard Chambre

Andrew Stotard iiijd

John Whipp iiijd

Alice Bradmedewe widow ijd

John Basse ijd

John Dakke iiijd

Stock of the said gild the above year

Robert Yerdley has xxs by pledge of Laurence Gregory – paid nothing

The said Robert has vjs viijd by pledge of William Godfrey – paid nothing

John Dak has xiijs iiijd by pledge of William Hawkes; of which he paid this day iijs iiijd – and owes xs. And for this he sought permission to pay the said xs by by pledge of aforesaid by means of the salary of the chaplain quarterly by equal portions before the feast of St Katherine virgin next following.

William Fawkes vjs viijd by pledge of William Hebbes of which he paid nothing this day but he has permission to pay annually xxd in issues of the office of bedell of the gild[111] until it shall have been fully paid.

---

[111] i.e. he will serve without payment until the said sum is paid

William Hawkes has xxs by pledge of John Dak of which he paid for increment for this day ixd; and he has permission to pay to the steward of the gild the said stock in support of the chaplain quarterly by equal portions before the feast of St Katherine next.

William Godfrey has xxs by pledge of William Templer And the said William Templer with the consent of the Alderman and brethren (*confratres*) etc and by pledge of John Yetson has permission to pay the said stock in the three years immediately following as appears in the Acts of the next preceding year[112] in equal portions. Of which he paid this day vjs viijd for one year. And he owes xiijs iiijd.

The same William Godfrey has vjs viijd by pledge of Robert Yerdley – paid nothing

The same William Godfrey has vjs viijd by pledge of John Honne which this John the said by pledge of has for his stock by pledge of the same William Godfrey xiijs iiijd ex gratia the Alderman with the consent of all the confratres has permission for all the aforesaid stock to be paid in support of the chaplain of the said gild namely each quarter of the year ijs vjd until the total of xxs of the said stock shall have been fully paid

William Hebbes has vjs viijd by pledge of William Fawkes – paid nothing

Thomas Dynnyell has iijs iiijd by pledge of John Yetson; paid increment iijd. And stock remains with the same Thomas by by pledge of as before

John Been' iijs iiijd by pledge of of Robert Yerdley – John paid nothing this day etc

John Basse xjs viijd; and permission was granted to him to pay annually xxd as in the preceding year

Dom John Capron has vjs viijd – he paid nothing this day

fol 19d

Stock for the same year millimo cccc° lxxxvj°

William Templer has stock of the same gild (xls *ins*) newly delivered by pledge of Henry Cok and John Palmer. Of which he paid for increment iijs. And the stock remains with the same William as before.

Henry Cok similarly has xls by pledge of John Yetson; of which he paid for increment iijs this day; and the stock remains as before

John Yetson has xls by pledge of Henry Cok of which paid for this day iijs increment. And stock remains in the hands of (*penes*) the same John as before

John Fissher has by pledge of John Yetson xiijs iiijd of which paid increment xijd. And stock remains by the said by pledge of as before

---

[112] this is evidence that the accounts often left spaces to be filled in at a later day

John Stede has in similar fashion by pledge of Henry Cok xls of which paid increment iijs. And stock remains as before.

Account of the providers for the feast

Thomas Dynnyell and John Fissher providers for the feast of this gild accounted for certain expenses incurred by them in the time of this account as can be more fully read in certain bills of these matters shown on his [sic] account and allowed xxviijs iiijd which they have received on the said account in the exchequer and were discharged quit

Account of steward

The abovesaid day and year John Yetson steward of the said gild accounted for such issues of his office for the past year, all accounts and allowances included, the same accountant by his bills shown on this account was in surplus xxvs ob which immediately he received in the exchequer. And was discharged quit

New Stock

The same day and year there remains in the hands of John Yetson the said steward in stock of the same gild delivered to him by the Alderman and confratres newly in the exchequer xxixs

fol 20

Staunford: Acts of the gild of St Katherine virgin and martyr anno dni millimo cccc° lxxxvij° and the third year of the reign of king Henry VII

Entries

Nicholas Vicars owes for his entry fine iijs iiijd
David Malpas armiger owes for same vjs viijd
Dom Edward Hoton vicar of Ryall iijs iiijd
John Wykes ijs iiijd
John Moreys iijs iiijd
John Gebon vs
John Been' iijs iiijd
Dom William Jerald xxd
John Stede xxd
John Nele owes xxd which paid this day xxd and quit
John Palmer xxd which paid and thus quit
Thomas Clopton xxd which paid and is quit
Nicholas Parker xxd which paid thus quit

Dom Robert Tailour vs

Richard Chambre vs

Andrew Stotard iijs iiijd of which paid this day xxd and owes xxd; paid and quit[113]

John Whippe owes iijs iiijd paid xxd and owes xxd; paid and quit

Alice Bradmedewe widow iijs iiijd which she paid[114] in the year following and quit

Thomas Stable vs

John Wasshingburgh vs of which paid this day xxd and he owes xld

Margaret Skynner widow vs paid xxd and owes xld

Humfrey Coton vjs viijd paid xxd and owes vs

Thomas Parnell vjs viijd paid xxd and owes vs

William Clerk vjs viijd paid xxd and owes vs

fol 20d

Waxshot anno domini millimo cccc^{mo} lxxxvij^o

William Broune merchant of the Calais Staple Alderman of this gild paid for the
  maintenance of the waxlights (ciriorum) this year iiijd

David Malpas armiger iiijd

Dom William Jerald ijd

Elizabeth Chapman widow ijd

Henry Cok iiijd

John Yetson iiijd

William Hawkes iiijd

Dom Robert Parnell iiijd

Dna anchoress iiijd

John Fissher iiijd

Robert Broune wever iiijd

Thomas Dynyell iiijd

+William Templer iiijd

Joan Clopton widow iiijd

+John Honne iiijd

William Godfrey baker iiijd

M Richard Wermouth iiijd

Robert Johnson iiijd

John Been' iiijd

---

[113] this and the next entry are unusual in that they record two payments which may not have been
made at the same time. The next entry records a payment made in the following year.

[114] probably 'paid' but it could be 'will pay' (sol'); elsewhere the text uses 'soluit' for 'paid'. These
entries may be an attempt to prevent entry payments going beyond the four years allowed to them
as many were doing.

William Fawkes iiijd
Robert Yerdley iiijd
+William Hebbes iiijd
John Billesby iiijd
Dom John Bothbroke Rector of Market Overton ijd
+M Richard Burton archdeacon of Worcester ijd
+Alice formerly wife of John Pykerell ijd
Nicholas Vicars iiijd
William Wareyn iiijd
Christopher Broune iiijd
William Sutton iiijd
M Robert Grymston iiijd
Dom Edward Hoton ijd
Thomas Philip iiijd
M Thomas Hikeham iiijd
John Wykes iiijd
Geoffrey Hampton iiijd
+John Moreys iiijd
+John Gebon iiijd
Richard Forster   iiijd
John Nele sen iiijd
John Palmer iiijd
Margar' Skynner iiijd

Fol 21
John Stede for the same maintenance of the waxlights iiijd
Thomas Clopton iiijd
Nicholas Parker iiijd
Dom Robert Tailour ijd
+Richard Chambre iiijd
Andrew Stotard iiijd
John Whipp iiijd
Alice Bradmedewe widow ijd
John Basse iiijd
John Dakke iiijd
Humfrey Coton iiijd
Thomas Parnell iiijd
William Clerk iiijd

Stock of this gild the abovesaid year

Robert Yerdley has xxs by pledge of Laurence Gregory

The same Robert has vjs viijd by pledge of William Godfrey

John Dak has xs by pledge of William Hawkes as is shewn more fully in the past year, of which he paid xld and he owes vjs viijd

William Fawkes had by pledge of William Hebbes – he had permission to pay annually xxd from the issues of his office of bedell of this gild until [sic]. Of which [he received] in his office xld and he owes iijs iiijd

William Hawkes has xxs by pledge of John Dak as appears in the last year past; of which he paid vjs viijd. And he now owes xiijs iiijd

+William Godfrey has xxs by pledge of William Templer, the which William Templer had permission to pay the aforesaid stock by pledge of John Yetson as in the past year, namely in the next iij years following; thus he paid immediately for one year. And he owes xiijs iiijd of which he paid this day vjs viijd And he owes vjs viijd

The same William Godfrey has vjs viijd by pledge of Robert Yerdley – nil

The same William Godfrey has vjs viijd by pledge of John Honne And the said John Honne in the same way by pledge of the same William xiijs iiijd paying as in the last past year

William Hebbes has vjs viijd by pledge of William Fawkes - nil

Thomas Dynyell has iijs iiijd by pledge of John Yetson - nil

John Been has iijs iiijd by pledge of Robert Yerdley - nil

+John Basse has xjs viijd and he had permission to pay as in the last past year.

fol 21d

Dom John Capron has vjs viijd – nil

[space]

William Templer has xls by pledge of Henry Cok and John Palmer; paid increment And stock remains by by pledge of as before.

Henry Cok has xls by pledge of John Yetson; paid increment; and stock remains by by pledge of as before

John Yetson has xls by pledge of Henry Cok, paid increment And stock remains as before

John Fissher has xiijs iiijd by pledge of John Yetson, paid increment And stock remains by by pledge of as before

John Stede has xls by pledge of Henry Cok paid increment And stock remains by by pledge of as before.

John Yetson has another xxixs of the remainder in the exchequer from the last past year which he paid this day into the exchequer and is discharged from this; quit.

Accounts of the providers

The same day and year John Fissher and John Palmer providers for the feast accounted for the issues of their office for the past year, all accounts and allowances included, the same accountants exceed xxiiijs ijd which they (paid *del*) received on this account and are quit

Election of officers

[14] The same day and year the commons elected into the office of Alderman William Broune as before

Into the office of providers of the feast John Palmer as before and Thomas Clopton new

Item into the office of steward John Yetson as before

Remainder

The same day and year the remainder in the exchequer xxxijs xd which were delivered to the said John Yetson steward on his account to be accounted for.

fol 22

Staunford. Acts of the gild of St Katherine virgin and martyr in the year millimo ccccmo lxxxviijo and the fourth year of the reign of king Henry VII

Entries

Nicholas Vicary owes up to now for entry iijs iiijd

David Malpas armiger vjs viijd

Dom Edward Hoton vicar of Ryall iijs iiijd

John Wykes owes iijs iiijd

John Moreys owes up to this day iijs iiijd and is pardoned

John Gebon owes vs and pardoned

John Been' owes for this day iijs iiijd

Dom William Jerald owes xxd

John Stede owes xxd which paid this day and thus quit

Dom Robert Tailour owes vs of which paid xxd and owes iijs iiijd

Richard Chambre owes vs

Andrew Stotard owes xxd which paid this day and thus quit

John Whip owes xxd which paid and thus quit

Alice Bradmedewe owes iijs iiijd which paid this day and is quit
Thomas Stable owes vs
John Wasshyngburgh owes iijs iiijd paid xxd and owes xxd
Margaret Skynner owes iijs iiijd paid xxd and owes xxd
Humfrey Coton owes up to this day vs
Thomas Parnell owes vs paid xxd and owes iijs iiijd
William Clerk owes vs paid xxd and owes iijxs iiijd

Waxshot

William Broune of Staunford merchant of the Calais Staple and Alderman of this
    gild paid to the maintenance of waxlights this year iiijd
David Malpas armiger arrears for v years iiijd
Dom William Jerald arrears for ij years paid this day viijd
Elizabeth Chapman widow paid for ij years iiijd
Elizabeth Cok for the current year ijd
John Yetson iiijd
William Hawkes paid iiijd
Dom Robert Pernell ijd
Dna anchoress ijd
John Fissher iiijd
Robert Broune wever iiijd
Thomas Dynyell ijd
William Templer iiijd
Joan Clopton widow ijd
William Godfrey arrears for five years iiijd
M Richard Wermouth paid this day for ij years iiijd

fol 22d
Robert Johnson to maintain the waxlights this year ijd
John Been' iiijd
William Fawkes paid for this year ijd
Robert Yerdley owes for five years iiijd
John Billesby owes for ij years (*ins in another hand* paid viijd)
John Bothbroke Rector of Market Overton owes for iij years ijd
Alice Pykerell iiijd
Nicholas Vicars owes for five years iiijd
William Wareyn owes for iiij years iiijd
Christopher Broune paid this day for the current year iiijd
William Sutton owes for ij years iiijd
M Robert Grymston paid this day ijd

Dom Edward Hoton for five years ijd
Thomas Philip paid for the current year iiijd
M Thomas Hikeham ijd
John Wykes arrears for iij years iiijd
Geoffrey Hampton paid for this day iiijd
Richard Forster   paid iiijd
John Nele iiijd
John Palmer iiijd
Margaret Skynner widow (ii *del*)ijd
John Stede iiijd
Thomas Clopton iiijd
Relict of Nicholas Parker ijd
Dom Robert Tailour ijd
Andrew Stotard iiijd
John Whip iiijd
Alice Bradmedewe widow ijd
Thomas Parnell iiijd
William Clerk iiijd
John Dak iiijd

Stock of this gild in the abovewritten year
Robert Yerdley has in stock xxs by pledge of Laurence Gregory nil
The same Robert has vjs viijd by pledge of William Godfrey nil
John Dak has vjs viijd by pledge of William Hawkes of which paid this day by the
  hands of the same William Hawkes iijs iiijd and owes iijs iiijd
William Fawkes had by pledge of William Hebbes iijs iiijd of which paid in the
  issues of his office of bedell of this gild this year xxd and owes xxd
William Hawkes has by pledge of John Dak xiijs iiijd of which paid increment and
  the said stock remains with the same William (*penes eundem Willielm*) by by pledge
  of as before
William Godfrey by pledge of William Templer has stock of this gild vjs viijd
  which the same William Templer the abovementioned by pledge of paid this day
  and hence quit
William Templer who has by pledge of Henry Cok and John Palmer xls, of which
  he paid increment iijs and of the stock by the hands of the said John Palmer xxs
  which remains in the exchequer and thus is quit. And because Henry Cok the
  other by pledge of is deceased, therefore the Alderman and brethren of special
  grace have given to the same William Templer permission to pay the said residue
  of xxs on his oath taken in person before the Alderman as follows – namely to
  pay to the steward ijs vjd of this sum in each quarter of the year until the residue

of the sum of xxs is fully paid and thus the said Henry Cok the abovementioned by pledge of shall similarly be quit of this.

fol 23

William Godfrey has vjs viijd by pledge of Robert Yerdley – nil

The same William Godfrey has vjs viijd by pledge of John Honne - nil; see more fully in the second year last past

William Hebbes has vjs viijd by pledge of William Fawkes

Thomas Dynyell has iijs iiijd by pledge of John Yetson

John Been has iijs iiijd by pledge of Robert Yerdley

Dom John Capron has vjs viijd - nil

Henry Cok has xls by pledge of John Yetson which paid this day into the exchequer with increment iijs and the stock shall remain in the exchequer and he is quit of this

John Yetson has by pledge of Henry Cok xls which paid this day with iijs increment; and immediately the said xls was delivered in stock to the said John Yetson and Andrew Stotard fissher, each of them being by pledge of for this for the other.

John Fissher has xiijs iiijd by pledge of John Yetson of which paid the same increment (*incr' tantum*)[115] and the stock was delivered by by pledge of as before.

John Stede has xls by pledge of Henry Cok; John Stede promised to pay the said stock before the feast of the Annunciation of BVM [25 March] next following, and the said John Stede took his oath to do this in person before the Alderman and the confreres.

Brethren newly admitted

The same day and year John Loryng and Elizabeth his wife were admitted into the confraternity of this gild and were sworn that they will pay for this admission and entry vjs viijd

John Thurlby and Elizabeth vjs viijd

John Cobbe and Agnes vjs viijd

Robert Clerk carpenter and Katherine vjs viijd

William Freman and Isabell vjs viijd

John Sylton and Isabell vjs viijd

William Richardson and Elizabeth vjs viijd

---

[115] this is the only indication that the 'increment' could vary. It is uniform throughout the accounts.

Account of providers for the feast

The same day and year John Palmer and Thomas Clopton providers for the feast accounted for the issues of their office and for outlay (*misis*) and expenses incurred by the said John and Thomas for the past year, all accounts and allowances included, as appears by a bill of certain particulars on this account shown, the said accountants are in surplus xxixs xjd ob which they have immediately received in the exchequer there and were discharged quit

fol 23d

For the support (exhibicionem) of the chaplain

The above day and year at (*apud*) the exchequer there was delivered to John Yetson steward of this gild for the support of the chaplain xxjs iiijd

And also the same steward received for the same from William Templer xxs stock being arrears as appears above (*inferius*) in the act made on that account, namely from now on in each quarter of the year ijs vjd until the same William Templer shall have fully paid the sum of xxs to him (the steward *ins*) as indicated above

[15] Election of officers

The same day and year the commons of this gild elected into the office of Alderman for the coming year William Broune as before

Item they elected into the office of steward John Yetson as before

Item into the office of providers for the feast Thomas Clopton as before and Andrew Stotard new

And into the office of bedell William Fawkes as before

Remainder

And the same day and year the remainder in the exchequer was delivered to Christopher Broune lxxiijs iiijd

fol 24

Staunford: Acts of the Gild of St Katherine virgin and martyr in the year of our Lord millimo cccc^mo lxxxix^o And the fifth year of the reign of king Henry vij^mi

[No heading Entry fines]

Nicholas Vicars owes for his entry iijs iiijd

David Malpace armiger owes for similar vjs viijd

Dom Edward Hoton vicar of Rihall owes iijs iiijd

John Wykes owes iijs iiijd

John Been owes vjs viijd

Dom William Jerald owes xxd

Dom Robert Tailyour owes iijs iiijd paid xxd and owes xxd

Margaret Skynner owes xxd paid and quit

Thomas Parnell owes iijs iiijd paid this day xxd paid and owes xxd

John Wasshyngburgh owes xxd paid this day and quit

William Clerke owes iijs iiijd paid xxd and owes xxd

John Lorynge owes vjs viijd paid xxd and owes vs

John Thurlby owes vjs viijd paid xxd and owes vs

Robert Clerk owes vjs viijd paid xxd and owes vs

John Shylton owes vjs viijd paid xxd and owes vs

William Freman owes vjs viijd paid xxd and owes vs

William Richardson owes vjs viijd paid xxd and owes vs

Waxshot

William Broune[116] of Staunford merchant of the Calais Staple and formerly
  Alderman of this Gild paid to the maintenance of the wax and lights this year
  [no sum]

David Malpace armiger arrears for vj years iiijd

Dom William Jerald iiijd

John Yetson iiijd

William Hawk iiijd

Dom Robert Parnell ijd

Dna anchoress ijd

John Fisscher iiijd

Robert Broune wever iiijd

Thomas Dynyell ijd

William Templer iiijd

Joan Clopton widow ijd

Magister Richard Warmouth ijd

Robert Johnson iiijd

John Been ijs [sic]

William Fawkes ijd

John Belesby iiijd

---

[116] If (as seems certain) this meeting was held in November 1489, William Broune was dead since
he died in April 1489. No payment is listed against his name. The full description and the word
'formerly' suggests this entry was a kind of memorial for him.

John Bothbroke Rector of Market Overton owes for iiij years [blank]
Alice Pikerell which paid and is quit [sic]

fol 24d
Nicholas Vicars iiijd
William Wareyn iiijd
Christopher Broune iiijd
William Sutton iiijd
M Robert Grymston ijd
Dom Edward Hoton arrears for vj years ijd
Thomas Philip iiijd
M Thomas Hikeham iiijd
John Wykes iiijd
Geoffrey Hampton iiijd
Richard Forster iiijd
John Nele iiijd
John Palmer iiijd
Margaret Skynner iiijd
John Stede iiijd
Thomas Clopton iiijd
Relict of Nicholas Parker iiijd
Dom Robert Tailour iiijd
Andrew Stotard iiijd
John Whipp iiijd
Alice Bradmedewe iiijd
Thomas Parnell iiijd
William Clerk iiijd
John Loryng iiijd
John Thurleby iiijd
(John Cobbe *del*)
Robert Clerke carpenter iiijd
William Freman iiijd
John Sylton iiijd
William Richardson iiijd

New brethren
M William Spenser and Margaret his wife admitted and will pay vjs viijd
John Cobbe and Agnes vjs viijd
Thomas Couper baker and his wife vjs viijd
Hugh Sutton smyth and his wife vjs viijd

Nicholas Billesdon and Katherine his wife vjs viijd

fol 25

The stock of the gild appears below

John Dak has iijs iiijd by pledge of William Hawkes; paid increment and stock
  remains as before

William Fawkes has xxd by pledge of William Hebbes which he paid in the issues
  of office of bedell and quit

Thomas Dynyell iijs iiijd by pledge of John Yetson; paid increment etc

William Hawkes has xiijs iiijd by pledge of John Dak; paid increment xijd (*tm?*)

John Bene has iijs iiijd

John Stede xls which he has promised to pay before the feast of the Annunciation
  BVM last past

John Fissher has xiijs iiijd by pledge of John Yetson. For which paid increment.
  And stock remains as before

John Yetson has xxs by pledge of Andrew Stotard paid increment and stock
  remains as before

Andrew Stotard has xxs by pledge of John Yetson for which paid increment and
  stock remains as before.

John Yetson has viijs iiijd by by pledge of[117]; of which he will pay next year xxd

William Templer has xxs will pay (*sol*) on his oath and nil

Robert Yerdley has xxvjs viijd of which paid xxs and the residue is pardoned and
  quit

William Godfrey has vjs viijd by pledge of John Honne

John Honne has xiijs iiijd by pledge of William Godfrey which paid and is quit

William Hawkes has xvijs by pledge of Christopher Broune; for which he paid the
  increment and stock remains as before

Account of the providers of the feast

The same day and year Thomas Clopton and Andrew Stotard providers for the
  feast account for expenses made by them, all accounts accounted, they were
  discharged quit.

---

[117] there is no sign of the origin of this stock which may be the reason for the failure to provide a
name for the 'by pledge of …'

Account of steward

The same day and year John Yetson steward of the lands of this gild accounted in similar fashion for the issues of his office for the past year and all accounts accounted for, the same steward was discharged quit

[16] Remainder

The same day and year Christopher Broune Alderman had lxxiijs iiijd of remainder which he paid this day into the exchequer And immediately there the same Alderman received on his account to be accounted for elsewhere lvs iijd

Remainder

The same day and year there was delivered to John Yetson steward xvjs viijd on his account to be answered for elsewhere

Election of officers

[16] The same day and year the commons elected into the office of Alderman Christopher Broune as before and Andrew Stotard as before into the office of provider of the feast and William Clerk for the coming year [sic]

fol 25d

Acts of the Gild of St Katherine virgin and martyr in the year of our Lord millimo ccccᵐᵒ lxxxxᵒ And the sixth year of the reign of king Henry VII

Entry fines

Nicholas Vicars owes for his entry iijs iiijd
David Malpas armiger , arrears for several years vjs viijd
Dom Edward Hoton vicar of Ryall owes iijs iiijd
John Wykes owes iijs iiijd
John Been owes vjs viijd of which paid xxd and owes xxd [sic]
Dom William Jerald owes xxd
Dom Robert Tailour owes xxd paid this day and thus quit
Thomas Parnell owes xxd paid this day and thus quit
William Clerk owes xxd paid this day and thus quit
John Loryng owes vs of which paid xxd and owes iijs iiijd
John Thurby [sic] owes vs of which paid xxd and owes iijs iiijd
Robert Clerke paid vs paid xxd and owes iijs iiijd
John Shilton owes vs paid xxd and owes iijs iiijd
William Freman owes vs paid xxd and owes iijs iiijd
William Richardson owes vs paid xxd and owes iijs iiijd

[*insertion mark — see below*]

Waxshott

Christopher Broun Alderman paid for maintenance of waxlights iiijd

David Malpas armiger owes for maintenance of lights, arrears for several years iiijd

Dom William Jerald owes ijd

John Yetson paid this day iiijd

William Hawkes paid iiijd

Dom Robert Parnell paid ijd

Donna anchoress paid ijd

John Fissher paid iiijd

Robert Broune wever paid iiijd

Thomas Dynyell ijd

William Templer iiijd

Joan Clopton widow ijd

Magister Richard Warmouth for the same ijd

John Been paid for several years ijs[118]

William Faux owes iiijd

John Belesby paid iiijd

John Bothbrok Rector of Market Overton for several years iiijd

Alice Pykerell iiijd

Nicholas Vicars iiijd

William Wareyn paid iiijd

William Sutton owes iiijd

M Robert Grymston for the same ijd

Dom Edward Hoton arrears for vij years ijd

Thomas Philip paid iiijd

M Thomas Hikeham ijd

John Wykes owes ijd

Geoffrey Hampton paid for the same iiijd

[119]*Entry fines* [marked with insertion mark in margin]

M William Spenser owes for entry vjs viijd of which paid xxd and owes vs

John Cobbe owes vjs viijd of which paid xld for ij years and owes iijs iiijd

Thomas Couper baker owes vjs viijd of which paid xxd and owes vs

---

[118] this is unlikely, as Been paid ijs the previous year, fol 24; it may be a copying error on the part of the clerk

[119] These four entries have been inserted at the bottom of this folio into the list of Waxshot which continues on the next folio

Hugh Sutton smyth vjs viijd paid xxd and owes vs
Nicholas Billesdon vjs viijd

fol 26

[120]Richard Forster paid iiijd
John Nele paid iiijd
John Palmer iiijd
Margaret Skynner ijd
John Stede iiijd
Thomas Clopton iiijd
Relict of Nicholas Parker ijd
Dom Robert Tailour ijd
Andrew Stotard iiijd
John Whipp iiijd
Alice Bradmedewe ijd
Thomas Parnell iiijd
William Clerk iiijd
John Loryng iiijd
John Thurleby iiijd
Robert Clerke carpenter iiijd
William Freman iiijd
John Sylton iiijd
William Richardson iiijd
M William Spenser iiijd
John Cobbe for ij years viijd
Thomas Couper baker iiijd
Hugh Sutton smyth iiijd
John Wasshyngburgh iiijd[121]
Nicholas Billesdon iiijd

New brethren
John Goylyn and Margaret his wife admitted into the fraternity of this gild and
    will pay vjs viijd
Thomas Peryman and Joan vjs viijd
Richard Joy and Elizabeth vjs viijd
Fr John Staunford admitted vjs viijd

---

[120] the list of waxshot begun on fol 25d is continued here
[121] different hand; JW written over erasure.

fol 26d

The Stock

John Dak has iijs iiijd by pledge of William Haux; increment iijd and stock remains as before

Thomas Dynyell iijs iiijd by pledge of John Yetson; increment iijd and stock remains

William Hawkes has xiijs iiijd by pledge of John Dak; increment xijd and stock remains

John Been has iijs iiijd

John Stede xls which he has promised to pay on his oath as in the last year, of which paid for increment iijs and stock remains as before

John Fissher has xiijs iiijd by pledge of John Yetson. For which he paid increment xijd. And stock remains as before

John Yetson has xxs by pledge of Andrew Stotard paid increment and stock remains as before

Andrew Stotard has xxs by pledge of John Yetson paid increment and stock remains.

John Yetson has viijs iiijd by pledge aforesaid of which he paid xxd

William Templer has xxs, to be paid on his oath as in preceding acts

William Godfrey has vjs viijd by pledge of John Honne

William Hawkes has xvijs by pledge of Christopher Broune

Account of the providers

The same day and year Andrew Stotard and William Clerk providers for the feast account for expenses made by them as appears by a bill of particulars made on this account xxiiijs ixd ob which they received in the exchequer and were discharged quit. And immediately there was delivered there to John Yetson steward for the support of the stipendiary chaplain xxs

Remainder

The same day and year John Wasshingburgh[122] delivered in a bag iij li xiiijs jd which remains in the hands of the said Alderman

---

[122] It seems that John Wasshynburgh was elected one of the providers for the feast at this meeting (see fol 28d) but no elections are recorded for 1490

fol 27

Staunford: Acts of the Gild of St Katherine virgin and martyr in the year of our Lord millimo cccc^{mo} lxxxxj^o And the 7th year of the reign of king Henry VII

Entry fines

Nicholas Vicars owes for his entry iijs iiijd

David Malpas armiger for similar arrears for several years vjs viijd

Dom Edward Hoton vicar of Ryall owes iijs iiijd

John Wykes iijs iiijd

John Been xixd

Dom William Geralde xxd

John Loryng paid xxd this day and owes xxd

John Thurleby paid xxd owes xxd

Robert Clerke paid xxd owes xxd

John Shilton paid xxd owes xxd

William Freman paid xxd owes xxd

William Richardson paid xxd owes xxd

M William Spenser paid xxd owes iijs iiijd

John Cobbe mercer paid xxd owes xxd

Thomas Couper baker paid xxd owes iijs iiijd

Hugh Sutton Smyth paid xxd owes iijs iiijd

Nicholas Billysdon paid xxd owes vs

John Goylyn paid xxd owes vs

Thomas Peryman paid xxd owes vs

Richard Joye furrour paid xxd owes vs

Fr John Parnell paid xxd owes vs

Brethren newly received

Magister John Manby pryor of St Leonard next to Staunford admitted into fraternity of this Gylde and sworn and paid for entry this day xxd and thus he owes according to ancient custom vs

William Bokenfelde and Katherine his wife admitted and will give vjs viijd

fol 27d

Waxshott follows

Christopher Broun Alderman paid for maintenance of wax and lights iiijd

David Malpas armiger owes arrears for several years iiijd

Dom William Jeralde owes ijd

John Yetson paid iiijd

William Hawkes paid iiijd

Dna anchoress paid ijd

John Fyssher pewterer paid iiijd

Robert Broun wever paid ijd

William Templer paid iiijd

Joan Clopton widow paid ijd

M Richard Warmouth Rector of the church of St George paid ijd

John Been taillour paid for this day iiijd

William Faux paid iiijd

John Belesby of Colyweston paid iiijd

Dom John Bougthbrok Rector of Market Overton owes for several years [blank]

Alice Pykerell owes iiijd

Nicholas Vycary owes ijd

William Sutton of [blank] owes iiijd

M Robert Grymston vicar of the church of St Martin paid ijd

Dom Edward Hoton arrears for viij years ijd

Thomas Phillipp paid for this day iiijd

M Thomas Hikeham Rector of the church of St Peter paid ijd

John Wykes owes for several years ijd

Geoffrey Hampton paid for this day iiijd

Richard Forster paid this day iiijd

John Nele iiijd

John Palmer paid iiijd

Margaret Skynner paid ijd

John Stede iiijd

Thomas Clopton paid iiijd

Dom Robert Taillour Rector of Brygcasterton paid ijd

Andrew Stodarde paid for this day iiijd

John Whippe paid iiijd

Alice Bradmedewe (owes *del*) (afterwards paid *ins*) ijd

Thomas Parnell paid iiijd

William Clerke paid iiijd

John Loryng paid iiijd

Waxshot continued (adhuc de *Waxshot)*

fol 28

Waxshot continued

John Thurleby paid this day for Waxshot iiijd

Robert Clerke paid iiijd

William Freman paid iiijd

John Sylton paid iiijd

William Richardson paid iiijd

M William Spenser paid iiijd

John Cobbe mercer paid iiijd

Thomas Couper baker paid iiijd

Hugh Sutton smyth paid iiijd

John Goylyn paid this day iiijd

Thomas Peryman paid iiijd

Richard Joy paid iiijd

Fr John Staunford of the order of Carmelites paid ijd

Nicholas Billesden paid todayiiijd

John Dacke [blank]

William Godfray [blank]

Thomas Dynyell for Matilda Dynyell for wax and maintenance of lights ijd

John Wasshyngburgh paid for this day iiijd

The stock of the Guylde appears below

John Dack has iijs iiijd by pledge of William Hawkes; for which paid gratuity (*ex devocione*) iijd and stock remains as before

Thomas Dynyell iijs iiijd by pledge of John Yetson; gratuity iijd and stock remains

William Hawkes has xiijs iiijd by pledge of John Dacke; gratuity xijd and stock remains

The same William Hawkes xvijs by pledge of Christopher Broune; gratuity xijd and stock remains

John Beene taillour has iijs iiijd; gratuity iijd and stock remains

John Fyssher pewterer has xiijs iiijd by pledge of John Yetson; paid gratuity xijd. And stock remains as before

+John Yetson has nothing for this day

[space]

+John Been taillour has iijs iiijd gratuity iijd and stock remains as before; +because it is written above

William Freman has xiijs iiijd delivered to him this day by pledge of John Shelton.

John Shelton has xiijs iiijd delivered to him this day (*ad hunc diem*) by pledge of William Freman.

William Bryghton has xxd delivered to him today (*hodie*) by pledge of John Cobbe mercer

John Thurleby has xxs delivered by pledge of Christopher Broun

Andrew Stodarde has xxs by pledge of John Yetson for which he paid gratuity xviijd.

William Templer has [blank]

fol 28d

Account of the providers for the feast

The same day and year came [blank] and John Wasshyngburgh providers for the entertainment and rendered account for expenses incurred by them this year as appears by a bill shown in this exchequer xxiiijs viijd which they received in the exchequer and thus they were discharged quit

Account of the steward

The same day and year John Yetson steward rendered account for the issues of his office this year last past and finished as appears by particulars contained in a certain bill total xliiijs And thus he was discharged quit

The charge of the steward

And afterwards there was delivered to the said John Yetson steward for the coming year for the wages (*stipend*) of the priest xvs; and he shall receive by order of the Alderman and confratres from Robert Broun tenant there for his rent for which he will respond xijs

Rendering accounts

M Christopher Broun Alderman of the Gylde answered (*pertulit*) here in the exchequer this day in cash counted out for iij li xiiijs jd which he received in his last account at the hands of John Wasshyngburgh which he paid and is quit

Receipts

And afterwards the said Master Alderman received in the exchequer in counted cash xxxviijs iiijd for which he will respond elsewhere. And afterwards he paid from the said sum to John Goylyn clerk of the gild for his wages for the past year xxd And thus there remains clear xxxvjs viijd

And in the following year the said M Christopher Broun delivered the said xxxvjs viijd into the exchequer – xxxvjs viijd and thus he is quit

[17] Election of officers

By common consent and assent of the brethren M Christopher Broun was elected
  Alderman for the coming year

Also they elected John Cobbe mercer and John Wasshyngburgh providers for the
  entertainment

And William Templer bedell

fol 29

**Staunfford: Acts of the Gylde of St Katherine virgin and martyr in the year
of our Lord millimo quadragent' nonagent' secundo And the eighth year
of the reign of king Henry VII**

Here follow the names of debtors for entry [fines]

Nicholas Vycaryes owes for his entry iijs iiijd

David Malpas armiger , arrears for several years vjs viijd

Dom Edward Hoton vicar of Royall owes iijs iiijd

John Wykes owes iijs iiijd

John Been taylour owes xixd

Dom William Jeralde vicar of Holywell owes xxd

John Loryng owes for this day xxd which paid and quit

John Thurleby xxd paid and quit

Robert Clerke wryght xxd paid and quit

John Shylton xxd paid and quit

William Freman xxd paid and quit

William Richardson owes for this day [blank]

M William Spenser paid this day xxd and owes xxd

John Cobbe mercer paid for this day xxd and quit

Thomas Couper baker paid xxd and owes xxd

Hugh Sutton smyth paid xxd and owes xxd

Nicholas Byllesden and Katherine his wife paid xxd and owe vs

John Goylyn paid for this day xxd and owes iijs iiijd

Thomas Peryman paid for this day xxd and owes iijs iiijd

Richard Joye furrer paid xxd and owes iijs iiijd

Fr John Parnell paid for this day xxd and owes iijs iiijd

M Dom John Manby pryor of St Leonard paid xxd and owes iijs iiijd

William Bokenffelde paid for this day xxd and owes vs

fol 29d

Waxshott Sunday feast of St Katherine [25 November] 8 Henry VII and anno domini millimo cccc^mo lxxxxij°

[17] M Christopher Broun Alderman of the Gylde paid for maintenance of wax and lights iiijd

M Nicholas Billesden paid for this day iiijd

M David Malpas armiger owes for several years iiijd

M Dom John Manby prior of St Leonards paid for this day ijd

M William Spenser iiijd

Thomas Philipp paid iiijd

M Thomas Ikham Rector of the church of St Peter Staunford ijd

M Richard Warmouth Rector of the church of St George paid ijd

M Robert Grymston vicar of the church of St Martin paid ijd

[7?] Dom Robert Taillour Rector of Brygge Casterton paid ijd

Dom William Jeralde vicar of Holywell paid for two years iiijd

Dom Edward Hoton vicar of Royall owes ijd

Dom John Bouthebroke Rector of Market Overton owes ijd

John Stede paid iiijd

Richard Forster paid for this day iiijd

John Thurleby paid for this day for maintaining lights iiijd

Margaret Skynner widow paid this day ijd

Geoffrey Hampton paid iiijd

John Cobbe mercer paid iiijd

John Goylyn paid this day iiijd

Thomas Couper baker paid iiijd

Thomas Parnell paid iiijd

John Loryng paid for maintaining wax and lights this year iiijd

Thomas Peryman paid iiijd

Thomas Clopton paid iiijd

John Palmer paid iiijd

Andrew Stodarde paid iiijd

John Fissher pewterer paid iiijd

John Yetson bocher paid iiijd

Joan Clopton widow paid ijd

John Byllesby of Collyweston paid iiijd

William Sutton iiijd

John Wykes ijd

John Whyppe paid for this day iiijd

William Templer paid for this day iiijd

fol 30
Waxshote continued

William Clerke kerver paid for this day for wax and maintaining lights as before
  iiijd
William Hawkes paid iiijd
William Faux paid ijd
Robert Clerke wryght paid for this day iiijd
Fr John Parnell paid to for this day ijd
John Wasshyngburgh paid for this day iiijd
William Freman paid for this day iiijd
John Shylton paid for this day iiijd
William Richardson alias Bryghton iiijd
Hugh Sutton smyth paid for the maintenance of the wax and lights iiijd
Richard Joye Furrer paid iiijd
William Godffraye iiijd
John Beene taillour paid for this day iiijd
John Wasshyngburgh iiijd
John Dakke iiijd
Thomas Dynyell iiijd
Robert Broun wever iiijd
William Bokenffelde paid for maintenance of wax and lights iiijd
Margaret former wife of Richard Herte paid this day ijd (*line inserted*)
William Bryghton iiijd
Alice Pykerell iiijd
Nicholas Vycary iiijd
Dom Robert Parnell Rector of the church of St Paul paid ijd
John Neele senior and Agnes his wife this day paid for two years vjd [sic]

Brethren newly [admitted]
Dom John Rydell co-monk[123] of St Leonards admitted into the confraternity of
  the Gylde and sworn and will pay according to ancient custom for entry vjs viijd
William Povy mason (and his wife *ins*) received and sworn and will give vjs viijd

---

[123] The accounts of St Leonards Priory suggest that at times, especially in the later Middle Ages, there were only two monks at St Leonards, one was the prior and the other a fellow monk (commonach'); I have translated this as 'co-monk'.

84

John Lytster and Isabella (his wife and Margaret formerly his wife *ins*) admitted
into the confraternity of the Gilde and will pay according to ancient custom in
four years vjs viijd

fol 30d

Account of the providers for the feast
John Cobbe mercer and John Wasshyngburgh providers for the feast account for
expenses incurred by them as appears by a bill of particulars on this account
xxijs xd which they received in the exchequer and thus they were discharged quit

Names of those who have stock
John Dakke has iijs iiijd by pledge of William Haux

Thomas Dynyell [blank]

William Hawkes has xiijs iiijd by pledge of John Dak

+The same William Hawkes xvijs by pledge of Christopher Broun, which paid
and is quit

John Bene taillour has iijs iiijd for which he paid gratuity iijd. And the chattells
remain as before

John Fyssher pewterer has xiijs iiijd by pledge of John Yetson. For which he paid
gratuity xijd. And stock remains as before

John Yetson [space]

William Freman has xiijs iiijd by pledge of John Shylton. For which he paid
gratuity xjd [sic]. And stock remains as before

John Shylton has xiijs iiijd by pledge of William Freman. For which he paid
gratuity xijd. And stock remains as before

William Brighton has xxd by pledge of John Cobbe mercer

John Thurleby has xxs by pledge of Christopher Broun; for which he paid gratuity
xijd and the stock remains as before

Andrew Stodarde has xxs by pledge of John Yetson for which he paid gratuity
xviijd. And stock remains as before

John Stede [space]

William Templer has xxs, of which there is allowed to him for the exercise of his
offices both of cook (*coci*) and of bedell for the year now elapsed iiijs. And thus
he owes up to the present xvjs

Thomas Peryman has xxvjs viijd newly delivered to him

fol 31

Account of the steward

The same day and year John Yetson steward renders account for xxvijs for cash (*denar*) received by him as appears in his last account; and also he renders account for certain particulars paid by him as appears by a bill shown here in the exchequer; sum total of expenses xxxixs vd. And all accounts and allowances included, there was delivered to him in the exchequer xijs xjd And thus he is quit

Delivered to the steward

And on this there was newly delivered to the said steward John Yetson for necessary expenses for the coming year to be incurred in his office xxs. And also he shall receive from the rents of the tenement of the gild of St Katherine xijs ; and further there was delivered to him for mending and sustaining the lights and wax in honour of St Katherine vijs viijd for which he will answer in his next account etc

[18] Election of officers

The same day and year the confratres of this gild elected into the office of Alderman for the coming year Christopher Broun as before
Item they elected into the office of steward John Yetson as before
Item providers for the entertainment John Cobbe and William Freman
And into the office of bedell and cook William Templer

fol 31d

Staunford: Acts of the gild of St Katherine virgin and martyr of the town of Staunford in the year of our Lord millimo lxxxxiijᵐᵒ And the ninth year of the reign of king Henry VII

For Entry fines

Nicholas Vicaryes still (*adhuc*) owes for his entry iijs iiijd
David Malpas armiger owes up to today (*ad huc diem*) vjs viijd
Dom Edward Hoton vicar of Royall owes iijs iiijd
John Wykes iijs iiijd
John Bene tayllour xixd
Dom William Jeralde perpetual vicar of Holywell owes xxd
William Richardson of [sic] owes up to today for his entry xxd
M William Spenser owes for entry xxd paid this day and quit of this
Thomas Couper baker xxd paid and quit

Hugh Smyth alias Sutton xxd paid and quit

Nicholas Byllesdon and Cateryne his wife owe nothing paid therefore they owe vs

John Goylyn paid for this day xxd and owes xxd

Thomas Peryman paid for this day xxd and owes xxd

Richard Joye furrer paid xxd and owes xxd

Fr John Parnell paid for this day xxd and owes xxd

M Dom John Manby prior of St Leonard paid xxd and owes xxd

Dom John Rydell co-monk of St Leonards nothing paid, therefore owes vjs viijd

William Bokenffelde paid for this day xxd and owes iijs iiijd

John Lytster and Isabell owe up to today for entry vjs viijd

William Povy mason paid nothing up to today for his entry and thus owes vjs viijd

Brethren newly admitted namely

[19] Fr Richard Lecke (sworn *ins*) prior of the order of St Augustine Staunford admitted into the confraternity of this gild and will pay according to ancient custom vjs viijd

Fr Richard Ravenell (sworn *ins*) friar minor admitted and will give vjs viijd

Dom William Ogle co-monk of St Leonards admitted vjs viijd

Reginald Loky and Isabella his wife of the parish of St George admitted similarly and sworn and will give for their entry according to ancient custom vjs viijd

Walter Feyrday glover and Agnes his wife admitted into fraternity of the gild [blank]

John Netlam of Royall and [blank] his wife admitted

fol 32

Waxshott

M Christopher Broun Alderman of the Gylde paid[124] for maintenance of wax and lights iiijd

M Dom John Manby Prior of St Leonards iiijd

M David Malpas armiger (paid nil but still owes for this day *ins*) iiijd

M William Spenser iiijd

+Dom John Rydell co-monk of St Leonards paid nothing for this day because he is abroad (*quia exivit de patria*)

M Thomas Philipp paid iiijd

M Nicholas Byllesdon nothing paid but (*sed*) owes iiijd

---

[124] this text (like others in this book) is confusing; at times the word 'soluit' is used, on rare occasions 'solvet' is used; and often simply 'sol' is used. I have tried to be consistent by assuming that 'sol' in this case means 'soluit'.

M (Thomas *ins*) Ickham Rector of St Peters ijd
M Richard Warmouth Rector of the church of St George paid ijd
M Robert Grymston vicar of the church of St Martin paid ijd
Dom Robert Taillour Rector of Brygge Casterton paid ijd
Dom William Jeralde vicar of Holywell ijd
John Stede of Staunford paid iiijd
John Lytster will pay (*solvet*) iiijd
Richard Forster paid (*soluit*) this day iiijd
John Thurleby iiijd
Margaret Skynner widow paid this day ijd
John Goylyn paid this day iiijd
Geoffrey Hampton paid for this day because alone (*quia solus*) ijd
John Cobbe mercer paid iiijd
Thomas Couper baker paid iiijd
Thomas Parnell paid iiijd
John Loryng paid iiijd
Thomas Peryman paid iiijd
Thomas Clopton paid iiijd
John Palmer paid iiijd
Andrew Stodarde paid iiijd
John Fissher pewterer paid iiijd
John Yetson bocher paid iiijd
John Byllesby of Collyweston paid iiijd
William Sutton iiijd
John Wykes ijd
William Clerke kervour paid for wax and maintaining lights as above (*supra*) iiijd

fol 32d

Waxshot continued (adhuc de Waxshotte)
William Haux paid for the maintenance of the wax and lights of the gild for this
    year iiijd
Robert Clerke wryght paid for this day iiijd
Fr John Parnell paid for this day ijd
John Wassyngburgh paid for this day iiijd
William Freman paid for this day iiijd
John Shilton paid for this day iiijd
Hugh Sutton smyth iiijd
Richard Joye Furrer iiijd
William Godffray iiijd

John Beene taillour paid for this day iiijd

John Whippe paid iiijd

William Templer paid iiijd

Wiliam Bokenffelde paid iiijd

William Povy paid iiijd

William Faux paid iiijd

William Bryghton iiijd

Matilda Dynyell paid ijd

Margaret Hobson ijd

fol 33

Stock of the same gild in the year before written

John Dakke has iijs iiijd by pledge of William Hawkes

Thomas Dynyell has iijs iiijd by pledge of John Yetson

William Hawkes has xiijs iiijd by pledge of John Dacke

The same William Hawkes xvijs by pledge of Christopher Broun, of which he is quit as appears above.

John Bene has iijs iiijd for which he paid gratuity iijd. And stock remains as before

John Fyssher pewterer has xiijs iiijd by pledge of John Yetson. For which paid xijd. And stock remains etc

William Freman has xiijs iiijd by pledge of John Shilton; paid (gratuity *ins*) xijd. And stock remains etc

John Shilton has xiijs iiijd by pledge of William Freman; paid xijd (gratuity *ins*). And stock remains as before

William Brighton has xxd by pledge of John Cobbe mercer

John Thurleby has xxs by pledge of Christopher Broun

Andrew Stodarde has xxs by pledge of John Yetson; paid gratuity xviijd. And stock remains as before.

John Stede has from old (*ex antiq*) xls. For which he paid in part payment xiijs iiijd. And thus he owes xxvjs viijd

Thomas Peryman has xxvjs viijd; paid gratuity ijs. And stock remains

William Templer has xvjs, of which there is allowed to him for the exercise of his office for the year now elapsed iiijs. And thus he still owes xijs

fol 33d

Adhuc de Acta of the gild anno ix° H vij°

Account of the providers for the feast

Sunday the first of December in the year of our Lord millimo cccc^{mo} nonagesimo
tercio [1493] John Cobbe and William Freman accounted for certain expenses
incurred by them in the past year namely in the time of this account as appears
by bills for such particulars on this account shown at this time xviijs iiijd which
they received in the exchequer. And they are discharged quit.

Account of the steward

The same day and year John Yetson steward of the gild accounted for the issues
of his office in the last year past, all accounts and allowances included, xvs ixd
which he received in the exchequer and he was discharged quit.

New Receipts

The same day and year there remains in the hands of John Yetson steward
delivered to him anew for necessary expenses for the coming year for which he
will respond elsewhere xviijs And in addition he shall receive by order of the
Alderman and the confratres of the gild from the tenement of St Katherine for
rent for the last Michaelmas term, namely for one quarter term to the feast of
the Nativity of our Lord next after the day of this account

[20] Election of officers for the following year

The same day and year Christopher Broun was elected into the office of
Alderman for the coming year as before
Item John Yetson was elected into the office of steward there as before
Item William Freman and Thomas Couper baker providers for the feast
And William Templer into the office of cook and bedell as before

fol 34

**Staunford: Acts of the gild of St Katherine virgin and martyr of the town of
Staunford in the year of our Lord millimo cccc^{mo} lxxxxiiij° And the tenth
year of the reign of king Henry VII**

For Entries

Dna Katarina Greye[125] wife of the said Lord [dm' dm'] le Greye owes for entry vjs viijd

Nicholas Vicary still owes for his entry iijs iiijd

David Malpas armiger vjs viijd

Dom Edward Hoton iijs iiijd

John Wykes iijs iiijd

John Bene taillour xixd

Dom William Jeralde vicar of Holywell xxd

William Richardson (alias Bryghton *ins*) for his entry xxd

Nicholas Billesdon and Katherine his wife vs

John Goylyn xxd which paid and thus quit

Thomas Peryman xxd which paid and thus quit

Richard Joy furrer xxd which paid and thus quit

Fr John Parnell xxd which paid and thus quit

Dom John Manby pryor of St Leonard xxd

Dom John Rydall co-monk of St Leonards vjs viijd

William Bekenfelde iijs iiijd (for entry xxd and xxd stock *del*)[126] of which paid xxd. And owes xxd

John Litster paid for this day xxd. And thus owes vs

William Povy mason to the present owes for his entry vjs viijd

Fr Richard Leke prior of the Austin site [*loci August*] of Staunford paid xxd. And owes vs

Fr Richard Ravenell of the friars minor of Staunford paid xxd. And owes vs

Dom William Ogle co-monk of St Leonard – nil

Reginald Loky paid for this day xxd. And owes vs

Walter Feyrday paid xxd. And owes vs

John Netlam of Ryall nil

New brethren

Dom Richard Purley Rector of the church of St Paul Staunfford admitted and sworn into the fraternity of the gild, and he will give for his entry according to ancient custom vjs viijd

William Jurden and Joan his wife and Margaret formerly (*nuper*) his wife (cum? Molle formerly (*nuper*) baker *ins*) admitted, will give vjs viijd

[127]And William Molle sometime (*quondam*) of Staunfford baker [blank]

---

[125] no admission for lord or lady Grey can be found

[126] The words 'for this day iijs iiijd (for entry xxd and xxd stock *del*)' are inserted in a different hand; the sums xxd and xxd are written above the deleted words 'entry' and 'stock'.

William Weste and Joan his wife admitted and sworn in similar fashion, will give vjs viijd of which paid for this day xxd And thus owe vs

William Hynkeley and Joan his wife admitted and sworn, will give for entry vjs viijd

Robert Crane and Agnes his wife and John Britton? formerly (*nuper*) of Undell and Elizabeth Crane formerly wife of Robert Crane admitted into the fraternity (v *del*) vjs viijd

Thomas Edward and [blank] his wife admitted etc; will pay vjs viijd

fol 34d

De Waxshott

Christopher Broun for maintenance of lights and wax [no sum]

Dom John Manby ijd

David Malpas armiger iiijd

William Spenser for maintenance of wax and lights iiijd

Thomas Philipp iiijd

Nicholas Billesdon paid iiijd

M Thomas Hykeham Rector of St Peters paid ijd

M Richard Warmouth paid ijd

M Robert Grymston paid ijd

Dom Robert Tailour Rector of Casterton ijd

Dom William Jaralde vicar of Holywell ijd

John Stede paid iiijd

John Litster paid iiijd

Richard Forster paid iiijd

(Item for his dyner this yer ijd *ins*)[128]

John Thurleby iiijd

Margaret Skynner widow paid ijd

John Goylyn paid iiijd

Geoffrey Hampton paid iiijd

John Cobbe mercer paid iiijd

Thomas Couper baker paid iiijd

Thomas Parnell paid iiijd

John Loryng paid iiijd

Thomas Peryman paid iiijd

---

[127] This whole line, which runs on from Jurden's entry, is inserted and no sum attached

[128] This is the only payment recorded for the dinner; it is not clear how these sums were collected or accounted for.

Thomas Clopton paid iiijd

John Palmer shomaker paid iiijd

Andrew Stodarde paid iiijd

John Fissher pewterer paid iiijd

John Yetson bocher paid iiijd

John Billesby of Collyweston paid iiijd

William Sutton iiijd

John Wykes ijd

William Clerke kervour paid iiijd

William Haux paid iiijd

Robert Clerke wright paid iiijd

Fr John Parnell paid ijd

John Wasshyngburgh paid iiijd

William Freman paid iiijd

John Shilton paid iiijd

Hugh Sutton smyth paid iiijd

Richard Joye furrour paid iiijd

William Godfray iiijd

John Bene taillour iiijd

John Whippe paid ijd

(John Netlam of Ryall *del*)

Fr Richard Leke prior etc ijd

Fr Richard Ravenell ijd

Dom William Ogle ijd

Reginald Loky paid iiijd

Walter Feyreday paid iiijd

William Templer paid iiijd

William Bokenfeld paid iiijd

William Povy ijd

William Faux paid ijd

William Brighton paid iiijd

Matilda Dynyell paid ijd

Margaret Hobson paid ijd

William Weste paid iiijd

[21] The vicary off Royall payd ffor waxshott for ix yer xviijd

William Waryn merchaunt iiijd

fol 35

Stock of this gild the said year

John Dakke has iijs iiijd by pledge of William Haux

Matilda Dynyell has by pledge of John Yetson iijs iiijd of which she paid to this day in part payment xvijd And she still owes xxiijd

William Haux has xiijs iiijd by pledge of John Dakke

The same William has xvijs by pledge of Christopher Broun which paid and quit as appears in the preceding[129]

John Bene taillour has iijs iiijd

John Fissher pewterer has xiijs iiijd And paid gratuity xijd, stock remains as before

William Freman has xiijs iiijd by pledge of John Shilton, paid gratuity xijd, stock remains as before

John Shilton has xiijs iiijd by pledge of William Freman; paid gratuity xijd; stock remains as before.

William Bryghton alias Richardson has xxd by pledge of John Cobbe mercer

John Thurleby has xxs by pledge of Christopher Broun

Andrew Stodard has xxs; he paid gratuity xviijd by pledge of John Yetson; stock remains as before.

John Stede still owes xxvjs viijd

Thomas Peryman had xxvjs viijd of which he paid in part payment vjs viijd, and ijs gratuity; and he still owes xxs

William Templer has xijs of which allowance is made to him for his offices of bedell and cook for this year now past iiijs. And thus he owes viijs

Accounts of the providers for the feast

Sunday the feast of St Andrew [30 November] in the foresaid year William Freman and Thomas Couper accounted for the certain expenses incurred by them as appears by bills shown in the exchequer, which amount to the sum of xxijs xjd ob; which they received in the exchequer, and thus they are discharged quit.

Account of steward

The account of John Yetson steward from the feast of St Katherine [25 November] in the ix° year of the reign of Henry VII for this day, namely Sunday the feast of St Andrew the Apostle [30 November 1494] in the x° year of the same king. He accounted for xviijs received by him in the exchequer in his last account. And also for ixs received by him from the farm of the tenement of

---

[129] see fol 30d

St Katherine for three quarters of the year ending at the feast of the Nativity next after this account; and it rendered to him no more for rent for that tenement because it was vacant for half a year and more etc. Sum in total of these receipts xxvijs, of which in expenses incurred by him as appears by particulars of payments xliijs jd. And thus there is owed to the same steward, all accounts and allowances included, xvjs jd. Which he received in the exchequer and so he is quit.

New receipts (Recept' de novo)

There remains in the exchequer in cash (*in peccun' num'at*) xiijs vjd which was delivered to the said John Yetson for which he will account elsewhere.

Item delivered to the same steward xvjd

Election of officers

[22] The same day they elected M Christopher Broun Alderman of the gild as before

John Yetson was elected as steward for the coming year

Thomas Couper baker and Hugh Sutton smyth were elected as providers for the feast

William Templer was elected into the office of cook and bedell for the coming year.

fol 35d

Staunfford: Acts of the gild of St Katherine virgin and martyr there in the year millimo cccc^mo lxxxxv° And in the xj year of the reign of king Henry VII

Entries

David Malpas armiger owes for his entry vjs viijd

Dom Edward Howton vicar of Royall owes iiis iiijd (marginal *desper*)

John Wykes owes (*desp*)

John Beene taillour owes iijs iiijd (*desp*)

Dom William Garald vicar of Holywell owes xxd

William Richardson alias Brighton owes xxd

Nicholas Billesden owes vs. And John Yedson paid the said vs. And he is quit

William Bokenfeld owes for this day xxd which paid; and quit

John Lytster owes vs of which paid xxd. And thus now owes iijs iiijd

William Povy mason paid for two years iijs iiijd And owes iijs iiijd

Fr Richard Leke prior of the Austin friars paid xxd. And owes iijs iiijd

Friar Richard Ravenell of the friars minor paid xxd; and still owes iijs iiijd
Reginald Lokhye [blank]
Walter Feyreday paid xxd; and still owes iijs iiijd
John Netlam of Royall [blank]
Dom Richard Purley Rector of St Paul [blank]
William Jurden paid xxd; and still owes vs
William Weste paid xxd; and still owes vs
William Hynckeley paid xxd; and still owes vs
Robert Crane paid to this day xxd; and still owes vs
Thomas Edwarde paid xxd; and still owes vs

Desperate [debts]
My lady Dam Kateryn Grey owes for her entry fine vjs viijd
Nicholas Vicary owes iijs iiijd
Dom John Manby owes xxd
Dom John Rydall owes vjs viijd
Dom William Ogle owes vjs viijd

fol 36

Waxshote this year
Christopher Broun Alderman of the gild paid for maintaining the lights this year
  iiijd
Thomas Edward iiijd
David Malpas armiger for the same iiijd
M William Spenser iiijd
William Waren merchaunt iiijd
Thomas Philipp iiijd
Nicholas Billesden iiijd
M Thomas Hykham ijd
M (*deletion*) Richard Warmouth ijd
M Robert Grymston ijd
Sir Robert Taillour ijd
Dom William Jeralde ijd
John Stede iiijd
Dom Richard Purley ijd
Fr Richard Leke prior of the Austins ijd
Robert Crane iiijd
William Jurden iiijd
Geoffrey Hampton ijd

John Lytster iiijd
John Goylyn iiijd
John Cobbe iiijd
Thomas Parnell iiijd responds by J Yedson
Thomas Peryman iiijd
(John Netlam *del*)
William Weste iiijd
William Hynkeley iiijd
Walter Feyreday iiijd
Fr Richard Ravenhill ijd
Dom Edward Hooton vicar of Royall ijd
M Margaret Skynner ijd [sic]
Margaret Forster ijd
John Thurleby iiijd
John Yedson iiijd
Thomas Couper baker iiijd
Thomas Clopton iiijd
John Fyssher pewterer iiijd
Andrew Stodard iiijd
John Palmer iiijd
John Billesby iiijd
Fr John Parnell ijd
Hugh Sutton smyth iiijd
Richard Joye furrour iiijd
John Loryng iiijd
John Wykes ijd
William Clerke kervour iiijd
Robert Clerke wryght iiijd
William Freman iiijd
William Godfray iiijd
John Shilton iiijd
John Wasshynburgh iiijd
John Whipp ijd
John Bene taillour iiijd
Reginald Loky iiijd
William Templer ijd
William Bokenfeld iiijd
William Povy ijd
William Faux ijd
William Bryghton iiijd

Matilda Dynyell ijd
Margaret Hobson ijd
William Sutton iiijd
Nicholas Vycary iiijd
John Dakke iiijd
William Haux iiijd
+ Richard Deye anno primo iiijd

fol 36d

Stock of the gild appears below
William Haux has xiijs iiijd by pledge of John Dak of which he has permission to
   pay annually ijs until the said sum of xiijs iiijd is paid
John Dak owes iijs iiijd by pledge of William Haux as appears in the preceding
   [year]
Matilda Dynyell owes xxiijd by pledge of John Yedson as in the preceding [year]
John Bene taillour owes iijs iiijd
John Fissher pewterer has xiijs iiijd; paid gratuity xxd and stock remains as before
William Freman has xiijs iiijd by pledge of John Shilton }
John Shilton has xiijs iiijd by pledge of William Freman } (paid jointly gratuity xxd
   written against both last two entries)
Andrew Stodard xxs of which paid in the exchequer xs and thus owes xs; nothing
   paid in gratuity (ex devocione)
John Stede owes xxvjs viijd
Thomas Pyryman has xxs of which paid in exchequer vjs viijd; paid gratuity xviijd
   and now owes xiijs iiijd
William Templer owes viijs of which allowed to him for his offices of cook and
   bedell this year iiijs. And thus owes iiijs.
William Bryghton owes xxd by pledge of John Cobbe
John Thurleby has xxs by pledge of Christopher Broun

Account of providers for the feast
The same day and year Thomas Couper and Hugh Sutton smyth providers for the
   feast accounted for expenses made by them as appears by a bill of particulars on
   this account made and shown here in the exchequer; total xxs jd ob. And quit

Account of the steward
And also John Yedson steward of the gild accounted in similar fashion for the
   issues of his office for the last year and all accounts and allowances included,
   the said steward was discharged for this quit

Remainder

And immediately there was delivered to the said steward from the remainder of
the cash in the exchequer at this account xvs vijd for which he will respond
elsewhere.

Brethren newly received

John Adewe shomaker and Amya admitted and sworn into fraternity and will give
vjs viijd

John Markeby and Elizabeth admitted and sworn vjs viijd

John Thomas and Katherine admitted and according to ancient custom will give
vjs viijd

John Hynkeley and Alys received admitted and sworn and will give vjs viijd

James Taillour alias Thistult(h *ins*)wayte and Alice admitted and sworn; will give
vjs viijd

Hugh Wade and Agnes admitted and sworn vjs viijd

Richard Dey and Elena admitted and swornvjs viijd

William Herryson (smyth *ins*) and Anabel admitted and sworn vjs viijd

Henry Yedson and Agnes admitted and sworn vjs viijd

John Parker glover and Joan admitted and will give according to ancient custom
vjs viijd

[23] Election

Thomas Philipp Alderman of the gild

John Yedson steward

Hugh Sutton and Robert Clerke wryght providers for the feast

William Templer cook and bedell

 officers for the following year.

fol 37

Staunford: Acts of the gild of St Katherine virgin and martyr there held (*habita*) millimo cccc^mo lxxxxvj° and the 12th year of the reign of King Henry VII

Entry fines

Dna (M *del*) Katherine Greye alias the said Dna Katherine (de la *ins*) Pole owes for
entry vjs viijd

David Malpas armiger owes for entry as appears in preceding [year] vjs viijd

Dom William Garalde vicar of Holywell owes for entry (*ingession*) as appears
before xxd; paid and quit

William Bryghton by pledge of J Cobbe xxd: he has day until the Nativity of our Lord next

John Lytster iijs iiijd of which paid xxd and thus now owes xxd

William Povy mason iijs iiijd

Fr Richard Leeke iijs iiijd

Fr Richard Ravennell iijs iiijd paid xxd and owes xxd

Reginald Loky vs paid xxd and now owes vs (not yet paid *ins*)[130]

Walter Feyreday iijs iiijd paid xxd and owes xxd

John Netlam of Royall vjs viijd

Dom Richard Purley vjs viijd; he has day to the Purification of BVM [2 February] next

William Jurden vs paid xxd and owes iijs iiijd

William Weste iijs iiijd paid xxd and owes xxd

William Hynkeley vs paid xxd and owes iijs iiijd

Robert Crane vs paid xxd and owes iijs iiijd

Thomas Edwarde vs paid xxd and now owes iijs iiijd

John Adewe vjs viijd (nil *in margin*)

John Markeby vjs viijd paid xxd and now owes vs

John Thomas vjs viijd paid xxd and owes vs

John Hynkeley vjs viijd paid xxd (not yet paid *ins*) and owes vjs viijd

James Thistultwayte vjs viijd paid xxd and owes vs

Hugh Wadye vjs viijd paid xxd and owes vs

Richard Dey vjs viijd paid xxd and owes vs

William Herryson smyth vjs viijd paid xxd (not yet *ins*) and owes vjs viijd [sic]

Henry Yedson vjs viijd paid xxd and owes vs

John Parker glover vjs viijd

Dom Edward Howghton vicar iijs iiijd

John Wykes iijs iiijd

John Bene taillour xixd[131]

Nicholas Vycary iijs iiijd

Received off my lady Grey for hyryng off the herse to Bytham for my lord Grey[132] and for devocion ijs vd

---

[130] This note helps to explain some of the ambiguous entries.

[131] error for xxd

[132] Henry lord Grey of Codnor who held half of the manor and castle of Castle Bytham died 18 April 1485; his wife was Katherine daughter of William lord Stourton and widow of Sir William Berkeley of Beverston, Glos (GEC). Katherine married (3rd) William de la Pole 5th son of the 2nd Duke of Suffolk; she died 1521, Burke's *Peerage* 106 edn, 1999 vol ii p 2021. I owe thanks to Adrian Channing for help with this identification.

fol 37d

Waxshot this year

Thomas Philipp Alderman of the gild paid for maintenance of the lights this year
iiijd

Christopher Broun merchant of the Calais staple paid for the same iiijd

Dna Katherine de la Pole for the same

David Malpas armiger iiijd

M William Spenser iiijd

William Waren merchaunt iiijd

Thomas Edwarde iiijd (wax *marg*)

Nicholas Billesden iiijd

John Stede iiijd

M Thomas Hykham ijd

M Richard Warmouth ijd

M Robert Grymston ijd

Dom Robert Taillour ijd

Dom William Jeralde ijd

Dom Richard Purley iiijd

Fr Richard Leke ijd

Fr Richard Ravenell ijd

Robert Crane iiijd

William Jurden iiijd

Geoffrey Hampton ijd

John Goylyn iiijd

John Litster iiijd (nil *ins*) nota *marg*

John Cobbe mercer iiijd

Thomas Peryman iiijd

Thomas Parnell iiijd

(John Netlam *del*)

William Weste iiijd

William Hynkeley iiijd

William Feyreday iiijd

Dom Edward Howghton ijd

 Margaret Skynner ijd

John Thurleby iiijd

John Yedson iiijd

Thomas Couper baker iiijd

Thomas Clopton iiijd

Andrew Stodard iiijd

John Fissher iiijd
John Byllysby iiijd
Margery Palmer iiijd
Fr John Parnell ijd
Hugh Sutton smyth iiijd
Richard Joye furrer iiijd
John Loryng iiijd
John Wykes jd [sic]
William Clerke kervour iiijd
Robert Clerke wryght iiijd
William Freman iiijd
William Godfray (iiijd *del*) (nil *ins bis*)
John Shilton iiijd
John Wasshyngburgh iiijd
John Whipp ijd
John Bene iiijd
Reginald Loky iiijd
William Templer ijd
William Bokenfeld iiijd
William Povy iiijd
William Faux iiijd
William Brighton iiijd
Matilda Dynyell ijd
Margaret Hobson ijd
(John Adewe del)
John Markeby iiijd
John Thomas iiijd
John Hynkeley iiijd
James Thistiltwayte iiijd
Hugh Wade iiijd
Richard Dey iiijd
(William Herryson smyth *del*) iiijd
Henry Yedson iiijd
John Parker glover ijd
John Dak iiijd
William Haux iiijd
William Sutton by John Yedson ijs quit[133]

---

[133] It would seem that William Sutton is paying off several years of arrears for his waxshot.

fol 38

Stock of the gild in the previous year namely millimo cccc^{mo} lxxxxvj^o

William Haux has xiijs iiijd by pledge of John Dak of which paid ijs

John Dak has iijs iiijd by pledge of William Haux

Matilda Dynyell owes xxiijd by pledge of John Yedson

John Bene taillour owes iijs iiijd

John Fyssher pewterer owes xiijs iiijd

William Freman owes xiijs iiijd by pledge of John Shilton

John Shilton owes xiijs iiijd by pledge of William Freman

Andrew Stodard owes xs paid this day xs and thus is quit

John Stede owes xxvjs viijd

Thomas Peryman owes xiijs iiijd

William Brighton owes xxd by pledge of John Cobbe

John Thurleby owes xxs by pledge of (Christopher *ins*) Broun

William Templer owes iiijs of which are allowed to him for his office of cook ijs
and for his office of bedell ijs for the past year. And thus quit.

Election of officers

[24] M Thomas Philipp Alderman of the gild

Robert Clerke and John Shylton providers for the feast

John Yetson steward

for the following year

Brethren and sisters newly admitted

Dna Agnes Leche anchoress admitted into membership[134] (*suffrag*) of the gild and
will give for entry vjs viijd

John Dycon formerly of Staunford deceased and Elizabeth Dycon living formerly
his wife this day admitted into confraternity of the gild and will give for entries
vjs viijd

Richard Bedwyn and Isabella vjs viijd of which paid xxd and thus owes vs

Alice wife of William Freman newly admitted into confraternity of the gild and
will pay for her entry according to the discretion of the Alderman and the
brethren ijs

Fr Hugh Broune of the order of Augustinians of Staunford admitted and will give
for his entry according to ancient custom vjs viijd

John Lee mercer vjs viijd

Robert Parsons and Margaret vjs viijd

---

[134] this may mean 'into the intercessions'

William Merys of the parish of Holy Trinity (and St Paul *ins*) and Elizabeth vjs viijd

fol 38d

Staunford: **Acts of the gild of St Katherine virgin and martyr in the parish of St Paul there held Sunday 26ᵗʰ November millimo cccc^mo lxxxxvij° and thirteenth year of the reign of King Henry VII**

Entry fines arrears for this day
Dna Katherine de la Pole owes for entry vjs viijd
David Malpas armiger vjs viijd
William Bryghton xxd by pledge of John Cobbe
John Lytster xxd
William Povy mason iijs iiijd
Fr Richard Leke xld which paid and quit
Fr Richard Ravenell xxd paid and quit
Reginald Loky vs
Walter Feyreday xxd paid and quit
John Netlam of Royall
Dom Richard Purley Rector of the church of St Paul vjs viijd paid xxd and owes
    vs
William Jurden iijs iiijd
William Weste xxd paid and quit
William Hynkeley iijs iiijd paid xxd and owes xxd
Robert Crane iijs iiijd paid iijs iiijd and thus quit
Thomas Edwarde iijs iiijd paid xxd and owes xxd
John Hynkeley bocher vjs viijd paid xld and owes iijs iiijd *(line squeezed in)*
John Markeby vs paid xxd and owes iijs iiijd
John Thomas vs paid xxd and owes iijs iiijd
James Thysteltwayte vs paid xxd and owes iijs iiijd
Hugh Wady vs paid xxd and owes xld
Richard Dey vs paid xxd and owes xld
Henry Yetson vs paid xxd and owes xld
Dna Agnes Leche anchoress vjs viijd paid xxd and owes vs
Elizabeth Dycons vjs viijd paid xxd and owes vs
Richard Bedwyn vjs viijd paid (xxd *del*) (xld *ins*) and owes (vs del) iijs iiijd
Alice wife of William Freman newly admitted [sic]
Fr Hugh Broun Augustinian vjs viijd paid xxd and owes vs
John Lee mercer vjs viijd paid xxd and owes vs

Robert Parsons vjs viijd paid xxd and owes vs
William Meyres vjs viijd paid xxd and owes vs
(John Hyckson owes *del*)

fol 39

Waxshott this year
Thomas Philipp Alderman of the gild paid for maintenance of the lights this year
 iiijd
Christopher Broun merchant of the staple paid for the same iiijd
Dna Katherine de la Pole
M William Spenser iiijd
William Waren
Thomas Edward iiijd
Nicholas Billesden iiijd
John Stede ijd
M Thomas Hickham ijd
M Richard Warmouth ijd
M Robert Grymston ijd
Dom Robert Taillour
Dom William Jaralde
Dom Richard Purley ijd
Fr Richard Leke ijd
Fr Richard Ravenell ijd
Robert Crane iiijd
William Jurden iiijd
Geoffrey Hampton ijd [*amended from* iiijd]
John Goylyn iiijd
John Lytster
John Cobbe mercer iiijd
Joan Peryman ijd
Thomas Parnell iiijd
John Netlam
William Weste iiijd
William Hynkeley iiijd
Walter Feyreday iiijd
Dom Edward Hughton
 Margaret Skynner ijd
John Thurleby
John Yetson iiijd

Thomas Couper baker iiijd
Thomas Clopton iiijd
Andrew Stodard iiijd
John Fissher iiijd
John Byllesby
Margeary [sic] Palmer ijd
Fr John Parnell ijd
Hugh Sutton iiijd
Richard Joy furrer iiijd
John Loryng iiijd
Dna Agnes Leche anchoress ijd
Elizabeth Dycons iiijd
Richard Bedwyn iiijd
John Lee (iiijd *del*) ijd
Hugh Wady iiijd
William Clerke kervour iiijd [*marg* nota]
Robert Clerke wryght iiijd
William Freman iiijd
John Shilton iiijd
John Wasshyngburgh iiijd
John Whipp ijd
William Templer ijd
William Bokenfelde iiijd
Richard Dey iiijd
Henry Yetson iiijd
William Meyres iiijd
Robert Parsons iiijd
Fr Hugh Brown ijd
John Wykes
William Bryghton
Margaret Hobson ijd
John Thomas iiijd
John Markeby iiijd
James Thistiltwayte ijd
Elena Haux ijd
John Hynkeley iiijd
Rawlen Loky

fol 39d

Stock of the gild written in the previous year (anno ante scripto)

William Haux has xiijs iiijd of which paid ijs as appears above and owes xjs viijd [sic]; and he is pardoned by the Alderman and brethren to the sum of viijs which he paid and is quit

John Dak has iijs iiijd by pledge of William Haux

Matilda Dynyell owes xxiijd by pledge of John Yetson

John Bene taillour owes iijs iiijd

John Fyssher pewterer xiijs iiijd of which paid gratuity xijd; he has day in the next account to pay the said xiijs iiijd by pledge of John Yetson, Andrew Stodard, Hugh Sutton, Roger Bedwyn etc

William Freman xiijs iiijd by pledge of John Shilton – he has day to pay at the feast of the Annunciation of BVM [25 March] next xxd And thus at each quarter in the year xxd until the said sum has been paid by the by pledge of of John Yetson, Richard Bedwyn and H Sutton

John Shylton xiijs iiijd by pledge of William Freman

John Stede owes xxvjs viijd 'payd' by Thomas Philipp and is quit

Thomas Peryman xiijs iiijd; paid gratuity viijd; by pledge of for the store (*staur*) M Robert Grymston

William Bryghton owes xxd by pledge of John Cobbe mercer

John Thurleby has xxs by pledge of Christopher Brown

Brethren and sisters newly admitted

M. Richard Cannell Alderman of Staunford merchant of the Calais staple and Alice his wife admitted into the membership of the gild and will give for entry as appears vjs viijd

David Cysell and Agnes[135] his wife in the same way admitted and will give for entry vjs viijd

Dom John Byrden Rector of the church of St Mary Staunford admitted and sworn in similar fashion vjs viijd

Laurence Cok and Elizabeth vjs viijd

---

[135] This entry poses a problem. The wife of David Cecil is usually given as Alice daughter of John Dycons, a prominent Stamford merchant and councillor; see e.g. S T Bindoff 1982 *The House of Commons 1509-1558* vols i-iii *Members* London: Secker and Warburg, etc. In his will of 1536-7 (see TNA/PRO PROB PCC 13 Adeane, 11/29/24; see also BL Cott. Charters iv 29), he talks about Jane his (second) wife (daughter of Thomas Roos of Dowsby, Lincs. While this register may be in error, this is unlikely; but although she is referred to several times, her name is not given again in these pages. The evidence for the name of Alice seems to come only from later pedigrees, visitations and antiquarians. For biography of David Cecil, see Alan Rogers, Parliamentary Representation of Stamford 1467 to 1509 (forthcoming).

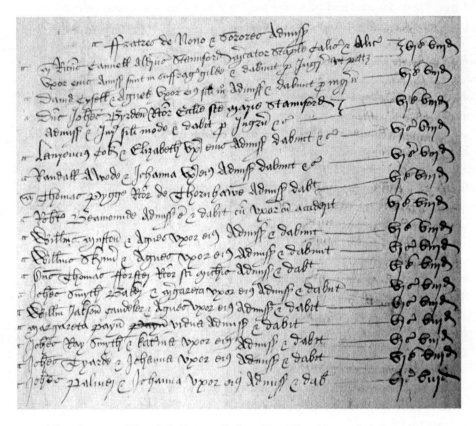

The admission of David Cecil, grandfather of Lord Burghley, and of Agnes his wife
(given in all pedigrees as Alice on the basis of notes compiled by Lord Burghley)

Randall a Wode and Joan vjs viijd
M Thomas Pygge Rector of Thornhawe vjs viijd
Robert Beaumonde with his wife cum acciderit vjs viijd
[24] William Muston and Agnes vjs viijd
William Skynner and Agnes vjs viijd
Dom Thomas Forster Rector of St Michael vjs viijd
John Smyth baker and Margaret vjs viijd
William Jakson candeler and Agnes vjs viijd
Margaret Payn (Payn *del*) widow vjs viijd
John Ray smyth and Katherine vjs viijd
John Tyarde and Joan vjs viijd
John Palmer and Joan vjs viijd

fol 40

Account

The account of John Shilton and Robert Clerke providers for the feast for certain expenses made by them for this day as appears by bills shown here totalling xviijs vd which they immediately received here in the exchequer and thus they were discharged quit

For rents

John Shilton tenant of the house (*domus*) of St Katherine paid this day in the exchequer xijs for his rent [due] for one whole year for the said house at Michaelmas before the day of this account etc

William Templer received here in the exchequer for the office of cook for the past year ijs
The same William received for the office of bedell for the past year ijs

Account

John Yetson steward of the gild rendered account for certain expenses made by him this year to the benefit of the gild namely for the wages of the priest and for certain obits for certain brethren of the gild deceased this year with certain other expenses as appears by a bill shown here in the exchequer to the sum of xxijs viijd which he immediately received and thus he was discharged quit

Note: And on this there was delivered newly to the said steward to be answered for elsewhere xxs

Remainder

And there remains in the exchequer certain particulars namely xxvjs viijd rendered for the debt of John Stede as appears above in the stock of the gild. Item xxs remains in the hands of M Thomas Philipp in the last account. And also now in this account there remains in the exchequer xxxijs – sum total of remainder iij li xviijs viijd And the said sum was delivered immediately to M Thomas Philipp Alderman of the gild to the benefit of the gild to be accounted elsewhere.

[25] Election of officers

M Thomas Philipp elected Alderman of the gild

John Yetton [Yetson] steward

John Shilton and Richard Joy furrer providers for the feast

for the following year etc

fol 40d

Staunford: Acts of the gild of St Katherine virgin and martyr in the parish of St Paul there held Sunday the feast of St Katherine virgin anno domini millimo ccccᵐᵒ lxxxxviijᵒ [25 November 1498] and the 14th year of the reign of King Henry VII

Entry fines

Dna Katherine de la Pole owes for entry vjs viijd

David Malpas armiger vjs viijd

William Bryghton by pledge of John Cobbe mercer xxd

John Lytster for entry xxd which paid and quit

William Povy mason iijs iiijd; he gave un spete de yron [nota *margin*][136]

Reginald Lokye vs

Dom Richard Purley vs paid (xxd *del*) (nil *ins*) [nota *margin*]

William Jurden iijs iiijd paid xxd and owes xxd

William Hynkeley xxd paid and quit

Thomas Edward xxd paid xxd and iiijd for le waxshott by the hand of Andrew Stodard and thus quit

John Hynkeley iijs iiijd

John Markeby iijs iiijd paid xxd and owes xxd

John Thomas iijs iiijd paid xxd and owes xxd

James Thysteltwayte iijs iiijd paid xxd and owes xxd

Hugh Wady iijs iiijd paid xxd and owes xxd

---

[136] the first occasion of payment in kind

Richard Dey iijs iiijd paid xxd and owes xxd
Henry Yetson iijs iiijd
Dna anchoress vs paid xxd and owes iijs iiijd
Elizabeth Dycons vs
Richard Bedwyn iijs iiijd paid xxd and owes xxd
Alice wife of William Freman [sic]
Fr Hugh Broun vs
John Lee mercer vs paid xxd and owes iijs iiijd
Robert Parsons vs paid xxd and owes iijs iiijd
William Meerys vs paid xxd and owes iijs iiijd
M Richard Cannell vjs viijd paid xxd and owes vs
David Cysell vjs viijd paid xxd and owes vs
Dom John Byrden vjs viijd paid iijs iiijd and owes iijs iiijd
Laurence Cok vjs viijd paid xxd and owes vs
Randall aWode vjs viijd
M Thomas Pygge vjs viijd paid xxd and owes vs
Robert Beamount vjs viijd paid xxd and owes vs

fol 41

Entries continued
William Muston vjs viijd paid xxd and owes vs
William Skynner vjs viijd paid xxd and owes vs
Dom Thomas Forster vjs viijd paid xxd and thus owes vs
John Smyth baker vjs viijd paid xxd and owes vs
William Jakson vjs viijd paid xxd and owes vs
Margaret Payn owes [blank]
John Ray smyth vjs viijd paid xxd and owes vs
John Tyarde vjs viijd paid xxd and owes vs
John Palmer vjs viijd paid xxd and owes vs
John Parker glover owes for entry as appears above vjs viijd

Names of those who have stock of the gild
John Dak has iijs iiijd by pledge of William Haux
Matilda Dynyell has xxiijd by pledge of John Yetson
John Bene has iijs iiijd
John Fissher has xiijs iiijd
William Freman has xiijs iiijd by pledge of John Shilton and others as before
John Shilton has xiijs iiijd by pledge of of William Freman
Joan formerly wife of Thomas Peryman has xiijs iiijd by pledge of M Robert
  Grymston; paid gratuity iiijd

William Bryghton alias Richardson [blank]. (*Nota ante* marg)
John Thurleby has xxs by pledge of Christopher Brown

Brethren newly admitted
William Bukston and Margaret admitted, sworn, will pay for entry vjs viijd
William Grenefelde and Joan vjs viijd
John Wattes peyntour and Margaret vjs viijd
William Clerke pewterer and Joan vjs viijd
Robert A Tales barbour and Agnes vjs viijd
Thomas Jakson shomaker and Margaret vjs viijd
John Palmer underbayly[137] and Joan vjs viijd [this line partly deleted "because above" *marginalia*]

fol 41d

Waxshote for maintenance of the wax and lights this year
M Thomas Philipp Alderman of the gild paid for maintenance of lights iiijd
M Christopher Broun merchant etc paid for the same iiijd
M William Spenser iiijd
M William Waren [blank]
Thomas Edwarde iiijd
Nicholas Billesden iiijd
John Stede ijd
M Thomas Hickham ijd
M Richard Warmouth ijd
M Robert Grymston ijd
Dom Robert Taillour pro eodem
Dom William Jarald pro consimil'
Dom Richard Purley
M Robert Crane iiijd
M Richard Cannell iiijd
M Thomas Pygge ijd
Dom John Byrdon ijd
Fr Richard Leeke ijd
Fr Richard Ravenell ijd
Fr Hugh Broune ijd
Geoffrey Hampton ijd
William Skynner iiijd

---

[137] this post is otherwise unknown; it may refer to the town rather than the gild.

William Jurden iiijd
Laurence Cokke iiijd
Robert Beamounde ijd
Randalff Wode
David Sycell iiijd
Dom Thomas Forster ijd
John Cobbe iiijd
John Goylyn iiijd
John Lytster ijd
John Tyarde iiijd
John Yedson iiijd
Margaret Skynner ijd
Dom Edward Houghton ijd
Thomas Couper iiijd
Thomas Clopton iiijd
Andrew Stodarde iiijd
John Thurleby
John Loryng iiijd
William Meyres paid iiijd
Dna anchoress ijd
Fr John Parnell ijd
Joan Parnell ijd
Joan Pyreman ijd (owes ijd *del*)
Hugh Wady iiijd
Hugh Sutton iiijd
John Fyssher iiijd
John Byllesby iiijd
Margery Palmer ijd
William Weste iiijd
Richard Joye furrer iiijd
William Hynkelely iiijd
John a Lee mercer ijd
Richard Bedwyn iiijd
John Wykys
Walter Feyreday iiijd
William Muston iiijd
John Smyth baker iiijd
William Jakson candeler iiijd
Margaret Payn
John Ray smyth iiijd

Henry Yetson iiijd
John Thomas iiijd
John Markeby iiijd
John Hynkeley owes iiijd
Helena Haux ijd
Margaret Hobson ijd
James Thystelthwayte ijd
Robert A Parsons iiijd
William Clerke kervour iiijd
William Freman
Robert Clerke wryght iiijd
William Templer ijd
John Shylton iiijd
John Wasshyngburgh iiijd
John Whyppe ijd
William Bokenfelde iiijd
Richard Dey ffissher iiijd
Rawlen Loky
William Richardson iiijd
John Palmer underbayly iiijd
John Parker glover

fol 42

Account

The account of John Shilton and Richard Joye furrer providers for the feast for certain expenses made by them this year for the benefit (*utilitat*) of the gild as appears by bills shown here this day in the exchequer and allowed xxs xd which they immediately received and were discharged quit

For receipt of rents

Memorandum that John Shilton tenant of the tenement of St Katherine paid to the Alderman of the gild for his rent due Michaelmas [29 September] last past xijs

Account

Account of John Yedson steward of the gild for certain particulars paid by him this year to the benefit of the gild as appears by a bill shown this day and allowed namely for the wages of the priest this year and also for other expenses as appears etc the price of which [came] to the sum of xxiijs ijd which he received and thus was discharged quit

Remainder

The same steward rendered account for xxs delivered to him in the last account which he took upon himself here in the exchequer. And in addition there was delivered to the said steward, with the said xxs, xxijs for which he shall answer - total xxijs [sic]

And at this time there remains in the hands of Thomas Philipp Alderman of the gild as appears in the last account iij li xviijs viijd. And of the remaining sums this day namely xls was delivered to the said Alderman. And thus there are now in his hands in total v li xviijs viijd

William Templer received this day for the office of cook and bedell for the past year iiijs

Election of officers for the following year

Thomas Philipp elected Alderman of the gild

Richard Joyee and William Bokenfelde providers for the feast

John Yetson steward of the gild

William Templer into the office of cook and will have for his wages xxd

William Richardson bedell for the following year and will have ijs

fol 42d

Staunford: Acts of the gild of St Katherine virgin and martyr held in the parish of St Paul Apostle in the town of Staunford Sunday the vigil of the feast of St Katherine virgin [24 November] the 15th year of the reign of King Henry VII and anno domini millimo cccc^mo lxxxxix^o

Entry fines

Dna Katherine de la Pole owes for entry vjs viijd

David Malpas vjs viijd

William Bryghton by pledge of J Cobbe xxd which paid in the office of bedell and quit

Reginald Loky vs

Dom Richard Purley Rector of Poules vs

William Jurden xxd

John Hynkeley iijs iiijd

John Markeby xxd paid and quit

John Thomas xxd paid and quit

James Thystyltwayte taillour xxd paid and quit

Hugh Wady xxd paid and quit

Richard Dey xxd paid and quit

Henry Hykson iijs iiijd

Dna anchoress iijs iiijd paid xxd and owes xxd

Elizabeth Dycons vs paid xxd and owes iijs iiijd

Richard Bedwyn xxd paid and quit

Alice wife of William Freman

Fr Hugh Broun Augustinian vs of which allowed to him for the celebration of
  masses in the chapel of St Katherine xxd and thus he owes iijs iiijd   (nota *marg*)

John Lee mercer iijs iiijd

Robert Parsons iijs iiijd paid xxd and owes xxd

William Meerys iijs iiijd

M Richard Cannell vs paid xxd and owes iijs iiijd

David Sycyll vs paid xxd and owes iijs iiijd

Dom John Byrden iijs iiijd paid xxd and owes xxd

Laurence Cok vs paid xxd and owes iijs iiijd

Randalff Wode vjs viijd

Dom Thomas Pygge vs paid xxd and owes xld

Robert Beamonde vs paid xxd and owes iijs iiijd

fol 43

entries continued

William Muston tayllour vs paid xxd and owes iijs iiijd

William Skynner vs paid xxd and owes iijs iiijd

Dom Thomas Forster vs paid xxd and owes iijs iiijd

John Smyth baker vs paid xxd and owes iijs iiijd

William Jakson candeler vs paid xxd and owes iijs iiijd

Margaret formerly wife of William Payn

John Ray smyth vs paid xxd and owes iijs iiijd

John Tyard bocher vs paid xxd and owes iijs iiijd

John Palmer underbayly vs paid xxd and owes iijs iiijd

John Parker glover vjs viijd

William Bukston sadeler vjs viijd paid xxd and owes vs

William Greneffeld taillour vjs viijd paid xxd and owes vs

John Wattes peyntour vjs viijd paid xxd and owes vs

William Clerke pewterer vjs viijd paid xxd and owes vs

Robert Atales barbour vjs viijd paid xxd and owes vs

Thomas Jakson shomaker vjs viijd paid xxd and owes vs

Names of those who have stock of the gild
John Dak has iijs iiijd by pledge of William Haux
Matilda Dynyell owes xxiijd by pledge of John Hykson
John Bene owes iijs iiijd
John Fyssher pewterer owes xiijs iiijd paid vjs viijd and owes vjs viijd
William Freman owes xiijs iiijd by pledge of John Shylton paid xs and owes iijs
    iiijd
John Shilton owes xiijs iiijd
Joan wife of Thomas Peryman owes xiijs iiijd by pledge of Maurice Bachyn paid
    iijs iiijd and owes xs
John Thurleby owes xxs by pledge of Christopher Broun

New brethren
Dom Robert Bates prior of St Leonards admitted, sworn into the membership of
    the gild vjs viijd
[26] Fr Thomas Harneys prior of friars preachers admitted vjs viijd
Fr William Henson prior of Carmelite friars vjs viijd
David Robynson bocher and Alice admitted and sworn vjs viijd
John Bassam barbour and Agnes admitted and sworn vjs viijd
Robert Cobbe wever and Joan vjs viijd
Maurice Bachyn admitted and sworn vjs viijd

fol 43d

Waxshot for maintenance of the wax and lights this year
Thomas Philipp Alderman of the gild paid for maintenance of wax iiijd
Christopher Broun armiger paid [blank]
M William Spenser paid iiijd
Dna [blank]
M Richard Cannell paid iiijd
Dna anchoress paid [blank]
Robert Crane paid iiijd
Nicholas Byllesdon iiijd
Thomas Edwarde
John Stede ijd
M Thomas Hykham ijd
M Robert Grymston ijd
Dom John Byrdon ijd

Dom Richard Purley
Dom Thomas Pygge ijd
Dom Thomas Forster ijd
Dom William Geralde
Dom Robert Taillour
Fr Richard Leeke ijd
Fr Richard Ravenell ijd
Fr Hugh Broun   ijd
Geoffrey Hampton ijd
William Skynner iiijd
Margaret Skynner
William Jurden iiijd
Laurence Cok iiijd
John Goylyn iiijd
John Lytster ijd
David Cysell iiijd
John Cobbe iiijd
John Tyard iiijd
Thomas Couper baker iiijd
Dom Edward Houghton
Robert Beamount ijd
John Thurleby
Fr John Parnell ijd
Randalff a Wode
John a Lee ijd
Hugh Wady iiijd
Thomas Clopton iiijd
Andrew Stoderde iiijd
John Loryng
William Merys ijd
Margery Hykson ijd
Hugh Sutton smyth iiijd
John Fyssher iiijd
John Byllysby iiijd
Richard Deye iiijd
Margery Palmer ijd
William Weste
Richard Bedwyn iiijd
John Ray smyth iiijd
William Bukston iiijd

William Grenefelde iiijd

Thomas Jakson shomaker iiijd

William Clerke pewterer iiijd

Robert A Tales iiijd

John Smyth baker iiijd

John Wattes peyntour iiijd

William Jakson candeler iiijd

John Wykes

Walter Feyreday iiijd

Margaret formerly wife of William Payn

John Palmer underbayly iiijd

James Thystelthwayte iiijd

Henry Hyckson

Joan Parnell ijd

Joan Pyryman ijd

William Hynkeley iiijd

William Muston taillour iiijd

William Templer ijd

John Thomas shomaker iiijd

John Hynkeley

John Markeby ijd

Robert A Parsons iiijd

John Shilton iiijd

John Wasshyngburgh iiijd

William Bokenfeld iiijd

John Whipp ijd

Rawlen Lokye

William Richardson iiijd

William Clerke kervour iiijd

Robert Clerke wryght iiijd

Helena Haux

Margaret Hobson paid ijd

Alice wife of W Freman

John Parker glover

[blank] wife of Richard Joye ijd

fol 44

Account of providers of the feast

The account of William Bokenfeld and William Templer providers for the feast for certain expenses made by them this year for the benefit of the gild as appears by bills shown here in the exchequer and allowed total of xxxiijs viijd ; and also they accounted for certain payments made and delivered by them namely to Margery wife of John Hyckson[138] formerly steward of the gild for certain expenses incurred by him this year and for the wages of the chaplain celebrating in the chapel of St Katherine there to the Nativity [Christmas] next after the receipt of this account and for other expenses to the benefit of the gild total viijs xd. Sum total of payments xxxijs vjd. Immediately [*in margin*].

From the Alderman of the gild received xs viijd. And from cash (*denariis*) at the general entertainment (*conviv'*) this day they received xiijs iijd[139] And also they received in the exchequer in full payment vijs vijd and thus they were discharged quit.

Account of the steward

To this account came Margery wife of John Hyckson formerly steward of the gild now deceased and she took upon herself (*pertulit*) and showed here in the exchequer a bill for certain expenses made by the said steward this year to the benefit of the gild and also she rendered account for xxijs received by her said husband as appears in the last year's account; and all accounts and allowances included as appears above in the account of the providers for the feast she was discharged quit; yet she is due to pay to the chaplain of the gild for his wages at the Nativity next etc ijs

Answering for the rents of the gild

At this account came [blank] the wife of John Shylton and paid for rent of the tenement of the gild due at Michaelmas last before the date of this account xijs

Remainder

And at this time there remains in the hands of M Thomas Phillipp Alderman of the gild as appears in the last account v li xviijs viijd And at this account he received xls. And thus now remains in his hands vij li xviijd viijd.

---

[138] see next account
[139] this may represent the payments for the dinner.

Remainder exonerated

And there was delivered at this account from the remaining sums in the exchequer to Andrew Stodard steward newly elected to the benefit of the gild for which he will answer elsewhere xxijs. And the said Andrew Stodard is exonerated for this sum in his next account following etc.

Election of officers for the coming year

M Thomas Philipp elected Alderman of the gild

Andrew Stodarde steward of the gild

William Bokenffelde and Walter Feyreday providers for the feast

William Bryghton bedell and will have for his labours ijs iiijd

William Templer into the office of cook of the feast and will have for his labours [blank]

fol 44d

Staunford: Acts of the gild of St Katherine virgin and martyr 1500 (*anno domini quingentesimo*) and the 16th (*sextodecimo*) year of the reign of King Henry VII in the parish of St Paul Apostle Sunday 29 November etc

Entry fines

Reginald Lokye owes for entry into the fraternity of the gild vs

Dom Richard Purley Rector owes vs

William Jurden xxd

John Hynkeley iijs iiijd paid xxd and owes xxd

Henry Hykson iijs iiijd

Dna anchoress xxd which paid and is quit

Elizabeth Dycons iijs iiijd

Alice (formerly *ins*) wife of William Freman owes for entry ijs

Fr Hugh Broun iijs iiijd

John Lee mercer iijs iiijd

Robert A Parsons xxd which paid and thus discharged quit

William Meerys iijs iiijd paid xxd and owes xxd

M Richard Cannell iijs iiijd paid xxd and owes xxd

David Cysell iijs iiijd

Rector of the church of St Mary xxd which paid and is quit

Laurence Cock iijs iiijd paid xxd and owes xxd

Randall a Wode vjs viijd

Rector Pygg iijs iiijd

Robert Beamount iijs iiijd paid xxd and owes xxd

William Muston tayllour iijs iiijd paid xxd and owes xxd

William Skynner iijs iiijd paid xxd and owes xxd

Rector of the church of St Michael iijs iiijd paid xxd and owes xxd

John Smyth baker iijs iiijd

William Jakson candeler iijs iiijd paid xxd and owes xxd

Margaret formerly wife of William Payn

John Ray smyth iijs iiijd paid xxd and owes xxd

John Tyarde Bocher iijs iiijd paid xxd and owes xxd

John Palmer underbayly iijs iiijd paid xxd and owes xxd

John Parker glover vjs viijd

William Bukston sadeler vs paid xxd and owes iijs iiijd

William Grenfelde taillour vs paid xxd and owes iijs iiijd

John Wattes peyntour vs paid xxd and owes iijs iiijd

fol 45

Entries continued

William Clerke pewterer owes for his entry vs paid xxd and owes iijs iiijd

Robert Attales barbour vs paid xxd and owes iijs iiijd

Thomas Jakson shomaker vs paid xxd and owes iijs iiijd

M prior of St Leonards vjs viijs   paid iijs iiijd and owes iijs iiijd

M prior of friars preachers vjs viijs   paid xxd and owes vs

M prior of friars Carmelites vjs viijs   paid xxd and owes vs

David Robynson bocher vjs viijs   paid xxd and owes vs

John Bassam barbour vjs viijs   paid xxd and owes vs

Robert Cobbe wever vjs viijs   paid xxd and owes vs

Maurice Bawchon vjs viijd paid xd and owes vs xd

Names of those who have stock of the gild

John Dak has iijs iiijd by pledge of William Hawx

Matilda Dynyell owes xxiijd by pledge of John Hykson

John Bene owes iijs iiijd

John Fyssher pewterer owes vjs viijd

William Freman owes iijs iiijd by pledge of John Shilton and paid ijs iiijd and owes
   xijd

John Shilton owes xiijs iiijd

Joan wife of M Thomas Pyryman owes xs

John Thurleby owes xxs by pledge of Christopher Broun paid xs and owes xs

Election of offices
Thomas Philipp elected Alderman of the gild
Walter Feyreday and William Clerke kerver elected providers of the feast
Andrew Stoderde elected into the office of steward of the gild
Richard Bedwyn elected as supervisor of the works and repairs to be made in (*infra*) the tenement of St Katherine etc
William Templer elected into the office of cook and he has agreed to exercise his office for the next feast [convivio] free for the said repairs etc
William Bryghton elected bedell.

fol 45d

Waxshot for maintenance of the wax and lights of this gild for the past (elaps') year
Thomas Philip Alderman of the gild paid for wax etc iiijd
Geoffrey Hampton Alderman of Staunford paid for the same (ii *del*) ijd
Christopher Broun armiger
Dna [blank] Wareyn
Dna Margaret Spenser iiijd
M Richard Cannell iiijd
Dna anchoress ijd
Robert Crane ijd
Nicholas Byllesden
Thomas Edwarde
John Stede ijd
M Thomas Hyckham ijd
M Robert Grymston ijd
M parson of seynt Maryes ijd
M parson of seynt Michells ijd
Rector of St Pauls Richard Purley
Vicar of Holywell
Prior of the Augustinian friars ijd
Fr Richard Ravenell ijd
Fr Hugh Broun
William Skynner iiijd
Margaret Skynner
William Jurdeyn iiijd
Laurence Cok iiijd
John Goylyn iiijd

John Lytster ijd
David Cysell
John Cobbe iiijd
John Tyarde iiijd
Thomas Couper baker iiijd
Vicar of Royall
Robert Beamount ijd
John Thurleby
Fr John Parnell ijd
John a Lee
Hugh Wady iiijd
Thomas Clopton iiijd
Andrew Stodarde iiijd
John Loryng
William Merys paid ijd
Margery Hykson ijd
Hugh Sutton smyth iiijd
John Fyssher pewterer iiijd
John Byllesby
Richard Dey iiijd
Margery Palmer ijd
Joan Weste iiijd
Richard Bedwyn iiijd
John Ray smyth iiijd
William Bukston iiijd (ijd amended to iiijd)
William Grenefelde iiijd
Thomas Jakson shomaker iiijd
Joan Clerke[140] iiijd
Robert A Tales iiijd
John Smyth baker iiijd
John Wattes peynter iiijd
William Jakson candeler iiijd
John Wykes
Walter Feyreday iiijd
John Palmer underbayly iiijd
James Taillour ijd
Henry Hykson

---

[140] She is, I think, the wife of William Clerke pewterer who later married George Trolopp; see fol 50; to be distingushed from William Clerke carver.

Joan Parnell ijd
Moreys Bachyn iiijd
William Hynkeley iiijd
William Muston iiijd
William Templer ijd
John Thomas iiijd
John Hynkeley iiijd
John Markeby iiijd
Robert a Parsons iiijd
John Shilton iiijd
William Bokynffeld iiijd
John Whipp ijd
(Rawlen Loky *written in margin*)
William Richardson iiijd
William Clerke kerver iiijd
Robert Clerke wryght iiijd
Margaret Hobson paid ijd
Isabell Joye ijd
The prior of St Leonards ijd
Prior of the friars preachers ijd
Prior of the friars Carmelite ijd
David Roberds bocher iiijd
John Bassam iiijd
Robert Cobbe wever iiijd

fol 46

Brethren newly admitted and sisters

[29] Dom John Rutkyn Rector of the church of Stretton admitted and sworn into
the fraternity of the gild; will give for his entry money vjs viijd paid xxd and
owes vs

[30] Dom Robert Brokenhurst Rector of the church of St Paul Staunford admitted
etc and will give vjs viijd for entry money paid xxd and owes vs

M Agnes Broun wife of Christopher Broun[141] armiger admitted etc and will give
[blank]

Thomas Hanford and Alice vjs viijd

John Burbage and Isabella vjs viijd

---

[141] This may be the second wife of Christopher Broun and if so may be from the Bedingfeld
family of Norfolk; see Visit Rut

John Lyryffax draper and Alice vjs viijd

William Inkersale baker and Joan vjs viijd

John Boston bocher and Margaret vjs viijd

Joan wife of William Templer received into the membership of the gild and will
give iijs iiijd

John Sharpe mercer and Agnes admitted into fraternity of the gild, will give for
entry money vjs viijd paid xxd and owes vs

Account

The account of William Bokynffelde and Walter Feyreday providers for the feast
rendered account for certain expenses made by them this year for the benefit of
the gild as appears by bills thus made and shown here in the court (*curia*) and
allowed in the exchequer (*scaccario*) up to the total of xxxijs vjd which they
received and thus are quit.

Account

The account of Andrew Stodard steward of the gild for certain expenses incurred
by him this year to the benefit of the said gild as appears by bills shown here in
the exchequer and allowed namely for celebrating certain obits of the brethren
of the gild this year and for the wages of the chaplain of the gild and other
necessary expenses as well as rendering account for xxijs remaining in his hands
as appears in the last account; the sum total of the particulars of the bills with
wax and his service (*factur*) xliijs vjd And thus the said steward is in surplus xxjs
vjd which he received and was discharged quit

Remainder

And there remains yet (*ad hunc diem*) in the exchequer, all allowances and accounts
included, xxxvijs ijd which immediately were delivered to Andrew Stodarde
steward of the gild and which will be accounted for elsewhere.

Remainder

And also there remains in the hands of Thomas Philipp Alderman of the gild vij li
xviiijs viijd as appears in the preceding account etc

Election of officers

Thomas Philipp elected Alderman of the gild

Andrew Stodarde steward of the gild

Walter Feyreday and William Clerke kervour providers for the feast

Richard Bedwyn elected supervisor of the repair works to the house of the gild

William Templer into the office of cook of the feast and he will give his wages to the said repairs

William Bryghton bedell

[fol 46d blank]

fol 47

Staunford: Acts of the gild of St Katherine virgin and martyr anno domini 1501 and the 17th year of the reign of King Henry VII

Entry fines

Reginald Lokye owes for entry into the fraternity of the gild vs

Dom Richard Purley formerly Rector[142] of St Pauls vs

William Jurden xxd (paid and quit *erased*)

John Hynkeley xxd paid and quit

Henry Hyckson iijs iiijd

Elizabeth Dycons widow iijs iiijd

Alice formerly wife of William Freman (xijd *del*) ijs

Fr Hugh Broun iijs iiijd

John Lee mercer iijs iiijd

William Meerys xxd

M Richard Cannell xxd which paid as appears in the next account following

David Cysell iijs iiijd which paid by his wife and is quit

Laurence Cok xxd paid and quit

Randalff a Wode vjs viijd

Rector Pygge iijs iiijd

Robert Beamount xxd paid and quit

William Muston xxd paid by his wife and quit

William Skynner xxd paid and quit

Rector of the church of St Michael xxd paid and quit

John Smyth baker iijs iiijd

William Jakson candeler xxd paid and quit

Margaret formerly wife of William Payn for entry vjs viijd

John Ray smyth xxd paid and quit

John Tyarde xxd paid and quit

John Palmer xxd paid and quit

---

[142] the term 'Rector' was used for most clergy although some of those listed here were in fact vicars. The term 'vicar' occurs occasionally.

John Parker (glover *ins*) vjs viijd
William Bukston iijs iiijd
William Greneffelde iijs iiijd paid xxd and owes xxd
John Wattes peyntour iijs iiijd paid xxd and owes xxd
William Clerke pewterer iijs iiijd
Robert Attales barbour iijs iiijd xxd paid and owes xxd
Thomas Jakson shomaker iijs iiijd xxd paid and owes xxd
M Robert Bates formerly prior of St Leonards iijs iiijd paid xxd and owes xxd
M prior of friars preachers Fr Thomas Harneys vs paid xxd and owes xld [sic]
M prior of friars Carmelites Fr William Henson vs paid xxd and owes xld
David Robynson bocher vs paid xxd and owes xld
John Bassam barbour vs paid xxd and owes xld
Robert Cobbe wever vs paid xxd and owes xld
Maurice Bawchyn vs xd
Dom John Rutkyn Rector of Stretton vs paid xxd and owes xld
Dom Robert Brokenhurst Rector of the church of St Paul vs paid xxd and owes
   xld
M [sic] Agnes wife of Christopher Broun armiger [blank]
Thomas Hanfford vjs viijd paid xxd and owes vs
John Burbage vjs viijd
John Leryfax vjs viijd paid xxd and owes vs
William Hynkelsale vjs viijd paid xxd owes vs
John Boston bocher vjs viijd paid xxd owes vs
Joan wife of William Templer owes iijs iiijd
John Sharpe mercer vs

fol 47d

Waxshot 1501
Thomas Philipp Alderman of the gild paid for maintenance of wax iiijd
Nicholas Byllesdon Alderman of Staunford paid iiijd
Christopher Broun armiger paid iiijd
Dna [blank] Waren
Dna Margaret Spenser ijd
M Richard Cannell iiijd
Dna anchoress
Robert Crane ijd
Thomas Edwarde
John Stede ijd
M Thomas Hykham ijd

M Robert Grymston ijd
M Rector of St Mary ijd
M Rector of St Michael ijd
Dom Richard Purley
Vicar of Holywell
Prior of the Augustinian friars ijd
Fr Richard Ravenell ijd
Fr Hugh Broun
William Skynner iiijd (*altered from ijd*)
Margaret Skynner ijd
William Jurden
Larence [sic] Cok iiijd
John Goylyn iiijd (*altered from ijd*)
John Lytster
David Cesell iiijd
John Cobbe iiijd
John Tyard iiijd
Thomas Couper baker iiijd
Vicar of Ryall
Robert Beamount ijd
John Thurleby
Fr John Parnell ijd
John a Lee ijd
Hugh Wady iiijd
Thomas Clopton iiijd
Andrew Stodard iiijd
John Loryng ijd
William Meerys
Margery Hykson ijd
Hugh Smyth iiijd
John Fyssher pewtrer iiijd
John Byllesby iiijd
Richard Dey iiijd
Margery Palmer ijd
Joan Weste
Richard Bedwyn iiijd
John Ray smyth iiijd
William Bukston
William Grenffelde iiijd
Thomas Jakson shomaker iiijd

Joan formerly wife of William Clerke
Robert Attales iiijd
John Smyth baker ijd
John Wattes peyntour iiijd
William Jakson candeler iiijd
John Wykes
Walter Feyreday iiijd
John Palmer iiijd
James Taillour ijd
Henry Hykson
Joan Parnell ijd
Maurice Bawchyn
William Hynkeley iiijd
William Muston iiijd
William Templer iiijd (stet *marg*)
John Thomas iiijd
John Hynkeley iiijd
John Markeby (iiijd *del*) ijd
Robert a Parsons iiijd
John Shilton iiijd
William Bokenffeld iiijd
John Whippe ijd
Rawlen Loky
William Richardson iiijd
(Agnes formerly wife of William Clerke kerver *del*)
William Clerke kerver iiijd
Robert Clerke wryght iiijd
Margaret Hobson ijd
Isabell Joye ijd
Dom Robert Bates formerly prior of St Leonards
Fr Thomas Harneys prior of the friars preachers ijd
Fr W Henson prior of the friars Carmelite ijd
David Roberts bocher iiijd
Dom John Ritkyn Rector of Stretton ijd
Dom Robert Brokenhurst Rector of St Paul ijd
Thomas Hanford iiijd
John Burbage
John Lyryffax iiijd
William Hynkersale iiijd
John Boston iiijd

John Sherpe mercer iiijd
[143]John Bassam barbour ijd (*altered from iiijd*)
Robert Cobbe wever iiijd
Geffrey Hampton iiijd
John Wasshyngburgh by hys wyff for iij yers behynde paied xijd. Item owes for
 this yer iiijd

fol 48

Stock of the gild
John Dak iijs iiijd by pledge of William Haux
Matilda Dynyell xxiijd by pledge of John Hykson
John Bene iijs iiijd by pledge of Robert Yerdeley
John Fissher pewterer vjs viijd by pledge of Andrew Stodard with others
The wife of William Freman xijd by pledge of John Shylton
John Shylton xiijs iiijd by pledge of W Freman
Maurice Bawchon and Joan his wife owe xs by pledge of M Robert Grymston
John Thurleby xs by pledge of Christopher Broun

Brethren and sisters newly admitted
Agnes wife of Thomas Philipp admitted will give [blank]
Richard Hardy and Alice his wife sworn and admitted will give vjs viijd
[31] Dom Thomas Folkelyn chaplain vjs viijd
Thomas Maidwell and Agnes vjs viijd
Fr Robert Legate prior of Carmelites of Northampton admitted into the
 membership of the gild will give vjs viijd paid xxd and owes vs
Henry Pypes and Isabella received and will give vjs viijd
John Parys and Amy his wife vjs viijd
Roger Gogh barbour and Margaret vjs viijd
Antony Hawe and Alice vjs viijd

Alice Bewshir widow among the living and William Bewshir among the dead
 were received (*inter vivos et* [WB] *inter mortuos recept' sunt*) into the fraternity of the
 gild and they will pay (*solvent*) according to ancient custom vjs viijd

Account
The account of Walter Feyreday and William Clerke kervour providers for the
 feast rendered account for certain expenses made by them this year for the

---

[143] the following four items are entered in a larger and more informal handwriting

benefit of the gild as appears by a bill shown here in the exchequer and allowed to the total of xxxiijs xd which they received and they have been discharged quit.

The account of Andrew Stodarde steward of the gild for certain payments and expenses made by him this year to the benefit of the said gild and paid as appears by bills shown here in the exchequer and allowed with the wages paid to the chaplain of the gild to the feast of the Nativity next and for celebrating the obit for the wife of John Bassam etc; the sum of the particulars xxxjs xjd, which he received immediately and thus he is discharged quit of this.

There remains for this day all accounts accounted for and allowed and paid etc ixs which immediately were delivered to Andrew Stoderd and which will be accounted for elsewhere.

fol 48d

The same Acts continued

Officers of the gild
Thomas Philipp elected Alderman of the gild
Andrew Stodard steward of the gild
William Clerke kervour and Richard Bedwyn providers for the feast
William Templer into the office of cook
William Bryghton bedell

fol 49

Staunford: Acts of the gild of St Katherine virgin and martyr anno domini 1502 and the 18th year of the reign of King Henry VII in the parish of St Paul there

Entry into the fraternity of the gild
Reginald Lokye owes for entry vs
Dom Richard Purley vs
William Jurden xxd
Henry Hyckson iijs iiijd
Elizabeth Dycons widow iijs iiijd
Alice formerly wife of William Freman ijs
Fr Hugh Broun iijs iiijd
John Lee mercer iijs iiijd

William Merys xxd which paid and quit

M Richard Cannell xxd paid and quit

Randalff a Woode vjs viijd

Parson Pygge iijs iiijd

John Smyth baker iijs iiijd

Margaret Payn vjs viijd

John Parker glover vjs viijd

William Bukston iijs iiijd

William Clerke pewterer iijs iiijd

William Greneffelde xxd paid and quit

John Wattes peyntour xxd paid and quit

Robert Attales barbour xxd paid and quit

Thomas Jakson shomaker xxd paid and quit

M Robert Bates formerly prior of St Leonards (iijs iiijd *del*) xxd paid and quit

Prior of friars preachers iijs iiijd paid xxd and owes xxd

Prior of friars Carmelites iijs iiijd paid xxd and owes xxd

David Robynson bocher iijs iiijd paid xxd and owes xxd

John Bassam iijs iiijd paid xxd and owes xxd

Robert Cobbe wever iijs iiijd paid xxd and owes xxd

Maurice Bawchon vs xd

Rector of Stretton in le Strete iijs iiijd paid xxd and owes xxd

Rector of the church of St Paul Staunford iijs iiijd paid xxd and owes xxd

M [sic] Agnes wife of Christopher Broun armiger iijs iiijd; paid and quit

Thomas Hanforde vs paid xxd and owes iijs iiijd

John Burbage vjs viijd

John Loryfax draper vs paid xxd and owes iijs iiijd

William Hynkelsale vs paid xxd owes iijs iiijd

John Boston bocher vs paid xxd owes iijs iiijd

Joan wife of William Templer owes for entry iijs iiijd; paid xxd and owes xxd

her for entries [sic]

fol 49d

Here for entries into fraternity of gild

John Sharpe mercer owes for entry vs paid xxd and owes iijs iiijd which paid and
    is quit [sic]

(respond per John Goylyn xld *marginalia*)

Agnes wife of Thomas Philipp owes for entry iijs iiijd

Richard Hardy owes for entry vjs viijd paid xxd and owes vs

The admission of Lady Margaret Beaufort of Collyweston near Stamford has been squeezed onto the page before the first main entry. William Elmes, who was Recorder of Stamford, Nicholas Trygge notary and William Radclyffe gentleman of Stamford, who were all closely associated with the household of Lady Margaret, and one of her servants, were admitted to the gild at the same time

Dom Thomas Folkelyn chaplain vjs viijd paid xxd and owes vs

Thomas Maidewell owes for entry vjs viijd paid xxd and owes vs

Fr Robert Legat etc vs paid xxd owes iijs iiijd

Henry Pypes vjs viijd

John Parys vjs viijd paid xxd and owes vs

Roger Gogh barbour vjs viijd paid xxd and owes vs

Anthony Hawe wryght vjs viijd

Alice Bewshir widow vjs viijd

Brethren and sisters admitted

[32] [144]Dna Margaret countess of Richmond and Derby and mother of king Henry
   VII admitted, paid iijs iiijd

M William Elmes and Elizabeth his wife received [sic] will give vjs viijd, paid and
   quit

M William Radclyff and Elizabeth his wife received and admitted and will give vjs
   viijd

M Nicholas Trygge and Joan his wife vjs viijd

[32] Richard Cotmount servant of the Countess of Richmond [blank] will give vjs
   viijd

[34] Dom John Stoderde Rector of Clypsham vjs viijd

Thomas Langar and Emma vjs viijd

Thomas Godeale and Agnes vjs viijd

William Pottell and Isabella vjs viijd

Edward Broune glover and Alice vjs viijd

William Tubman bocher and Emma vjs viijd

Elizabeth Sabyn widow received [blank]

Joan wife of William Merys vjs viijd

Fr Christopher Ryder of the order of Carmelites received, will pay vjs viijd

Alice wife of John Bassam iijs iiijd

John Moreton and Elizabeth vjs viijd

fol 50

Waxshot for the maintenance of the wax and lights of the said gild in the year millimo ccccc^{mo} ij^o

Thomas Phillipp Alderman of the gild paid for wax iiijd

Christopher Broun armiger and Alderman of the borough of Staunford iiijd

Dna [blank] Wareyn

Dna Margaret Spenser ijd

---

[144] This line is squeezed in between heading and first line of entry

Richard Cannell iiijd
Dna anchoress ijd
Robert Crane
Thomas Edward
John Stede ijd
M Thomas Hyckham ijd
M Robert Grymston ijd
Rector of St Mary ijd
Rector of St Michael ijd
Dom Richard Purley
Prior of the Augustinian friars ijd
Fr Richard Ravenell ijd
Fr Hugh Broun
William Skynner iiijd
Margaret Skynner ijd
William Jurden
Wife of Laurence Cok
John Goylyn iiijd
John Lytster ijd
David Cysell iiijd
John Cobbe iiijd
John Tyarde iiijd
Thomas Couper iiijd
Vicar of Ryall
Robert Beamont ijd
John Thurleby
Fr John Parnell ijd
John a Lee ijd
Hugh Wadye iiijd
Thomas Clopton iiijd
Andrew Stodarde iiijd
John Loryng ijd
William Merys ijd
Margery Hyckson ijd
Hugh Smyth iiijd
John Fyssher iiijd
John Byllesby iiijd
Richard Dey iiijd
Margery Palmer ijd
Joan West ijd

Richard Bedwyn iiijd
John Ray smyth iiijd
William Bukston
Geoffrey Hampton ijd
Nicholas Byllesden iiijd
William Grenefelde iiijd
Thomas Jakson shomaker iiijd
Joan wife of Trolopp
Robert Attales iiijd
John Smyth baker ijd
John Wattes peyntour iiijd
William Jakson candeler iiijd
John Wykes
Walter Feyreday iiijd
John Palmer iiijd
James Taillour ijd
Henry Hykson
Joan Parnell ijd
Maurice Bawchon iiijd
William Hynkeley iiijd
William Muston iiijd
William Templer iiijd
John Thomas shomaker iiijd
Wife of John Hynkeley
John Markeby iiijd
Robert a Parsons iiijd
John Shylton iiijd
William Bokenffeld iiijd
John Whipp ijd
Rawleyn Loky
William Richardson iiijd
W Clerke kervour iiijd
Robert Clerke kervour iiijd
Margaret Hobson ijd
Isabell Joye ijd
Dom Robert Bates ijd
Prior of the friars preachers ijd
Prior of the friars Carmelite ijd
David Roberts Bocher iiijd
Rector of Stretton ijd

Rector of St Paul ijd

Thomas Hanford iiijd

John Burbage

John Lyryffax iiijd

William Hynkersale iiijd

John Boston iiijd

John Sharpe (deceased *ins*) wife of iiijd

John Bassam iiijd

Robert Cobbe wever iiijd

John Wasshyngburgh

Richard Hardy iiijd

Dom Thomas Folkelyn ijd

Thomas Maidwell iiijd

Prior of the Carmelites of Northampton ijd

Henry Pypes

John Parys iiijd

Roger Gogh barbour iiijd

Anthony Hawe

Alice Bewshyr

Wife formerly of William Freman

Wife formerly of William Clerke pewterer because above (*ante*) now M George Trolopp[145]

fol 50d

Account

The account of William Clerke kervour and Richard Bedwyn providers for the feast for certain expenses made this year for the benefit of the gild as appears by particulars contained in a certain bill shown here in the exchequer and allowed, namely the total of the particulars [146]extend to xljs iiijd which they received and have been discharged. Quit.

The account of Andrew Stoderd steward of the gild for certain payments and expenses made by him to the benefit of the said gild this year as appears by bills shown here in the exchequer and allowed with the wages paid to the chaplain of the gild extending to the sum of xxxvs vjd, with ixs for which he is charged on

---

[145] this is Joan formerly wife of William Clerke pewterer and now wife of George Trolloppe
[146] A new hand takes over at this point.

the account of the preceding year. And thus remains in exchequer iiijs xd which immediately were delivered to him and which will be accounted for elsewhere.

fol 51

Staunford: Acts of the gild of St Katherine virgin and martyr held in the common hall of the said gild on Sunday after the said feast, 26 November in the 19th year of the reign of King Henry VII and anno domini millimo ccccc^{mo} iij^o

Brethren newly admitted
William Darley and Alice his wife owes vjs viijd
Robert Stevenson and Emma owes vjs viijd
Margery Belton widow owes iijs iiijd
Edward Story and Elizabeth owes vjs viijd
Dom Robert Shepehay Rector of the church of St Paul owes vjs viijd
Henry Abney vjs viijd
Katherine wife of William Grenefelde [blank]

Entry of brethren and sisters
Dna Margaret Richmunde mother of the king and countess of Richmond and
    Derby owes for her entry xvjd
William Radclyff and Elizabeth vs
Nicholas Trygge and Joan vs
M Robert Barnard master of the college of Fodrynghay vjs viijd which paid and
    quit
M Christopher Calcott perpetual fellow of the said college vjs viijd; paid xxd and
    owes vs
M [blank] Hud fellow of the same college vs
Thomas Hanford xxd
Richard Hardy iijs iiijd
Dom John Rutkyn Rector of the church of Stretton xxd paid and quit
Dom John Stoderd Rector of church of Clypsam vs
William Hynkersale xxd
Dom Thomas Folkelyn chaplain iijs iiijd
Thomas Goodale vs
Elizabeth Sabyn widow vs
Thomas Langar and Emma vs
William Tubman and Emma owe vs
Edward Brown glover and Alice owe vs

John Loryfax owes for same iijs iiijd paid and quit
Joan wife of William Templer paid xxd and thus quit
Fr William Henson prior of the house of Carmelite friars owes xxd paid and quit

to here for entry money

fol 51d
John Bassam xxd paid and quit
Alice his wife ijs vjd
John Parys iijs iiijd
John Boston xxd
Johyn Cob wever xxd paid and quit
Richard Cotmount vs
Fr Thomas Hernes prior of the friars preachers xxd paid and quit
Emma wife of Robert Beaumund is admitted into sisterhood. But she paid
    nothing for her entry because her husband paid in his entry as appears in Acts of
    the gild of the preceding year 1497 and 13th year of Henry VII
Thomezona Berecok widow for her entry money vs
Dom Robert Brokenhurste xxd paid and quit
Roger Gowgh iijs iiijd
Thomas Maydewell owes iijs iiijd
Fr Christopher Ryder vs
John Moreton vjs viijd of which paid in service as bedell xxd and owes vs

Account
The account of Andrew Stoterde steward of the lands of the gild for certain
    payments and expenses made by him to the benefit of the said gild this year.
    The said accountant is charged with iiijs xd as appears in the last account of the
    preceding year
And delivered to him this year in the exchequer xxvs viijd which makes a total of
    xxxs vjd of which he will account in the next year.

Account
Account of the said Andrew made xj° December millimo ccccc^mo iij° and xix year
    of Henry VII. The said Andrew spent (*exposuit*) for repairs for the preceding
    two years as appears by bills shown here in the exchequer xxs ix ob which were
    allowed to him, and thus he owes ixs iiijd ob which will be accounted elsewhere.

Account

The account of Thomas Phelipp Alderman of the gild of St Katherine for certain cash spent by him for repairs to the benefit of the gild as appears by bills shown here in the exchequer and allowed to him extending to the sum of viij li xviijs viijd of which he has in his hands as appears in his account for the year 1500 and 16th year of Henry VII vij li xviijs viijd And thus there is owed to him xxs

fol 52

Waxshot for the maintenance of the wax and lights of the said gild in the year 1503
[35] Thomas Phelipp Alderman of the gild paid for wax ijd[147]
Nicholas Billesdon and wife ijd [sic]
Christopher Brown and wife iiijd
Dna Waren ijd
Dna Margaret Spenser ijd
Richard Canell and wife iiijd
The anchoress ijd
Robert Crane ijd
Thomas Edwarde and wife iiijd
John Stede ijd
M Thomas Hikham ijd
M Robert Grymston ijd
Parson of the church of St Mary ijd
Dom Thomas Forster ijd
Dom Richard Purley ijd
Dom Henry Wykes ijd
Prior of the Augustinian friars ijd
Fr Ravenell ijd
Fr Hugh Brown ijd
William Skynner iiijd
Margaret Skynner ijd
William Jorden iiijd
wife Cokke ijd
Margaret Goylyn ijd
John Lister ijd
David Cecill iiijd

[147] It would seem that his wife died this year; he pays ijd until 1509 when Maria Spendluff widow (admitted at reduced rate of iijs iiijd in 1507) was described as Maria Spendluff alias Phelip; she seems to have become his (second?) wife just before he died in 1509. After his death Marre Phelip occurs regularly until 1517.

John Cob iiijd
John Tyarde iiijd
Thomas Cowper baker iiijd
Vicar of Ryall
Robert Beamund iiijd
John Thurleby
Joan Parnell ijd
John a Lee iiijd
Hugh Wady iiijd
Thomas Clopton iiijd
Andrew Stoderd iiijd
John Loryng ijd
William Merys iiijd
Margery Hikson ijd
Hugh Smyth iiijd
John Fyssher pewtrer iiijd
John Billesby iiijd
Richard Dey iiijd
Margery Palmer ijd
John Ray smyth   iiijd
Elizabeth Bedwyn ijd
William Bukston
William Grenefeld ijd
Thomas Jacson shomaker iiijd
Joan wife of George Trolop
Robert Atles iiijd
John Smyth baker ijd
John Watts peyntour iiijd
William Jacson candeler iiijd
John Wykes
Walter Fayreday iiijd
John Palmer iiijd
James Taylour ijd
Henry Hikson iiijd
Joan Parnell ijd
Maurice Bawchon iiijd
William Muston iiijd
William Templer iiijd
John Thomas iiijd
William Hynkley iiijd

John Markeby iiijd

Robert Parsons iiijd

John Shilton iiijd

William Bokenfeld iiijd

John Whipp ijd

Raulins Lok ijd

William Richardson iiijd

William Clerke kervour iiijd

Robert Clerke wryght iiijd

Margaret Hobson ijd

Isabella Joy ijd

prior of the friars preachers ijd

prior of the friars Carmelite ijd

David Bocher iiijd

Robert Bocher ijd

Rector of the church of Stretton ijd

Thomas Hanford iiijd

John Burbage iiijd

John Loryfax iiijd

William Hynkersale iiijd

John Boston iiijd

wife Sharp ijd

Fr Robert Legat ijd

John Bassim iiijd

Richard Hardy iiijd

Thomas Folkelyn chaplain ijd

Thomas Maydewell iiijd

John Parys iiijd

Roger Gowgh iiijd

Antony Howe iiijd

Dna Margaret Richmond ijd

William Elmes and his wife iiijd

William Radclyff iiijd

Nicholas Trygge iiijd

Richard Cotmount ijd

John Stoderd parson of the church of Clypsam ijd

M [blank] Calcott of Fodrynghey ijd

M [blank] Hode ijd

Thomas Langar iiijd

William Potell iiijd

Edward Brown glover iiijd
William Tubman iiijd
Elizabeth Sabyn widow ijd
Thomas Godeale iiijd
John Moreton iiijd

fol 52d

Acts of this [gild] continued

[36] Election of officers
Thomas Phelipp is elected Alderman for the following year
Richard Fyssher and William Grenefeld as provisioners (*garniannos*)
Andrew Stoderd as steward of the lands

fol 53

Acts of the gild of St Katherine virgin held on Sunday[148] after the feast of St Katherine virgin, namely the last day of November [30 November] in anno domini 1504 and the 20th year of the reign of King Henry VII

Brethren and sisters newly admitted
[37] Cecily lady Welles second daughter of king Edward IV was admitted and owes vjs viijd for her entry which is paid and she is quit
Thomas Williams and Agnes his wife vjs viijd
Robert Haddon and [blank] his wife vjs viijd
Walter Servi [blank] servant of the king's mother vjs viijd
Alexander Gibson and Alice vjs viijd
Dna Margaret White anchoress at the Nuns admitted vjs viijd
Robert Marbery admitted vjs viijd
[38] Dom William Fyssher vicar of the collegiate church of Leicester admitted vjs viijd

[No heading or marginalia but Entry fines]
Dna Margaret countess of Richmond and Derby owes xvjd which paid and is quit
Margery Belton widow vjs viijd; paid and quit
Roger Gowgh iijs iiijd; paid xxd and owes xxd

---

[148] this date is odd, for the Sunday after the feast of St Katherine in 1504 (20 Henry VII) was 1 December.

Richard Hardy iijs iiijd; paid xxd and owes xxd

William Radclyffe owes vs; paid xxd and owes iijs iiijd

Nicholas Trygge owes vs; paid xxd and owes iijs iiijd

Dom Thomas Folkelyn chaplain owes iijs iiijd; paid xxd and owes xxd

Elizabeth Sabyn widow owes vs; paid xxd and owes iijs iiijd

Robert Stevenson and Emma his wife vjs viijd; paid xxd and owes vs

Edward Story and Elizabeth his wife vjs viijd; paid xxd and owe vs

William Darley and Alice owe vjs viijd; paid xxd and owes vs

Thomas Goodale vs; paid xxd owes iijs iiijd

Thomas Hanford owes xxd; paid and is quit

William Hynkersale owes xxd; paid and quit

Alice wife of John Bassam ijs vjd; paid xd and owes xxd

Edward Brown glover and Alice owe vs; paid xxd and owe iijs iiijd

Thomezona Berecok widow owes vs; paid xxd and owes iijs iiijd

William Tubman and Emma owe vs; paid xxd and owes iijs iiijd

John Boston owes xxd; paid and quit

Thomas Maydewell owes iijs iiijd; paid xxd owes xxd

Thomas Langar and Emma vs; paid xxd owe iijs iiijd

Richard Cotmounte domestic servant of the king's mother owes vs paid xxd and
  owes iijs iiijd

Henry Abney owes vjs viijd paid xxd and owes vs

Dom Robert Shephey Rector of St Paul's church Staunford owes vjs viijd   paid
  xxd and owes vs

M Christopher Calcott perpetual fellow of the college of Fodringhey owes vs; paid
  xxd and owes iijs iiijd

M [blank] Hud fellow of the same college owes vs; paid xxd and owes iijs iiijd

Dna Margaret White anchoress at the Nuns vjs viijd; paid xxd and owes vs

Robert Marbery gent vjs viijd; paid xxd owes vs

Dom William Fyssher vicar of the new collegiate church at Leicester vjs viijd; paid
  xxd and owes vs

note at bottom of page more in the other part

fol 53d

Dom John Stoderd Rector of the church of Clypsam for this day vs

John Parys for this day vs

John Moreton owes vs paid in the service of bedell xxd and owes iijs iiijd

Stock of the gild

Andrew Stoderd xijd by pledge of William Freman paid vjd and owes vjd

John Shilton vjs viijd of the store of the gild for this day
Joan formerly wife of John Peryman owes xs by pledge of Maurice Bawchon
John Thurleby xs by pledge of Christopher Brown
Matilda Denyell xxiijd by pledge of John Hikson

Election of officers
Thomas Phelipp is elected Alderman for the coming year
William Grenefeld and John Shilton as provisioners
Andrew Stoderd as steward of the lands
Nicholas Trygge as clerk
Thomas Morton as bedell

Account
The account of Richard Fyssher and William Grenefeld providers for the entertainment for expenses about the entertainment incurred by them as appears by particulars in certain bills shown here in the exchequer and allowed the which expenses extend to the sum of xxxviijs

Account of steward of lands
The account of Andrew Stoterd steward of the lands of the gild for certain payments made by him to the benefit of the said gild this year xxxvjs vd

Remainder
And there remains for this day in the hands of Andrew Stoderd xls xjd to be accounted for elsewhere.

fol 54

Waxshot for the maintenance of the wax and lights of this gild the year millimo ccccᵐᵒ iiijᵒ
Thomas Phelipp Alderman of the gild paid for wax ijd
Nicholas Billesdon and wife iiijd
Christopher Brown and wife iiijd
Dna [blank] Waren
Dna Margaret Spenser ijd
Richard Canell and wife iiijd
anchoress
Robert Crane
Thomas Edward and wife
M Thomas Hikham ijd
Rector of the church of St Mary ijd

Dom Thomas Forster ijd
Dom Richard Purley
Dom Henry Wykes
Fr Hugh Brown
W Skynner iiijd
W Jorden
wife of Laurence Cokke ijd
Margaret Goylyn ijd
John Lister
David Cecill iiijd
John Cob iiijd
John Tyarde iiijd
Thomas Coper baker iiijd
Robert Beamunt
John Thurleby
Joan Parnell
John a Lee ijd
Hugh Wady iiijd
Thomas Clopton iiijd
Andrew Stoterd iiijd
W Merys
Margery Hykson ijd
John Fyssher pewtrer iiijd
John Billesby
Richard Dey iiijd
Margery Palmer ijd
John Ray smyth
Elizabeth Bedwyn ijd
W Grenefeld iiijd
Thomas Jacson shomaker iiijd
Robert Atales iiijd
John Smyth baker
John Watts peynter
William Jacson candeler iiijd
John Wykes
Walter Fayreday iiijd
James Taylour ijd
Henry Hykson
Maurice Bawchon
William Muston iiijd

William Templer iiijd
John Thomas iiijd
William Hynklay iiijd
John Markeby
Robert Parsons iiijd
John Shilton iiijd
W Bokenfeld iiijd
Raulins Lok
William Richardson
William Clerke kervour iiijd
Robert Clerke wryght
Margaret Hobson ijd
Isabella Joy
Prior of the friars preachers ijd
Prior of the friars Carmelite ijd
David Bocher ijd
Robert Bocher
Rector of the church of Stretton
Thomas Hanford iiijd
John Burbage
John Loryfax iiijd
William Hynkersale iiijd
John Boston iiijd
Fr Robert Legatt
John Bassam iiijd
Richard Hardy iiijd
Thomas Folkelyn chaplain ijd
Thomas Maydewell iiijd
John Parys
Roger Gowgh iiijd
Antony Hawe
Dna Margaret countess of Richmond
William Elmes and his wife
W Radclyff iiijd
Nicholas Trygge iiijd
Richard Cotmount ijd
Master Christopher Calcott
M [blank] Hode
Thomas Langar iiijd
W Potell

fol 54d

Edward Brown glover iiijd

William Tubman iiijd

Elizabeth Sabyn widow

Thomas Goodeale iiijd

John Moreton iiijd

Cecily lady de Welles

Thomas Williams and wife

Robert Haddon and wife

Walter [blank] servant of the king's mother

Alexander Gibson and his wife

Dna anchoress at the Nuns

Robert Marbury

Dom William Fyssher vicar of the New collegiate church at Leicester

William Darley and wife iiijd

Thomezone Berecok widow

(Thomas Langar and wife *del*)

Henry Abney (servant of lord de Ryvers *ins*) ijd

Robert Shephay Rector of St Paul's ijd

(John *del*) Washyngburght and owes for five years and for the preceding year[149]

Dom John Stoterd Rector of church of Clyppesham

Edward Story iiijd

fol 55

Acts of the gild of St Katherine virgin held in the common hall of that fraternity on Sunday the last day of November in anno domini millimo ccccc^{mo} v^o [150] and the 21st year of the reign of King Henry VII

Brethren newly admitted

Robert Martyndale and Joan his wife admitted, will give vjs viijd

John Wallys and Margaret his wife vjs viijd

Robert Stede and Margaret his wife vjs viijd

William Rankell and Joan his wife vjs viijd

John Dalton and Alice his wife vjs viijd

Maurice Johnson and Alice his wife vjs viijd

Mathew Milling and [blank] his wife vjs viijd

---

[149] This is on two lines and appears to be inserted; marginal note 'nota'

[150] this day is correct for 1505; see footnote 94

Roger Beele and Joan his wife vjs viijd

Robert Cave and Elizabeth his wife vjs viijd

George Robynson bocher and Margaret his wife vjs viijd

Henry Lay bocher and Alice his wife vjs viijd

Thomas Stannerd and Margaret his wife vjs viijd

William Wryght and Margaret his wife vjs viijd

Christopher Palfreyman and Joan his wife vjs viijd

Katherine wife of William Grenefeld admitted iijs iiijd [sic]

Richard Hodgeson and Joan his wife vjs viijd

[No heading or marginalia but Entry fines]

William Radclyffe owes iijs iiijd; paid xxd and owes xxd

Nicholas Trygge owes iijs iiijd; paid xxd and owes xxd

Robert Haddon vjs viijd paid xxd and owes vs

Agnes Goodale owes iijs iiijd; paid xxd and owes xxd

Richard Hardy owes xxd which paid and is quit

Elizabeth Sabyn owes iijs iiijd; paid xxd and owes xxd

Dom Thomas Folkelyn owes xxd which paid and is quit

Robert Stevenson vs paid xxd and owes iijs iiijd

Alice wife of John Bassam owes xxd paid xd and owes xd

Ralph Lokhey owes vs paid ijs vjd and owes ijs vjd

William Darley owes vs paid xxd and owes iijs iiijd

Edward Story baker owes vs paid xxd and owe iijs iiijd

Thomas Maydewell owes xxd which paid and is quit

Edward Brown owes iijs iiijd paid xxd and owes xxd

William Tubman owes iijs iiijd paid xxd and owes xxd

fol 55d

Thomezona Berecok owes vs; paid xxd and owes iijs iiijd

Alexander Gybson vjs viijd paid xxd and owes vs

Dom Robert Sheppey Rector of St Paul's church owes vs paid xxd and owes iijs iiijd

Dom William Fyssher owes vs paid xxd and owes iijs iiijd

Roger Gowgh owes xxd which paid and is quit

Thomas Willyams owes vjs viijd paid xxd and owes vs

Katherine wife of William Grenefeld owes iijs iiijd paid xxd and owes xxd

John Paryssh owes iijs iiijd paid xxd and owes xxd

John Moreton owes vs paid xxd and owes iijs iiijd

Stock of the gild

John Shilton vjs viijd of the store of the gild

Maurice Bawchon and Joan his wife xs

John Thurleby xs by pledge of Christopher Brown

Matilda Denyell xxiijd by by pledge of John Hykson

John fyssher pewtrer vjs viijd by by pledge of Andrew Stoderd

Election of officers

Thomas Phelipp is elected Alderman for the following year

Andrew Stoderd as steward

John Shilton and William Jacson candeler as provisioners

Robert Stede as bedell and he will have for his labour ijs vjd

Account

The account of William Grenefeld and John Shilton providers for the entertainment for expenses about the entertainment incurred as appears by particulars in certain bills shown here in the exchequer and allowed, the which expenses extend to the sum of xxvijs viijd which they received here in the exchequer and thus are quit.

Account

The account of Andrew Stoderd steward of the lands of the gild for certain payments made by him to the benefit of the said gild this year. The same is charged with xls xjd from the charge of the account of the previous year.

And for rents of one tenement in the tenure of John Gibson xviijs

Total lviijs xjd; of which he seeks to be allowed for certain payments made this year by him to the benefit of the gild as appears by bills shown here in the exchequer and allowed lvs xjd. Item there is allowed to him for eight latezes [lattices?] for the said tenement xvjd. And thus he owes xxd which he paid and is quit. And there remains in the exchequer this day xlixs vjd of which paid to Thomas Phelipp Alderman for repairs made by him

fol 56

as appears in his account made in the year millimo ccccc^mo iij° and the 19th year of the king together with vjs viijd paid to him by John Shilton this day xxs; and of which payment also to Thomas Coper to the benefit of one woman (*Mulieris*) formerly staying with John[151] Whipp for reward xiijs iiijd; and thus accounting

---

[151] the text suggests Joan but it is almost certainly John since John Whipp's wife was Matilda. John Whipp was tenant in one of the gild's properties.

for all things there remains for this day xxijs xd. Which immediately has been delivered to Andrew Stoderd steward of the lands which shall be accounted for elsewhere. And thus between the said Thomas Phelipp and the said gild is quittance today.

Waxshot for the maintenance of the wax and lights of the said gild in the year millimo ccccc^mo v^o

Thomas Phelipp ijd

Nicholas Billesdon and wife iiijd

Christopher Brown and wife iiijd

Dna [blank] Waren

Dna Margaret Spenser ijd

Richard Canell and wife iiijd

Dna anchoress

Robert Crane

The wife of Thomas Edward

M Thomas Hikham

Rector of the church of St Mary ijd

Dom Thomas Forster ijd

Dom Richard Purley

+Dom Henry Wykes

Fr Hugh Brown

William Skynner and wife iiijd

W Jorden

Margaret Goylyn

John Lister iiijd

David Cecill iiijd

John Cob iiijd

John Tyard

Thomas Coper baker iiijd

Robert Beamond iiijd

John Thurleby

Joan Parnell ijd

John Lee iiijd

Hugh Wady ijd

Thomas Clopton iiijd

Andrew Stoderd iiijd

William Meyres

Margery Hykson ijd

John Fyssher pewtrer iiijd

John Billesby iiijd

Richard Dey iiijd
Margery Palmer ijd
John Ray smyth iiijd
Elizabeth Bedwyn
W Grenefeld iiijd
Thomas Jacson shomaker iiijd
Robert Tales iiijd
John Smyth baker ijd
John Watts peynter
William Jacson candeler iiijd
John Wykes
Walter Fayreday iiijd
James Taylour ijd
Henry Hikson
Maurice Bachon
W Muston iiijd
W Templer iiijd
John Thomas iiijd
W Hynklay iiijd
John Markeby
Robert Parsons iiijd
John Shilton iiijd
William Bokenfeld iiijd
Raulinns Lokky ijd
W Richardson
W Clerke kervour
Robert Clerke wryght

fol 56d
Margaret Hobson
Isabella Joy
Prior of the friars preachers ijd
Prior of the friars Carmelite ijd
David Bocher ijd
Robert [blank] bocher
Rector of the church of Stretton ijd
Thomas Hanford iiijd
John Burbage
John Loryfax iiijd
W Hynkersale iiijd

John Boston iiijd
Fr Robert Legatt
John Bassam iiijd
Richard Hardy iiijd
Dom Thomas Folkelyn ijd
Thomas Maydewell iiijd
John Parys iiijd
Roger Gowgh iiijd
Antony Hawe
Dna Margaret countess of Richmond
The wife of William Elmes
William Radclyff iiijd
Nicholas Trygge iiijd
Richard Cotmount
Master Christopher Caldecote
M Hode
Master of the college of Fodrynghay
William Potell
Edward Brown glover iiijd
William Tubman iiijd
Elizabeth Sabyn
Thomas Godale ijd
John Moreton ijd
Cecily lady de Wellys
Thomas Willyams and wife iiijd
Robert Haddon and wife iiijd
Walter [blank] servant of the king's mother
Alexander Gibson and his wife iiijd
Dna anchoress at the nuns
Robert Marbury gent
Dom W Fyssher vicar of the Newark Leicester
William Darley and wife iiijd
Thomezone Berecok ijd
Thomas Langar and wife
Henry Abney
Dom Robert Shephay ijd
Margery Belton ijd
Edward Story and wife iiijd

fol 57

Acts of the gild of St Katherine virgin held in the common hall there on Sunday the penultimate day of November [29 November] the 22nd year of the reign of King Henry VII and anno domini millimo cccccᵐᵒ vjᵒ

Brethren newly admitted

Thomas Lacy and Agnes vjs viijd

John Thorneff and Katerina vjs viijd

Dom Thomas Richardson chaplain vjs viijd [*marginal* but not sworn]

Dom John Forster Rector of the parish church of St George and Elena Owdeby his sister vjs viijd which paid

Robert Herryson shomaker and Margaret vjs viijd

Fr Robert Staunford of the order of friars preachers vjs viijd

Fr Richard Thorpe of order of friars Carmelite vjs viijd

Thomas Grace and [blank] his wife vjs viijd which paid and they are quit

[No heading but Entry fines][152]

William Radclyffe and Elizabeth owe xxd which paid and quit

Nicholas Trygge xxd which paid and is quit

John Wallys and Margaret his wife owe vjs viijd paid xxd and owe vs

Robert Haddon vs paid xxd and owes iijs iiijd

Agnes Goodale xxd

Elizabeth Sabyn xxd

Henry Lay and Alice his wife vjs viijd paid xxd and owe vs

William Tubman owes xxd which paid and is quit

Dom John Forster Rector of the parish church of St George and Elena Owdeby his sister owe vjs viijd which paid and they are quit

Alexander Gibson and Alice his wife owe vs paid xxd and owe iijs iiijd

Edward Story iijs iiijd paid xxd and owes xxd

William Rankell and Joan his wife vjs viijd paid xxd and owe vs

Robert Stevenson iijs iiijd paid xxd and owes xxd

John Dalton and Alice his wife vjs viijd   paid xxd and owes vs

Alice wife of John Bassam owes xd which paid and is quit

Christopher Palfreyman and Joan his wife owe vjs viijs paid xxd and owe vs

Edward Brown glover owes xxd which paid and is quit

Robert Martyndale and Joan his wife vjs viijd   paid xxd and owe vs

George Robynson bocher and Margaret his wife vjs viijd paid xxd and owe vs

---

[152] the next line runs on without a break – no heading or marginalia

fol 57d

Katherine wife of William Grenefeld owes xxd which paid and is quit

Raulins Lokky owes ijs vjd paid and quit

William Darley owes iijs iiijd paid xxd and owes xxd

Thomezona Bercok owes iijs iiijd; paid xxd and owes xxd

Dom Robert Shephey Rector of the church of St Paul owes iijs iiijd paid xxd and
  owes xxd

Thomas Willyams owes vs paid xxd and owes iijs iiijd

John Parys xxd

John Moreton iijs iiijd

Maurice Jonson and Alice owe vjs viijd paid xxd and owe vs

Mathew Mylling and his wife vjs viijd

Roger Bele and Joan his wife vjs viijd paid xxd and owe vs

Thomas Stannard and Margaret his wife vjs viijd paid xxd and owe vs

William Wryght of Gretford and Margaret his wife vjs viijd paid xxd and owe vs

Richard Hodgeson and Joan his wife vjs viijd paid iijs iiijd and owe iijs iiijd

Dom William Fysssher owes iijs iiijd paid xxd and owes xxd

William Meyres owes for entry xxd as appears anno domini millimo ccccc^{mo} j^o

Fr Robert Legatt owes iijs iiijd which paid and quit

Robert Stede and Margaret his wife vjs viijd paid xxd in the office of bedell and
  owe vs

Stock of the gild

John Shilton vjs viijd of the store of the gild

Maurice Bawchon and Joan his wife xs

John Thurleby xs by pledge of Christopher Brown

Matilda Denyell xxiijd by by pledge of John Hykson

John Fysssher pewtrer vjs viijd of which paid in the office of the cook this year xxd
  and in vessels (vasis) [blank] called le pewtre xxd and thus he owes iijs iiijd

Election of officers

Thomas Phelipp is elected Alderman for the following year

Nicholas Trygge as clerk of the gild

William Jacson candeler and Thomas Clopton as provisioners

Andrew Stoderd as steward of the lands

fol 58

The account of John Shylton and William Jacson providers for the entertainment for expenses about the entertainment incurred which extends as appears by bills shown here in the exchequer and allowed to the sum of xxxiijs xd ob which they received and they were discharged quit.

The account of Andrew Stoderd steward of the lands of the gild for certain payments made by him to the benefit of the gild

The same accountant responds for xxijs xd delivered to him in the exchequer the previous year on the day of his account and for xviijs for the rent of one tenement in the tenure of John Gibson

Sum total of the charge xls xd

Of which he petitioned for allowance for certain payments made this year by him to the benefit of the gild, namely for the wages of the chaplain, certain obits and other necessities as appears by bills shown here in the exchequer and allowed xls xd

Item he petitions allowance for vs for (rents *del*) decay of rents of the said tenement this year (namely for the space of *del*) which it was agreed would be allowed. And thus there is owed to the said Andrew vs, which were delivered immediately to him from the cash paid by Thomas Grave[153]. And thus he is quit

And delivered to Nicholas Trygge (clerk of the gild *ins*) for his wages ijs
And to Robert Stede bedell ijs vjd

And remains for this day in the exchequer lxiiijs ijd which immediately were delivered to Andrew Stoderd steward to be accounted for elsewhere.

fol 58d

Waxshott for the maintenance of the wax and lights of the said gild in the year millimo ccccc^mo vj^o
Thomas Phelipp ijd
Nicholas Billsdon and wife iiijd
Christopher Brown and wife
Dna Agnes Waren
Dna Margaret Spenser ijd
Richard Canell and wife
Dna anchoress

---

[153] Thomas Grave (Cranc?) is not otherwise known

Rector of the church of St Mary ijd
Dom Thomas Forster ijd
William Skynner iiijd
John Lister ijd
John Cob and wife iiijd
John Tyarde and wife iiijd
Thomas Coper and wife iiijd
Robert Beaumount iiijd
John Thurleby
Joan Parnell ijd
John a Lee iiijd
Agnes Wady ijd
Thomas Clopton iiijd
Andrew Stoderd iiijd
William Meyres
Margery Hikson ijd
John Fyssher pewtrer iiijd
John Billesby iiijd
Richard Dey iiijd
Margery Palmer ijd
John Ray smyth iiijd
William Grenefeld iiijd
Thomas Jacson shomaker iiijd
Robert Tales iiijd
John Smyth baker ijd
John Watts peyntour
William Jacson candeler iiijd
Walter Fayreday iiijd
James Taylour ijd
Henry Hykson
Maurice Jonson[154]
William Muston iiijd
William Templer
John Thomas ijd
William Hynklay iiijd
Robert Parsons iiijd
John Shilton iiijd

---

[154] error for Maurice Bawchon; Maurice Johnson had just been admitted and his name occurs in thie list below, fol 57

William Bokenfeld
Raulins Lok ijd
William Richardson
William Clerke viijd
Robert Clerke wryght
Margaret Hobson
Prior of the friars preachers ijd
Prior of the friars Carmelite ijd
David Roberds ijd (ijd *marg*)
Rector of the church of Stretton
Thomas Hanford iiijd
John Loryfax iiijd
William Hynkersale iiijd
John Boston iiijd
Fr Robert Legate
John Bassam iiijd
Richard Hardy iiijd
Thomas Folkelyn chaplain ijd
Thomas Maydewell iiijd
John Parys
Roger Gowgh
Dna Margaret countess of Richmond
Elizabeth the wife of William Elmes
William Radclyff iiijd
Nicholas Trygge iiijd

fol 59

Richard Cotmount
Master of the college of Fodringhay
Edward Brown glover iiijd
William Tubman iiijd
John Moreton
Dna Cecily lady de Welles
Thomas Willyams and wife iiijd
Robert Haddon and wife iiijd
Walter servant of the king's mother
Alexander Gibson and Alice his wife iiijd
Dna anchoress at the Nuns
Robert Marbury
Dom William Fyssher vicar of the Newark Leicester

William Darley and wife iiijd
Thomezone Berecok ijd
Thomas Langar and wife
Henry Abney
Dom Robert Shephay ijd
Edward Story and wife iiijd
Robert Martyndale and wife iiijd
John Wallys and wife iiijd
Robert Stede and wife iiijd (in office of bedell *ins*)
William Rankell and wife iiijd
John Dalton and wife iiijd
Maurice Jonson and wife iiijd[155]
Mathew Mylling and wife iiijd
Roger Bele and wife iiijd
George Robynson and wife iiijd
Henry Lay and wife iiijd
Thomas Stannerd and wife iiijd
William Wryght of Gretford and wife iiijd
Christopher Palfreyman and wife iiijd
David Cecill and wife iiijd
Robert Stevenson and wife iiijd
Robert Cob wever
Fr John Parnell ijd

fol 59d

Acts of the gild of St Katherine virgin held in the common hall there on Sunday after that feast xxviij day of November anno domini millimo ccccc^{mo} vij^o and the 23rd year of the reign of King Henry VII

Brethren newly admitted
John Adew and Christiana his wife admitted and will give vjs viijd
John Selby and Agnes vjs viijd
John Warde and Joan vjs viijd
Thomas Crosse and Agnes vjs viijd
Joan Loky wife of Raulin Loky iijs iiijd
Maria Spendluff widow iijs iiijd

---

[155] see note 100

[No heading but Entry fines]
John Walles and Margaret his wife owe vs paid xxd and owe iijs iiijd
Robert Haddon vs paid xxd and owes iijs iiijd
Agnes Goodale xxd
Elizabeth Sabyn xxd which paid and she is quit
Henry Lay and Alice his wife vs paid xxd and owe iijs iiijd
Alexander Gibson and Alice his wife owe iijs iiijd
Edward Story xxd which paid and is quit
William Rankell and his wife vs paid xxd and owes iijs iiijd
Robert Stevenson xxd which paid and is quit
John Dalton and Alice his wife vs paid xxd and owe iijs iiijd
Christopher Palfreyman and Joan his wife owe vs
Robert Martyndale and Joan his wife vs paid xxd and owe iiijs iiijd
George Robynson and Margareta his wife vs paid xxd and owe iiijs iiijd
William Derley xxd paid and quit
Thomezona Bercok xxd
Dom Robert Shephey owes xxd
Thomas Williams owes iijs iiijd paid xxd and owes xxd
John Paryssh xxd
John Moreton iijs iiijd
Maurice Jonson owes vs which paid and is quit

fol 60
Mathew Milling and [blank] his wife vjs viijd paid xxd and owe vs
Roger Bele and Joan his wife vs paid xxd and owe iijs iiijd
Thomas Stannerd and Margaret his wife vs paid xxd and owe iijs iiijd
William Wryght and Margaret his wife vs paid xxd and owe iijs iiijd
Richard Hodgeson and Joan his wife iijs iiijd paid xxd and owe xxd
Dom William Fyssher xxd
William Meyres xxd
Robert Stede and Margaret his wife vs paid xxd and owe iijs iiijd
Thomas Lacy and Agnes his wife vjs viijd paid xxd and owe vs
John Thorneff and Katherine his wife vjs viijd paid xxd and owe vs
Dom Thomas Richardson chaplain vjs viijd
Robert Herryson shomaker vjs viijd
Fr Thomas Staunford of the order of friars preachers vjs viijd
Fr Richard Thorpe of the order of friars preachers vjs viijs   paid xxd and owes vs

Stock of the gild
John Shilton vjs viijd

Maurice Bawchon and Joan his wife xs
John Thurleby xs by pledge of Christopher Brown
Matilda Denyell xxijd by by pledge of John Yetson
John Fyssher pewtrer iijs iiijd

Election of officers
Thomas Phelipp is elected Alderman of the gild
Andrew Stoterd as steward of the lands
Thomas Clopton and William Hynkley as providers for the entertainment
Nicholas Trygge as clerk of the gild
Robert Stede as bedell

The account of William Jakson and Thomas Clopton providers for the entertainment for expenses about the entertainment incurred this year which extends to the sum of xvijs jd which they received in the exchequer and thus they received as quit.

fol 60d

The account of Andrew Stoderd steward of the lands of the gild for certain payments made by him this year to the benefit of the gild
The same accountant responds iij li iiijs ijd remaining in the hands of the said accountant at the last account; and for xviijs for the rent of one messuage called Saint Kateryns hall; and for vijs for the rent of one cottage formerly of John Whypp
Total of the charge iiij li ixs ijd
Of which he petitioned for allowance of decay of the said tenement and cottage this year pro descu tenement[156] xxvs
Item he petitions allowance for xliijs laid out by him this year for the benefit of the gild as appears by bills shown here in the exchequer and allowed[157]
And this he owes for this day xxjs ijd. And remains (further *ins*) for this day in the exchequer iijs li xvijs which immediately were delivered to Andrew Stoderd to be accounted for elsewhere.

Waxshott for the maintenance of the wax and lights of the said gild in the year millimo ccccc^mo vij^o
Thomas Phelipp ijd

---

[156] meaning uncertain
[157] *nota* is inserted in the margin twice against this and the next item

Christopher Brown and wife
Dna [blank[Waren
Dna Margaret Spenser ijd
Richard Canell and wife iiijd
Dna anchoress
Rector of the church of St Mary ijd
Dom Thomas Forster ijd
Fr Hugh Brown
William Skynner iiijd
John Cob iiijd
John Tyard iiijd
Thomas Coper baker iiijd
Robert Beaumund
John Thurleby
Joan Parnell iiijd
John a Lee iiijd
Hugh Wady ijd
Thomas Clopton iiijd
Andrew Stoderd iiijd
William Meyres
Margery Hykson ijd
John Fyssher pewtrer ijd
John Billesby ijd
Richard Dey iiijd
Margery Palmer ijd
John Ray smyth
William Grenefeld iiijd
Thomas Jacson iiijd
Robert Tales iiijd
John Smyth baker ijd
William Jacson candeler iiijd

fol 61
Walter Faireday iiijd
James Taylour ijd
Henry Hikson
Maurice Bawchon
John Thomas ijd
William Hynklay ijd
Robert Parsons iiijd

John Shilton iiijd
Raulins Loky ijd
William Richardson
William Clerke
Robert Clerke wryght iiijd
Margaret Hobson
Prior of the friars preachers ijd
Prior of the friars Carmelite ijd
David Roberds bocher
Rector of the church of Stretton
Thomas Hanford iiijd
John Loryfax iiijd
William Hynkersale iiijd
John Boston
Fr Robert Legate
John Bassam iiijd
Richard Hardy iiijd
Dom Thomas Folkelyn ijd
Thomas Maydewell iiijd
John Parys
Roger Gowgh
Dna Margaret countess of Richmond
The wife of William Elmes
William Radclyff iiijd
Nicholas Trygge iiijd
Richard Cotmunt
M[aster] of the college of Fodringhey
Edward Brown glover iiijd
Elizabeth Sabyn widow
William Tubman iiijd
Thomas Williams iiijd
Cecily lady de Welles
Robert Haddon iiijd
Walter [blank] servant of the king's mother
Alexander Gibson
Anchoress at the Nuns
Robert Marbery
Dom William Fyssher vicar of the Newark Leicester
William Derley iiijd
Thomezone Bercok ijd

Thomas Langar
Henry Abney
Dom Robert Shephey ijd
Edward Story iiijd
Robert Martyndale iiijd
John Walles iiijd
Robert Stede iiijd
William Rankell iiijd
John Dalton iiijd
Maurice Jonson iiijd
Mathew Milling
Roger Bele iiijd
George Robynson iiijd
Henry Lay iiijd
Thomas Stannerd iiijd
William Wright of Gretford
Christopher Palfreyman iiijd
David Cecill iiijd
Robert Stevynson iiijd

fol 61d
Robert Cob wever
Fr John Parnell
Thomas Lacy iiijd
John Thorneff iiijd
Dom Thomas Richardson
Dom John Forster and Elena Owdeby his sister iiijd
Robert Herryson shomaker
Fr Robert Staunford of the friars preachers ijd
Fr Richard Thorpe of the order of Carmelites ijd
Fr Christopher Ryder ijd

fol 62

Acts of the gild of St Katherine virgin held in the common hall there on Sunday after the feast of the said virgin xxvj day of November anno domini anno domini millimo ccccc^{mo} viij^o and the 24th year of the reign of King Henry VII

Brethren newly admitted

Henry Parsons and [blank] his wife admitted; will give vjs viijd

Fr John Tynnell prior of the convent of the friars preacher of Staunford admitted; will give vjs viijd

Dom John Harrop Rector of the church of St Paul Staunford admitted; will give vjs viijd

Thomas Wordington of Fodringhay admitted; will give vjs viijd

John Nettilham and Elizabeth his wife vjs viijd

Thomas Waters and Agnes his wife vjs viijd

William Graunt and [blank] his wife vjs viijd

Richard Pulter of Norburgh armiger and Anna his wife vjs viijd

John Byrde of Helpiston and [blank] his wife vjs viijd

Anna Wittlibury widow vjs viijd of which paid xxd and owes vs

[No heading but Entry fines]

Mathew Milling alias Millys vs of which paid xxd and owes iijs iiijd

John Wallys and Margaret his wife owe iijs iiijd paid xxd and owes xxd

Robert Haddon iijs iiijd paid xxd and owes xxd

Agnes Goodhale xxd

Henry Lay and Alice his wife iijs iiijd paid xxd and owe xxd

Alexander Gibson and Alice his wife owe iijs iiijd

William Rankell and [blank] his wife iijs iiijd paid xxd and owe xxd

John Dalton and Alice his wife iijs iiijd paid xxd and owe xxd

Christopher Palfreyman and Joan his wife owe vs paid iijs iiijd and owe xxd

Robert Martyndale and Joan his wife iijs iiijd paid xxd and owe xxd

George Robynson and Margaret his wife iijs iiijd paid xxd and owe xxd

Thomezona Berecok xxd

(Dom Robert Shephey chaplain owes xxd which paid and is quit *del*)

fol 62d

Thomas Williams owes xxd which paid and is quit

John Paryssh xxd

John Moreton iijs iiijd

Roger Bele and Joan his wife iijs iiijd

Thomas Stannerd and Margaret his wife iijs iiijd paid by John Shilton xxd and owe xxd

William Wright and Margaret his wife iijs iiijd paid xxd and owes xxd

Richard Hodgeson and Joan his wife xxd which paid and is quit

Dom William Fyssher xxd

William Meyres xxd

Robert Stede and Margaret his wife iijs iiijd paid in his fee as bedell xxd and owe
xxd

Thomas Lacy and Agnes his wife vs paid xxd and owe iijs iiijd

John Thorneff and Katerina his wife vs

Dom Thomas Richardson chaplain vjs viijd

Robert Herryson shomaker vjs viijd

[28] [158]Fr Robert Staunford of the convent of the order of friars preachers
Staunford vjs viijd

Fr Richard Thorpe of the order of Carmelites there vs paid xxd and owes iijs iiijd

John Addew and Christiana his wife vjs viijd paid xxd and owe vs

John Selby and Agnes his wife vjs viijd paid xxd and owe vs

John Warde and Joan his wife vjs viijs paid xxd and owe vs

Thomas Crosse and Agnes his wife vjs viijs paid xxd and owe vs

Joan Lokky wife of Raulin Lokky iijs iiijd

Maria Spendluff widow iijs iiijd paid xd and owes ijs vjd

Thomas Wordington of Fodringhay vjs viijd paid xxd and owes vs

fol 63

Stock of the gild
John Shilton vjs viijd
Maurice Bawchon and Joan his wife xs
John Thurleby xs by pledge of Christopher Brown
Matilda Denyell xxijd by by pledge of John Yetson
John Fyssher pewtrer iijs iiijd

Election of officers
Thomas Phelipp is elected Alderman
Andrew Stoterd as steward of the lands
Thomas Coper baker and Robert Stevynson as providers for the entertainment
Nicholas Trygge clerk of the gild
Robert Stede as bedell
John Selby owes xls by pledge of Robert Martyndale and John Shilton [sic]

The account of Thomas Clopton and William Hinklay providers for the
entertainment for moneys about the entertainment this year laid out by them
which extends to the sum of xxvs xd which they received and thus they were
discharged as quit.

---

[158] this and the next entry are bracketed in the same hand as the marginal number

167

The account of Andrew Stoderd steward of the lands of the gild for certain payments made by him this year to the benefit of the gild

The same accountant responds for arrears of his last account iiij li xviijs

Item for the issues of one messuage called Saint Kateryns hall leased this year for viijs – viijs.

Item for the issues of one cottage in the parish of St Paul of William Radclyff for five quarters viijs ixd

Total charge v li xiiijs ixd

Of which he petitioned for allowance of certain payments made by him to the benefit of the gild this year as appears by bills here in the exchequer shown and so allowed iijs li ijd ob

And thus he owes up to today liiijs vjd ob

And remains for this day iiijs viijd delivered to the said steward to be accounted for elsewhere

fol 63d

Waxshot for the maintenance of the wax and lights of the said gild in the year millimo ccccc^mo viij^o

Thomas Phelipp ijd
Christopher Brown
Dna anchoress
Robert Crane
Dom John Byrden ijd
Dom Thomas Forster ijd
Fr Hugh Brown
William Skynner
John Lister
John Cob iiijd
John Tyarde iiijd
Thomas Cowper iiijd
Robert Beaumount
John Thurleby
Joan Parnell ijd
John a Lee iiijd
Agnes Wady ijd
Thomas Clopton iiijd
Andrew Stoderd iiijd
William Meres

Margery Hikson ijd
John Fyssher pewtrer iiijd
John Billesby ijd
Richard Dey iiijd
Margery Palmer ijd
John Ray smyth
William Grenefeld iiijd
Thomas Jacson iiijd
Robert Talys iiijd
John Smyth baker
John Watts peynter
William Jacson candeler iiijd
Walter Faireday iiijd
James Taylour ijd
Henry Hikson
Maurice Bawchon
William Muston
Katerina Thomas ijd
Robert Parsons iiijd
Dom Robert Shephey ijd
John Shilton iiijd
William Richardson iiijd
Raulins Lokky iiijd
William Clerke iiijd
Robert Clerke wright iiijd
Margaret Hobson
Fr John Tynnell ijd
The prior of the order of Carmelites ijd
David Roberds ijd
Rector of the church of Stretton
Thomas Hanford iiijd
John Loryfax iiijd
William Hynkersale iiijd
John Boston
Fr Robert Legat
John Bassam iiijd
Richard Hardy iiijd
Dom Thomas Folkelyn ijd
Thomas Maidwell iiijd
John Parys

Roger Gowgh
Dna Margaret countess of Richmond
Elizabeth Elmes
William Radclyff iiijd
Nicholas Trygge iiijd
Richard Catmount
M Robert Barnard

fol 64
Edward Brown glover iiijd
William Tubman iiijd
John Moreton ijd
Thomas Williams iiijd
Robert Haddon iiijd
Alexander Gibson
Dna Margaret White anchoress at the Nuns
Robert Marbery
Dom William Fyssher
William Darley iiijd
Thomas Langar
Henry Abney
Edward Story ijd
Robert Martyndale iiijd
John Wallys iiijd
Robert Stede iiijd
William Rankell
John Dalton iiijd
Maurice Jonson iiijd
Mathew Milling iiijd
Roger Bele
George Robynson iiijd
Henry Lay iiijd
Thomas Stannerd iiijd
William Wright
Joan Palfreyman ijd
David Cecill iiijd
Robert Stevenson iiijd
Robert Cob wever
Fr John Parnell ijd
Thomas Lacy iiijd

John Thorneff

Dom Thomas Richardson

Dom John Forster

Robert Herryson

Fr Robert Staunford ijd

Fr Richard Thorp ijd

Fr Christopher Ryder

John Addew iiijd

John Selby iiijd

John Warde iiijd

Thomas Crosse iiijd

Maria Spendluff ijd

fol 64d

Acts of the gild of St Katherine virgin held in the common hall there on Sunday the feast of the said St Katherine xxv November anno domini millesimo quingentesimo nono [1509] and the first year of the reign of King Henry VIII

Brethren newly admitted

[159]Mathew Witton and Joan his wife admitted, will give vjs viijd (of which paid xxd and owes vs *ins*)

Fr William Clyff of the convent of the order of friars minor Staunford admitted and vjs viijd

Dom Richard Bardeney abbot of the monastery of Crowland admitted vjs viijd

Fr William Maltby abbot of the monastery of Brune [Bourne] admitted vjs viijd

Dom Robert Parow prior of the monastery of Spaldyng admitted vjs viijd

Dom Henry Thew prior of the house of St Leonards by Staunford vjs viijd

M Henry Nettilham vicar of Ryall admitted vjs viijd

[No heading but Entry fines]

Mathew Millyng alias Millys iijs iiijd of which paid xxd and owes xxd

John Wallys xxd which paid and is quit

Robert Haddon xxd which paid and quit

Agnes Goodhale xxd

Henry Lay and his wife xxd which paid and he is quit

Alexander Gybson and his wife owe iijs iiijd

---

[159] a marginal sign of emphasis

William Rankell and his wife xxd which paid and quit
John Dalton and his wife xxd which paid and quit
Joan Palfreyman xxd
Robert Martyndale and his wife xxd which paid and quit
George Robynson and his wife xxd which paid and quit
Thomezona Berecok xxd
John Parys xxd
John Moreton iijs iiijd
Roger Bele iijs iiijd paid xxd and owes xxd
Thomas Stannerd and his wife xxd which paid and quit
William Wright and his wife iijs iiijd paid xxd and owes xxd
Dom William Fyssher xxd
William Meyres xxd
Robert Stede and his wife xxd which are paid in his fees and so quit
Thomas Lacy and his wife iijs iiijd paid xxd and owes xxd

fol 65
John Thorneff and his wife vs paid xxd and owes iijs iiijd
Dom Thomas Richardson chaplain vjs viijd
Robert Herryson shomaker vjs viijd
Fr Robert Staunford vjs viijd
Fr Richard Thorp iijs iiijd paid xxd and owes xxd
John Addew and his wife vs paid xxd and owes iijs iiijd
John Selby and his wife vs
John Warde and his wife vs paid xxd and owes iijs iiijd
Thomas Crosse and his wife vs paid xxd and owes iijs iiijd
Joan Lokky iijs iiijd
Maria Spendluff alias Phelipp ijs vjd paid xd and owes xxd
Thomas Wordington of Fodrynghay vs
Henry Parsons and his wife vjs viijd paid xxd and owes vs
Fr John Tynnell vjs viijd paid xxd and owes vs
Dom John Harropp vjs viijd paid xxd and owes vs
 John Nettilham and his wife vjs viijd paid xxd and owes vs
Thomas Waters and his wife vjs viijd paid xxd and owes vs
William Graunt and [blank] his wife vjs viijd
Richard Pulter of Norburgh armiger and Anna his wife vjs viijd
John Byrde of Helpiston and his wife vjs viijd
Anna Wittelbery vs

Election of officers
Nicholas Tryg is elected into the office of Alderman for the following year
Robert Stevynson and John Bassam into the providers for the entertainment
Andrew Stoderd as steward of the lands
Robert Stede as bedell

The account of Thomas Coper and Robert Stevynson providers for the entertainment for certain moneys (before *del*) about the entertainment this year laid out by them which extend to the sum of xxixs viijd which they received in the exchequer and so there is quittance between them and the gild.

The account of Andrew Stoderde steward of the lands for payments made by him this year to the benefit of the gild

The same responds for liiijs vjd ob for arrears from the last

fol 65d
account and for iiijs viijd delivered to him by the Alderman. And for the issues of one messuage called Santkateryns hall leased this year to John Selby for xiijs iiijd. And for vjs viijd for the issues of one cottage formerly of John Whippe and now of William Radclyff thus leased this year to Elizabeth Roger.
Sum total of the charge iijli xixs ijd ob

Of which he petitioned for allowance of certain payments made by him this year for repairs, lights, the sustenance of the chaplain, obits of the brethren and other necessities of the gild which extend to the total of xxxvs jd
Of which he petitions for allowance of vs from the rent of a cottage now in the tenure of Elizabeth Roger for iij quarters of the year on account of the tenement being in decay

Stock of the gild
John Shylton owes vjs viijd of which paid xijd and owes vs viijd.
Maurice Bawchon and Joan his wife owe xs for which Robert Stede bedell has one other ewer weighing xxx li worth vs
John Thurleby owes xs by pledge of Christopher Brown
Matilda Denyell owes xxijd by pledge of John Yetson
John fyssher pewtrer owes iijs iiijd
John Selby owes xls by pledge of Robert Martyndale and John Shilton

And remains this day xls which were delivered into the hands of Nicholas Trig Alderman

Md that le stuff of John Selby[160] was appraised at xvs iijd

fol 66

Waxshot for the maintenance of the wax and lights of the said gild in the year anno domini millimo ccccc^{mo} ix°

[no sums at all this year]
Thomas Phelipp
Christopher Brown
Dna [blank] Waren
Dna Agnes Leche anchoress
Dom John Byrden Rector of the church of St Mary
Dom Thomas Forster
Fr Hugh Brown
William Skynner
John Cob
John Tyard
Thomas Cowper baker
Robert Beaumount
John Thurleby
Joan Parnell
John a Lee
Agnes Wady
Thomas Clopton
Andrew Stoderd
Margery Yetson
John Byllesby
Richard Dey
Margery Palmer
The wife of John Ray smyth
William Grenefeld
Thomas Jacson
Robert Talys
John Smyth baker

---

[160] He was tenant in the gild hall (fol 65d) and had just died.

William Jacson candeler
Walter Fairedey
James Thistilwhayte taylour
Maurice Bawchon
John Thomas
Robert Parsons
John Shilton
Raulins Lokky
William Richardson
William Clerke
Robert Clerke wrigth
Margaret Hobson
The prior of the friars preachers
Thomas Lacy
John Thorneff
Dom Thomas Richardson
Dom John Foster and Elena his sister
Robert Herryson shomaker
Fr Robert Staunford of the order of friars preachers
Fr Richard Thorp of the order of the carmelites
Fr Christopher Rider
John Addew
Agnes wife of John Selby
John Warde and his wife
The prior of the Carmelite friars
David Roberd bocher
Rector of the church of Stretton
Thomas Hanford
John Loryfax iiijd
William Hynkersall
John Boston
Fr Robert Legatt
John Bassam
Richard Hardy
Dom Thomas Folklyne
Thomas Maydewell
John Parys
Roger Gowgh
William Radclyff
Nicholas Trygge

The wife of William Elmes
M Robert Barnard Master of the college of Fodrynghey
Edward Brown glover
Elizabeth Sabyn widow
William Tubman
Thomas Williams
Robert Haddon
Walter [blank] former servant of the lady countess of Richmond
Alexander Gubson
The anchoress at the Nuns
Dom William Fyssher vicar of the collegiate church of Newark Leicester
William Derley
Thomas Langar
Thomezona Beroke
Henry Abney
Dom Robert Shiphey
Edward Story
Robert Martyndale
John Walles iiijd
Robert Stede
William Rankell
John Dalton
Maurice Jonson
Mathew Millyng
Roger Bele
George Robynson
Henry (Lacy *del*) Lay
Thomas Stannerd
William Wrigth of Gretford
Joan Palfryman
David Cecyll
Robert Stevynson
Robert Cob wever
Fr John Parnell
Thomas Crosse and wife
Joan Loky
William Muston
Marre wife of Thomas Phelypp
Thomas Wordyngton of Fordrynghey
Henry Parsons

Fr John Tynnell prior of the convent of the order of friars preachers Staunford

Dom John Harropp Rector of the church of St Paul

John Nettilham

Thomas Waters

William Graunt

Richard Pulter of Northburgh armiger and Anna his wife

John Byrde of Helpiston and his wife

Anna Wittilbery widow

fol 66d

161 Acts of the gild of St Katherine virgin held in the common hall on Sunday xxiiij° day of November anno domini anno domini millimo cccccᵐᵒ xᵒ and the second year of the reign of King Henry VIII

Brethren newly [admitted]

Robert Hundesley and his wife admitted and will give vjs viijd of which paid xxd and owe vs

Richard Wryght similarly and will give iijs iiijd

Richard Clapoll and his wife vjs viijd

William Spenser and Janne hys wyffe vjs viijd

John Welles of Uffyngton and his wife vjs viijd

Thomas Welles of Eston and his wife vjs viijd

Thomas Tampon of Eston and his wife vjs viijd

Entry fines

Mathew Melles owes xxd

Alexandre Gebson and his wife iijs iiijd

Joan Palfreman xxd

John Morton iijs iiijd

Thomezana Bercoke xxd

Roger Bell xxd

William Wryght xxd

Dom William Fescher xxd

Thomas Lacy xxd which paid and is quit

John Thorneff iijs iiijd paid xxd and owes xxd

Dom Thomas Rychardson chaplain vjs viijd

---

161 At this point there is a marked change of hand and of style with much English.

Fr Robert Staunford vjs viijd

Fr Richard Thorpe xxd

John Adew iijs iiijd paid xxd and owes xxd

John Warde iijs iiijd paid xxd and owes xxd

Thomas Crosse iijs iiijd paid xxd and owes xxd

Joan Lokky iijs iiijd

Maria Phelep xxd paid xd and owes xd

Thomas Wordyngton of Fodrynghay vs

Harre Parsons vs

Fr John Tennell vs paid xxd and owes iijs iiijd

Dom John Harrope vs paid xxd and owes iijs iiijd

John Nettylham vs

Thomas Waters vs

William Graunt and wife vjs viijd

Richard Pulter armiger vjs viijd

John (Bry *del*) Byrde vjs viijd

Anne Wettylbere vs

Mathew Wetton vs paid xxd and owes iijs iiijd

Fr William Clyff vjs viijd paid xxd and owes vs

Dom Richard Bardeney abbot of the monastery of Crowland vjs viijd paid xxd
   and owes vs

Dom Robert Boston prior of Spaldyng vjs viijd

Dom Henry Thew prior of St Leonards vjs viijd which paid and is quit

M Henry Nettylham vicar of Ryall vjs viijd paid xxd and owes vs

fol 67

Election of officers

William Radclyff Alderman for thys yer; steward of the lands Thomas Couper
   baker; Stewards of the fest John Bassam and William Muston; Robert Sted
   bedell

Waxschott thys yer xvjs vjd Resaved for the dener [dinner] thys yer xjs vjd

The accompte of Robert Stevenson and John Bassam Stewards of the fest for the
   morow spech and the dener as ytt ys showed by a bell therof made the qwech ys
   to the sum of xxixs xjd the qwech was payd on the chekour and so they er quite.

The accompt of Joan Stodart lat the wyffe of Andrewe Stodart for diverse ressatts
   that sche hayth ressaved to the profett of the geld; Ferst for the arrareges of the

last accompt xxxixs jd ob And alsso with xiijs iiijd for the geld hall. Item for anoder tenement that Elyzabeth Roger dwells in vjs viijd. And iijs iiijd delyvered by the Alderman. The holle sume ys iij li ijs vd ob wherof sche axes to be alowed as ytt aperes by a bell for the prest wages and oder thyngs xxxiiijs. Item for the Dekaye of the halle for thys yer vijs iiijd and so sche owes yett xxjs jd ob The qwech ys payd at thys day on the Chekour And so sche ys quite.

Stock of the gild
fferst John Schelton owes vs viijd the qwech ys payd at thys day and so he ys quite.
John Thurlbe owes xs plege Christopher Brown
Mawde Denyell owes xxijd plege John Yetson
John Fescher pewterer owes iijs iiijd
John Selby[162] owes xls plege Robert Martyndall and John Schelton
Robert Stede owes for a brass potte vs wherof he hayth payd thys yer by hys wages ijs iiijd and so he owes yett ijs viijd
Nicholas Trygge owes sens the last yer xls

Md that ther remannes at thys accompt all thyngs rekynned ljs iiijd the qwech ys delyvered to Thomas Couper steward of the lands as stor of the geld.

yet Waxscotte
fferst William Radclyff Alderman iiijd
Christopher Brown
Thomas Phelep
Dame Alyzabeth Waren
Dame Augnes Lech
Sir John Byrdon ijd
Sir Thomas Foster ijd
Fr Hew Brown
William Skynner iiijd
John Cobbe iiijd
John Tyard
Thomas Couper baker iiijd
Robert Beaumount
John Thurlby
Joan Parnell
John Lee iiijd

---

[162] Although John Selby had died, his sureties owed this sum.

Augnes Wady ijd
Thomas Clopton
Andrew Stodard ijd
Margery Yetson ijd
John Belesby
Richard Day
Margery Palmer ijd
The wyff of John Ray smith ijd
William Grenefeld iiijd
Thomas Jacson iiijd
Robert Taylles iiijd
William Jacson candeller iiijd
Walter Fayreday iiijd
James Thystylwhayte ijd
Morres Bawchon
John Thomas ijd
Robert Parsons iiijd

fol 67d
John Schelton ijd
Rawlyn Lokky
William Rychardson ijd
William Clerke ijd
Robert Clerke wryght
Margaret Hobson
The pryor of the blake freres ijd
Thomas Lacy ijd
John Thorneff
Sir Thomas Rychardson
Sir John Foster
Ellyn Foster ijd
Robert Haryson
Fr Robert Staunford
Fr Richard Thorpe
Fr Christopher Rydar
John Adew iiijd
John Ward iiijd
The pryor of Whytte freres ijd
Davy Roberts
Thomas Hannford iiijd

John Lerefaxe iiijd
William Hynkkersall iiijd
John Boston
Fr Robert Legatt
John Bassam
Richard Harde iiijd
Sir Thomas Fokeleyn ijd
Thomas Maydwell iiijd
John Parys
Roger Gowgh iiijd
Nicholas Trygge ijd
M Robert Barnard
Edward Brown glover iiijd
William Tubman
Thomas Wyllyams iiijd
Robert Haddon
Alexander Gebson
The ankores of the Nonnes
Sir William Fescher of Leycester
William Darley iiijd
Thomas Langer
Sir Robert Schepey ijd
Andrew Stodard
Robert Martyndall iiijd
John Walles iiijd
Edward Store iiijd
Robert Sted iiijd
William Rankell iiijd
John Dalton iiijd
Morres Johnson
Roger Belle
George Robynson iiijd
Harre Ley iiijd
Thomas Stannard
William Wryght of Gretforth
Joan Palfreman
Davy Cessell
Robert Stevenson iiijd

Robert Cobbe vev' [sic[163]]
Fr John Parnell
Thomas Crosse iiijd
Joan Loky
William Muston iiijd
Marre Phelep ijd
Thomas Worthyngton of Fodrynghay
Harre Parsons iiijd
Sir John Harrope
John Netylham
Thomas Watters
William Graunte
Richard Pulter
John Byrde
Anna Wettylbere
Mathew Wetton iiijd
Fr William Clyff
The abbot of Crowland
The pryore of Spaldyng
The pryor of Sent Lenards ijd
M Herre Nettylham of Ryall
William Spenser iiijd
Robert Hundesley ijd
Richard Wryght iiijd
Richard Claypoll iiijd
John Welles of Uffyngton
Thomas Welles of Eston iiijd
Thomas Tampon

fol 68

Acts of the gild of St Katherine virgin held in the common hall on Sunday xxviij[164] day of November anno domini anno domini millimo ccccc^mo xj^o and the third year of the reign of King Henry VIII

Entry fines
fferst Alexander Gebson iijs iiijd

---

[163] for 'wever'
[164] Sunday in 1511 (3 Henry VIII) was 30 November.

Joan Palframan xxd

John Morton iijs iiijd

Roger Belle xxd

William Wryght xxd

Sir William Fescher xxd

Sir Thomas Rychardson of Barnake vjs viijd

Fr Robert Staunford vjs viijd

Fr Richard Thorpe xxd

Fr John Tennell (xxd *del)* iijs iiijd paid xxd and owes xxd

Sir John Harrope iijs iiijd

John Netylham vs

Thomas Watters (iijs iiijd *del)* vs paid xxd and owes iijs iiijd

Richard Pulter armiger vjs viijd

John Byrde vjs viijd

Anna Wettylbere vs

Mathew Wetton iijs iiijd paid xxd and owes xxd

The pryore of Spaldyng vjs viijd

M Harre Nettylham vs paid xxd and owes iijs iiijd

William Spenser vjs viijd paid iijs iiijd and owes iijs iiijd

Robert Hundesley vs   paid xxd and owes iijs iiijd

Richard Wryght iijs iiijd paid xxd and owes xxd

Richard Claypolle vjs viijd   paid xxd and owes vs

John Welles vjs viijd paid xxd and owes vs

Thomas Welles vjs viijd paid xxd and owes vs

Thomas Tampon vjs viijd

Harre Parsons vs paid iijs iiijd and owes xxd

(Robert Saundes iijs iiijd *del*)

New brethren

fferst Thomas Jakson and will give iijs iiijd

Robert Saunde and will give iijs iiijd

The Eleccion of offecers

fferst the alderman William Radclyff; steward of the lands John A Lee; Stewards
 of the fest William Muston and Thomas Jakson; bedell Robert Sted

Stock money

fferst John Thurlbe owes xs plege Christopher Brown

Mawde Denell owes xxijd plege John Yettson

John Fescher owes iijs iiijd

John Selbe owes xls plege Robert Martyndall and John Schelton

Robert Sted owes for a brasse pott ijs viijd the qwech ys payd by hys wedg'[165] and so he ys qwytt

Nicholas Trygge owes sens the last yer xls

Md ther remannes at thys day all thyngs accompted liiijs the qwech was delyvered to John A Lee steward of the lands to the behuffe of the geld.

fol 68d

The accompt of Thomas Cowper baker steward of the lands; fferst he ys charged with xijs for the halle. Item for anoder hows that Robert Herde dwelles in vjs viijd. And alsso he ys charged with ljs iiijd that leffte at the last accompt and so the (sayd *del*) hoolle charge ys iij li xs wherof he axes allowance for the prest, for obbetts, for waxe makyng as ytt aperes by a bell therof made xls vijd. And so he owes yett xxixs vd. Alsso he axes allowance of vjs of the geld halle for the halffe a yer ys nott to Crystymasse And alsso he axes for Robert Herds hows for halffe a yer iijs iiijd And so he owes yett to the geld xxs jd, the qwech ys payd at thys tym and so he qwytte et quietus est

Md that thys ys the accompte of John Bassam steward of the ffest for dyvers thyngs layd owte by hym at thys day as ytt a peres (at t *del*) by a bell therof made whech extendes to the sume of xxvjs xjd, the qwech ys payd on the exchechour and so he ys qwytte et quietus est.

ffor Waxschotte
fferst William Radclyff Alderman iiijd
Christopher Brown
Marre Phelepe
Dna Augnes Lech ijd
Sir John Byrdon ijd
Sir Thomas Foster ijd
William Skynner
John Cobbe iiijd
John Tyard iiijd
Thomas Couper baker iiijd
Robert Beamont
John Thurlby
Joan Parnell

---

[165] i.e. wages [as bedell]

John ALee iiijd
Augnes Wade ijd
Thomas Clopton
Joan Stodart ijd
John Bellesbe
Richard Day
Margery Palmer ijd
The wyff of John Raye smith
William Grennefeld iiijd
Thomas Jakson iiijd
Robert Taylles iiijd
William Jakson iiijd
Walter Fayrday iiijd
James Thystyllwhayt ijd
Morres Jonson
John Thomas ijd
Robert Parsons iiijd
John Schelton
Rawllyn Lokhey ijd
William Rychardson ijd
William Clerke
Robert Clerke wryght
Fr (John *del*) (William *ins*) Hennson ijd
Sir Thomas Rychardson
John Thorneff
Sir John Foster
Ellyn Foster
Edward Store iiijd
Richard Hoggeson iiijd
Robert Haryson
Fr Robert Staunford
Fr Richard Thorpe
Fr Christopher Rydare
John Adew
John Warde
The pryore of the Whytte freres
Davy Roberts
Thomas Hannford
John Lerefaxe iiijd
William Inkersall

John Boston
Fr Robert Legatte
John Bassam
Richard Harde
Sir Thomas Fokleyn ijd
Thomas Maydwell iiijd
John Parysche
Roger Gowgh iiijd
Joan Trygge ijd
M Robert Barnard
Edward Brown glover iiijd
William Tubman
Thomas Wylliams
Robert Haddon
Alexander Gebson
The ankores of the Nunes
Sir William Fescher of Leycester
William Darley iiijd
Thomas Langer
Sir Robert Schepey ijd
Joan Stodard nothing because before [nil quia an']
Robert Martyndall iiijd
John Walles iiijd
Robert Sted
William Rankell iiijd
John Dalton
Morres Johnson
Roger Beelle
Fr John Tynnell ijd

fol 69
George Robynson iiijd
Harre Lee iiijd
Thomas Stannerd
William Wryght of Gretford
Joan Palfreman
Davy Cessell
Robert Stevenson
Robert Cobbe vever [sic]
Thomas Crosse

William Muston iiijd
Thomas Worthyngton of Fodrynghay
Harre Parsons iiijd
Sir John Harrope
John Netylham
Thomas Watters
William Graunte
M Richard Pulter armiger
John Byrde
Augnes Lacy ijd
Anna Wettylbere
Mathew Wetton ijd
The abbott of Crowlande
The pryore of Spaldyng
The pryore of Sent lenards
M Harre Nettylham of Ryall ijd
William Spenser iiijd
Robert Hundesley ijd
Richard Wryght iiijd
Richard Claypoll iiijd
John Welles of Uffyngton
Thomas Welles of Eston
Thomas Tampon of Eston
Robert Sande iiijd
John Morton ijd

Acts of the gild of St Katherine held in the common hall on Sunday xxviij day of November anno domini millimo cccccᵐᵒ xijᵒ and the fourth year of the reign of King Henry VIII

fferst for Entres money[166]
fferst Alexander Gybson iijs iiijd
Joan Palfreman xxd
John Morton iijs iiijd
Roger Beylle xxd
William Wryght xxd
Sir William Fescher xxd

---

[166] this heading squeezed in

Sir Thomas Rychardson vjs viijd
Fr Robert Staunford vjs viijd
Fr Richard Thorpe xxd
Fr John Tynnell xxd which were paid and is quit
Sir John Harrope iijs iiijd
John Nettelham vs
Thomas Watters iijs iiijd
Richard Pulter armiger vjs viijd
John Byrde vjs viijd
Anna Wettylbery vs
Mathew Wetton xxd which paid and is quit
Dam Robert Boston pryore of Spaldyng vjs viijd
M Harre Nettylham iijs iiijd paid xxd and owes xxd
William Spenser iijs iiijd
Robert Hundesley iijs iiijd paid xxd and owes xxd
Richard Wryght xxd which paid and is quit

fol 69d

Richard Claypolle vs paid xxd and owes iijs iiijd
John Welles vs
Thomas Welles vs
Thomas Tampon vjs viijd
Harye Parsons xxd which paid and is quit
Thomas Jakson wyff iijs iiijd paid xxd and owes xxd
Robert Saunde iijs iiijd

Brethren newly [admitted]
M Harre Bownde is admitted and will give vjs viijd
Allis the wyffe of Mathew Wetton and will give iijs iiijd
Robert Moraunt and Allis hys wyff and will give vjs viijd

The Eleccion of offecers
fferst the alderman William Radclyff; steward of the lands John A Lee; Stewards
   of the fest Thomas Jakson and Richard Hoggeson; bedell Robert Sted

Stock money
fferst John Thurlby oweth xs plege Christopher Brown
Mawde Deneyll oweth xxijd plege John Yettson
John Fescher oweth iijs iiijd
John Selbe oweth xls plege Robert Martyndall and John Schelton

Nicholas Trygge oweth xls the weche ys in the Aldermannes hands

The accompte of John Lee steward of the lands; ferst he ys charged with liiijs that leffte at the last accompt. Alsso he ys charged with xijs for the geld halle and alsso with vjs viijd for Robert Herds howse And so the holle charge ys at thys day iij li xijs viijd wherof he axesse alowaunce for the dekay of the geld halle thys yer xijs and so he owes yet lxs viijd. Alsso he axesse alowaunce for obbetts, reparacions and oder thyngs as ytt a perres by a bell therof made xxxvijs xjd. And so he owes yett xxijs ixd

Md that (ys *del*) thys ys the accompte of Willyam Muston steward of the fest for dyvers thyngs layd owte by hym as ytt aperres by a bell therof made the whech exstendes to the sum of xxviijs ijd the qwech at thys day [is paid] and so the said William ys qwytte et quietus est. .

Md that all thyngs Rekynned and accompted ther remannes xxviijs xd; the weche ys delyvered to John Lee steward of the lands to the profite of the Gelde.

fol 70

ffor Waxeschotte
fferst William Radclyff iiijd
Christopher Brown
Mare Phelepe
Dna Augnes Lech ijd
Sir John Byrdon ijd
Sir Thomas Foster ijd
William Skynner
John Cobbe iiijd
John Tyard iiijd
Thomas Couper baker iiijd
Robert Beamont
John Thurlby
John Lee iiijd
Augnes Wade ijd
(Thomas Clopton *del)*
Joan Stodard ijd
John Bellesbe
Richard Day
Margery Palmer ijd

William Grenfeld iiijd
Thomas Jakson iiijd
Robert Tayllys iiijd
William Jakson iiijd
Walter Fayrday iiijd
James Thystylwhayte ijd
Morres Johnson iiijd
John Thomas ijd
Robert Parsons iiijd
Robert Saunde iiijd
Rawlyn Lokhey ijd
William Rychardson ijd
William Clerke
Robert Clerke
Fr William Hennson ijd
Sir Thomas Rychardson
John Thorneff
Sir John Foster   } iiijd
Ellen Foster   }
Edward Store iiijd
Richard Hoggeson iiijd
Robert Haryson
Fr Robert Staunford
Fr Richard Thorpe
Fr Christopher Rydare
John Adew
John Ward
Fr John Kyrton
Davy Roberts
Thomas Hannford
John Lerefaxe iiijd
William Inkersall
John Boston
Richard Wryght iiijd
Fr Robert Legate
John Bassam
Richard Harde
Sir Thomas Fokleyn ijd
Thomas Maydwell iiijd
John Parysche

Roger Gowght iiijd
Joan Trygge ijd
M Robert Barnard
Edward Brown glover iiijd
Thomas Wylliams
William Tubman
Robert Haddon
Alexander Gebson
The ankeres of the Nunes
Sir William Fescher of Leycester
William Darley iiijd
Thomas Langer
Sir Robert Scheppey ijd
Joan Stodard
Robert Martyndall iiijd
John Walles iiijd
Robert Sted
William Rankell iiijd
John Dalton
Morres Johnson
Roger Beyll
Fr John Tynnell ijd
George Robynson iiijd
Harre Lee
Thomas Stannard
William Wryght of Gretford
Joan Palfreyman
Davy Cessyll
Robert Stevenson
Robert Cobbe vener [sic]
Thomas Crosse
William Muston iiijd
Sir Thomas Worthyngton of Fodrynghay
Harre Parsons iiijd
Sir John Harrope
John Netlam
Thomas Watters
William Graunte
M Richard Pulter
John Byrde

Augnes Lacy
Anna Wettylbery
Mathew Whetton ijd
The abbott of Crowland
The pryore of Spaldyng
M Harre Netylham ijd
William Spenser iiijd
Robert Hundesley ijd
Richard Claypoll iiijd
John Welles
Thomas Welles
Thomas Tampon
(Robert Sande ijd *del*)
John Morton ijd

fol 70d

**The acts of the geld of sent Kateren the yer of owre lord anno m¹ vᶜ and xiij
and the vth yer of kyng harre the viijth**

fferst for Entres money
fferst Alexander Gebson iijs iiijd
Joan Palfreyman xxd
John Morton iijs iiijd
Roger Beyll xxd
William Wryght xxd
Sir William Fescher xxd
Sir Thomas Rychardson vjs viijd
Fr Robert Staunford vjs viijd
Fr Richard Thorpe xxd
Sir John Harope iijs iiijd
John Netylham vs
Thomas Waters iijs iiijd paid xxd and owes xxd
Richard Pulter armiger vjs viijd
John Byrde vjs viijd
The pryore of Spaldyng vjs viijd
M Harre Nettylham xxd
William Spenser iijs iiijd paid xxd and owes xxd
Robert Hundesley xxd
Richard Claypoll iijs iiijd paid xxd and owes xxd

John Welles of Uffyngton vs

Thomas Welles of Eston vs paid iijs iiijd and owes xxd

Thomas Tampon vjs viijd

Thomas Jakson wyff xxd which paid and she is quit

Robert Saunde iijs iiijd paid xxd and owes xxd

Joan Lokey iijs iiijd which paid and she is quit

M Harre Bownde vjs viijs paid xxd and owes vs

Alice the wyff of Mathew Wetton iijs iiijd paid xxd and owes xxd

Robert Moraunt vjs viijd paid xxd and owes vs

Brethren newly [admitted]

fferst Sir William Bawchon vecare of Talyngton and schall pay vjs viijd which paid
and is quit

Rauffe Wryght and Joan hys wyff and schall pay vjs viijd

The Eleccion of offecers

fferst William Radclyff alderman; steward of the lands M John Lee; Stewards of
the fest Richard Hoggeson and Mores Johnson; bedell Robert Sted

Md that thys ys the accompt of Thomas Jakson steward of the fest for dyvers
thyngs layd owte by hym as yt aperes by a bell therof made the qwech exstendes
to the sume of xxijs vd ob, the qwech ys payd and so he ys qwytte.

Md that (the *del*) thys ys the accompte of John Lee steward of the lands; ferst he ys
charged with xxviijs xd of the arrears of the laste yer. And alsso with xijs for the
geld halle and with vjs viijd for Robert Herd howse. And so he owes at thys day
xlvijs vjd, wherof he axes to be alowed for the prest, reparacions and oder
thyngs as ytt aperres by a bell therof made xlixs iijd.   And so the sayd John lee
ys in a surplesege all thyngs rekynned xxjd, the qwech ys payd at thys day and so
he ys qwytte.

Md that all thyngs rekynned and accompted at thys day ther remannes xiijs iijd,
the qweych ys delyvered to John A Lee steward of the lands. Item delyvered to
the same John Lee after the rekynnyng for Thomas Welles of Eston iijs iiijd and
viijd for Waxschott

fol 71

ffor Waxschott

fferst William Radclyff Alderman iiijd

Christopher Brown
Marre Phelype
Dna Augnes Lech ijd
Sir John Byrdon ijd
Sir Thomas Foster
William Skynner
John Cobbe
John Tyard
Thomas Couper baker
Robert Beamont
John Lee
Augnes Wade
(Thomas Clopton *del*) William Inkersalle
Joan Stodart
John Bellesbe
Richard Daye
Margery Palmer
William Grennfeld
Thomas Jakson
Robert Tayllys
William Jakson
Walter Fayrday
James Thystylwhayt
Mores Johnson
John Thomas
Robert Parsons
(John Schelton *del*) Robert Saunde
Rawlyn Lokley
William Rychardson
William Clerke
Robert Clerke wryght
Fr William Henson
Sir Thomas Rycharson
John Thorneff
Sir John (Richard *del*) Foster
Ellyn (F *del*) Odby
Edward Storee
Richard Hoggeson
Robert Haryson
Fr Robert Staunford

Fr Richard Thorpe
Fr Christopher Rydare
John Adew
John Warde
Fr John Kyrton
Davy Roberts
Thomas Hannford
John Lerefaxe
John Boston
Richard Wryght
Fr Robert Ledgate
John Bassam
Richard Harde
Sir Thomas Foklyn
Thomas Maydwell
John Parisch
Roger Gowgh
Joan Trygge
M Robert Barnard
Edward Brown glover
Thomas Wyllyams
Robert Haddon
Alexander Gebson
The ankeres of the Nunes
Sir William Fyscher of Leycester
William Darley
Thomas Langer
Sir Robert Schepey
Robert Martyndall
Joan Stodart
John Walles
Robert Sted
William Rankell
John Dalton
Morres Johnson
Roger Beyll
Fr John Tynnell
George Robynson
Harre Lee
Thomas Stannerd

William Wryght of Gretforth
Joan Palfreyman
Davy Cessyll
Robert Stevenson
Robert Cobbe
Thomas Crosse
William Muston
Sir Thomas Worthyngton of Fodrynghay
Harre Parsons
Sir John Harrope
John Nettylham
Thomas Waters
William Graunte
M Richard Pulter
John Byrde
Augnes Lacy
Mathew Wetton
The abbot of Croland
The pryour of Spaldyng
M Harre Nyttylham
William Spenser
Robert Hundesley
Richard Claypoll
John Welles of Uffyngton
Thomas Welles of Eston
Thomas Tampon
M Harre Bownde
Robert Morraunt

Stock money
fferst John Thurlby oweth xs plege Christopher Browne
Mawde Daneyll oweth xxijd plege John Yetson
John Fescher oweth iijs iiijd
John Selby oweth xls plege Robert Martyndall and John Schelton
Item in the aldermannes hannds xls that N Trygge hade

fol 71d

The acts of the geld of sent Kateryn the yer of owre lord a m^l v^c and xiiijth the vjth yer of (owre _del_) kyng harre the viijth

fferst for Entres money
fferst Alexander Gebson iijs iiijd
Joan Palfreyman xxd
John Morton iijs iiijd
Roger Beell xxd
William Wryght xxd
Sir William Fescher xxd
Sir Thomas Rychardson vjs viijd
Fr Robert Staunford vjs viijd
John Nettylham vs
The pryore of Spaldyng vjs viijd
M Harre Nettylham xxd
Thomas Tampon vjs viijd
M Harre Bownd vs
Robert Moraund vs
The abbott of Corland [Crowland] Dam [sic] John Welles (ys _ins_) admytted and must pay vjs viijd the wech ys to the geltyng[167] of sent Kateryn and so he ys qwytte
[_erasure William Spenser?_] The warden of the Gray freres vjs viijd
William Frend vjs viijd

ffor Waxschott
fferst William Radclyff Alderman
Christopher Brown
Mare Phelyp
Dna Augnes Lech
Sir John Byrdon
Sir Thomas Foster
William Skynner
John Cobbe
Joan Tyard
Thomas Couper
Robert Beamont

---

[167] probably the gilding of the statue of St Katherine

John a Lee
Augnes Wade
William Ynkersall
Joan Stodart
Richard Day
Margery Palmer
William Grenfeld
Thomas Jakson
Robert Taylles
William Jakson
Walter Fayrday
James Thystylwhayt
Morres Jonson
John Thomas
Robert Parsons
Robert Sandwayth
Rawlyn Lokkey
William Rychardson
Robert Clerke wryght
Fr William Henson
Sir Thomas Rychardson
John Thorneff
Sir John Foster
Ellyn Odby
Edward Store
Richard Hoggeson
Fr Richard Thorpe
John Adew
John Ward
Fr John Kyrton
Davy Roberts
Thomas Hannford
John Lerefax
John Boston
Richard Wryght
John Bassam
Richard Harde
Sir Thomas Foklyn
Thomas Maydwell
John Parisch

Roger Gowght
Joan Trygge
M Robert Barnard
Edward Brown glover
Thomas Wylliams
Robert Haddon
Alexander Gebson
The ankeres of the Nunnes
Sir William Fescher
William Darley
Thomas Langers wyff
Sir Robert Schepey
Robert Martyndall
Joan Stodart
John Walles
Robert Sted
William Rankell
John Dalton
Roger Beyll
Fr John Tennell

fol 72
Harre Lee
George Robynson
Thomas Stannard
William Wryght of Gretforth
M Davy Cessyll
Joan Palffreyman
Robert Stevenson
Robert Cobbe
Thomas Crosse
William Muston
Sir Thomas Worthyngton of Fodrynghay
Harre Parsons
John Nettylham
Thomas Watters
William Graunte
William Spenser
Augnes Lacy
Mathew Wetton

The pryore of Spaldyng
The abbott of Crowland
M Harre Netylham
Robert Hundesley
Richard Claypoll
John Welles of Uffyngton
Thomas Welles of Eston
Thomas Tampon
M Harre Bownd
Robert Moraunt
The warden of the Grayfrerres
William Frend

The Eleccion of offecers thys yer
fferst William Radclyff alderman; steward of the lands John A Lee; Stewards of the fest Mores Johnson and John Lerefax; bedell Robert Sted

The new Breder thys yer
fferst Dom John Welles abbott of the monestare of Crowland and schall pay vjs viijd the qwech ys geffen to the payntyng of sent Kateryn and so he ys qwytte
[blank for name] the warden of the Grayfreres and schall pay vjs viijd
William Frend and schall pay in lyke manner vjs viijd

Md that thys ys the accompte of John A Lee steward of the lands: fferst he ys charged with xvijs iijd of the last (accompt). Alsso he ys charged with xijs for the geld hall and alsso with vjs viijd of anoder hows. And so the holle charge ys nowe xxxvs xjd; wherof he axes to be alowed for the prest, obbetts and other thyngs as ytt aperes by a bell therof made to the sume of xxxs vjd ob. And so the sayd John alee oweth yet to the geld clerly vs iiijd ob, the wech ys payd. And so the sayd John ys qwytte et quietus est.

Md that thys ys the accompte of Richard Hoggeson steward of the fest for dyvers thyngs layd owte by hym as ytt a perres by a bell therof made the qwech exstends to the sume of xixs ijd ob, the qwech he ys payd.

Md that all thyngs rekynned and accompted at thys day ther remannes clerly xxijs vd the qwech delyvered to John A Lee steward of the geld to the next accompte wherof payd to the kokke [cook] xd and so he oweth yett xxjs vijd

Stock money

fferst John Thurlby oweth xs plege Christopher Brown

Mawde Daneyll oweth xxijd plege John Yettson

John Fescher oweth iijs iiijd

John Selbe oweth xls plege Robert Martyndall and John Schelton

Item in the aldermans hands xls that N Trygge hade

fol 72d

The acts of the geld of sent Kateryn in the yer of owre lord a m^l v^c and xvth the vijth yer of kyng harre the viijth

fferst for Entres money[168]

fferst Alexander Gebson iijs iiijd

John Morton iijs iiijd

Roger Beyll xxd

William Wryght xxd

Sir William Fescher (vjs viijd *del*) xxd

Sir Thomas Rychardson vjs viijd

Fr Robert Staunford vjs viijd

John Netylham (iijs iiijd *del*) vs of which paid xxd and owes iijs iiijd

Joan Palfreman xxd paid and quit

The pryore of Spaldyng vjs viijd

M Harre Netylham xxd

Thomas Tampon vjs viijd

M Harre Bownde vs

Robert Morraunt vs

The warden of the Gray freres vjs viijd of which paid xxd and owes (vjs *del*) vs

Kateryn the wyffe of Mores Johnson iijs iiijd of which paid xd and owes ijs vjs

William Frend vjs viijd

ffor the Waxschott

fferst William Radclyff Alderman

Christopher Brown

Mare Phelepe

Dna Augnes Lech

Sir John Byrdon

---

[168] This heading is squeezed in

Sir Thomas Foster
William Skynner
M John Cobbe
Joan Tyard
Thomas Couper
Robert Beamont
John a Lee
Augnes Wade
William Ynkersall
Joan Stodart
Ellyn Day
Margery Palmer
William Grenfeld
Thomas Jakson
Robert Taylles
William Jakson
Walter Fayrday
James Thystylwhayte
Morres Johnson
John Thomas
Robert Parsons
Robert Sandwayth
Rawlyn Lokkey
William Rychardson
Robert Clerke wryght
Fr William Henson
Sir Thomas Rychardson
John Thornyffe
Sir John Forster
Ellyn Odbye
Edward Store
Richard Hoggeson
Fr Richard Thorpe
John Adew
John Ward
Fr John Kyrton
Davy Roberts
Thomas Hanndforth
John Lerefaxe
John Boston

Richard Wryght
John Bassam
Richard Harde
Sir Thomas Fokleyn
Thomas Maydwell
John Parische
Roger Gowght
Joan Trygge
M Robert Barnard
Edward Brown glover
Thomas Wyllyams
Robert Haddon
Alexander Gebson
The ankeres of the Nunes
Sir William Fescher
William Darley
Thomas Langers wyffe
Sir Robert Schepey
Robert Martyndall
Joan Stodart
John Walles
Robert Sted
William Rankell
John Dalton
Roger Beyll
Fr John Tennell
Harre Lee
George Robynson
Thomas Stannarde
William Wryght
M Davy Cessyll
Joan Palfreman

fol 73
Robert Stevenson
Robert Cobbe
Thomas Crosse
William Muston
Sir Thomas Worthyngton of Fodrynghay
Harre Parsons

John Netylham
Thomas Waters
William Graunte
William Spenser
Robert Draper
Mathew Wetton
The pryore of Spaldyng
The abbott of Crowland
M Harre Netylham
Robert Hundesley
Augnes Claypoll
John Welles of Uffyngton
Thomas Welles of Eston
Thomas Tampon
M Harre Bownd
Robert Morraunt
The warden of the Gray freres
William Frend

The new Breder
fferst M doctour Roston and schall pay vjs viijd of which paid xxd and owes vs
M Sir Stevyn Scherpe pryore of Newsted and schall vjs viijd
M Hew Phelepe and Margete hys wyfe vjs viijd of which paid xxd and owes vs
Sir Hewe Gee and schall pay vjs viijd
Robert Draper and schall pay iijs iiijd because his was syster before [sic]
Robert Thomson and Margett hys wyffe and schall pay vjs viijd
M John Johnson parson of Uffyngton and schall pay vjs viijd

The Eleccion of offecers
fferst William Radclyff alderman; steward of the lands John A Lee; Stewards of
the fest John Lerefaxe and Edward Brown; bedell Robert Stede

Md that thys ys the accompt of John A Lee steward of the lands: ferst he ys
charged with xxjs vijd of the last accompte. Alsso he ys charged with xijs for the
geld halle and alsso with vjs viijd for anoder hows agayns star layn end. And so
the holle charge ys nowe xls iijd; wherof he axes to be alowed for the prest,
waxe and dekayes with oder thyngs as ytt aperes by a bell theroff to the sume of
xxxjs xjd. And so the sayd John alee owes yett viijs iiijd.

Md that thys ys the accompte of Morres Johnson steward of the fest for all thyngs layd owte by hym as ytt aperes by a bell therof made, the qwech extends to the sume of xxjs ijd the qwech ys payd and so he ys qwytte et quietus est.

Md that all thyngs rekynned and accompted at thys day ther remannes xijs ixd the qwech ys delyvered to John A Lee steward of the landes to the next accompte

The stoke money
fferst John Therlbe oweth xs plege Christopher Brown
Mawde Daneyll oweth xxijd plege John Yetson
John Fescher oweth iijs iiijd
John Selbe oweth xls plege Robert Martyndall and John Schelton
Item in the aldermans hands xls that N Trygge hade

fol 73d

The acts of the geld of sent Kateryn the yer of owre lord a m^l v^c and xvj and the viijth yer of kyng harre the viijth

fferst for Entres money
fferst Alexander Gebson iijs iiijd
Item of John Morton iijs iiijd
Item of Roger Beyll xxd
Item of William Wryght xxd
Item of Sir William Fescher xxd
Item of Sir Thomas Rychardson vjs viijd
Item of Fr Robert Staunford vjs viijd
Item of John Nettylham iijs iiijd
The pryour of Spaldyng vjs viijd
M Harre Nettylham xxd which paid and is quit
Thomas Tampon vjs viijd
M Harre Bownde vs
Item of Robert Morande vs paid iijs iiijd and owes xxd
Item of Kateryn the wyffe of Mores Johnson ijs vjd paid xd and owes xxd
Item of William Frende vjs viijd
M Doctour Roston vs
M pryour of Newsted vjs viijd
Item of Hewe Phelepe vs paid xxd and owes iijs iiijd
Item of Sir Hew Gee vjs viijd paid xxd and owes vs
Item of Robert Draper iijs iiijd paid xxd and owes xxd

Item of Robert Thomson vjs viijd paid xxd and owes vs
M John Johnson vjs viijd paid xxd and owes vs

Brethren newly [admitted]
fferst M John Russell chaunter of Fodrynghay and schall pay vjs viijd
Item M George Kyrkham and Cessyll hys wyffe and schall pay vjs viijd
Item of Thomas Foldyngton and Alice hys wyffe and schall pay vjs viijd
Fr John Eyake warden of the Gray Freres and schall pay vjs viijd

ffor Waxshotte
fferst William Radclyff
Christopher Browne
Mare Phelepe
Dna Augnes Lech
Sir John Byrdon
Sir Thomas Foster
Augnes Skynner
M John Cobbe
Joan Tyard
Thomas Couper
Robert Beamont
John a Lee
Augnes Wade
William Inkersall
Joan Stodarte
Ellyn Day
William Grenfeld
Thomas Jakson
M Walter Fayrday
James Thestylwhayte
Mores Johnson
John Thomasse
Robert Parsons
Robert Sandwaytt
Rawlyn a Lokkey
William Rychardson
Robert Clerke
Fr William Henson
Sir Thomas Rychardson
John Thornney

Ellyn Odby
Edward Story
Richard Hoggeson
Fr Richard Thorpe
John Adew
John Warde
Fr John Kyrton
Davy Roberts
Thomas Hannforth
John Lerefaxe
John Boston
Richard Wryght
John Bassham
Richard Harde
Sir Thomas Fokleyn
Thomas Maydwell
John Parisch
Roger Gowght
Joan Trygge
M Robert Barnard
Edward Brown glover
Thomas Wyllyams
Robert Haddon
Alexander Gebson
The ankeres at the Nunes
Sir William Fescher
Thomas Langer wyffe
Sir Robert Schepey
Robert Martyndall
John Walles

fol 74
Robert Sted
William Rankell
Roger Belle
Fr John Tennell
Harre Ley
George Robynson
Thomas Stannard
William Wryght

M Davy Cessyll
Robert Steveson
Robert Cobbe
Thomas Crosse
William Muston
Sir Thomas Worthyngton of Fodrynghay
Harre Parsons
John Nettylham
Thomas Waters
M Doctour Roston
The pryore of Newsted
M John Johnson
William Graunte
Jane Spenser
Robert Draper
Mathew Wetton
The pryour of Spaldyng
The abbott of Crowland
M Harre Nettylham
Robert Hundesley
Augnes Claypolle
John Welles of Uffyngton
Thomas Welles of Eston
Thomas Tampon
M Harre Bownde
Robert Moraund
William Frend
Sir Hew Gee
Robert Tomson

The Eleccion of offecers
fferst William Radclyff alderman; steward of the lands Robert Martyndall; Stewards of the fest Edward Brown and Thomas Crosse; bedell Robert Sted

Md that thys thys [sic] ys the accompt of John Lerefax steward of the fest for dyvers thyngs layd owte by hym as ytt aperes by a bell therof made xxs iiijd the wech ys payd and so he ys qwytte et quietus est

Md that thys ys the accompt of John A Lee steward of the lands: ferst he ys charged with xijs viijd[169] of the last accompt. Alsso he ys charged with xijs for owre geld halle. Alsso he ys charged with vjs viijd for Thomas Taverners hows. (Suma *del*) Sum total xxxjs iiijd; wherof he axes to be alowed as ytt aperes by a bell therof made xxixs iiijd. And so the sayd John oweth yett to the geld ijs id. The qwech ys payd on the Chekkore and so he ys qwytte.

The stoke money
fferst John Therlbe oweth xs plege Christopher [sic]
Item Mawde Daneyll owethe xxijd plege John Yetson
Item John Fescher oweth iijs iiijd
Item John Selbe owetht xls plege Robert Martyndall and John Schelton
Item in the aldermans hands that N Trygge hade xls

Md that all thyngs rekynned and accompted ther remannes xvijd the whech ys
 delyvered to Robert Martyndall steward of the landes

fol 74d

**The acts of the geld of sent Kateryn the yer of owre lord a m^l v^c and xvij
 and the (ix *ins*) yer of kyng harre the viijth**

fferst for Entres money
fferst Alexander Gebson iijs iiijd
Item John Morton iijs iiijd
Item Roger Beyll xxd
Item William Wryght xxd
Item Sir William Fescher xxd
Fr Robert Staunford vjs viijd
Item John Nettelham iijs iiijd
Item the pryour of Spaldyng vjs viijd
Thomas Tampeon vjs viijd
Item William Frend vjs viijd
Item M Doctour Roston' vs
Item M pryore of Newsted vjs viijd paid xxd and owes vs
Item Robert Morraunt xxd which paid and is quit
Item Kateryn the wyffe of Morres Johnson xxd which paid and she is quit
Item Sir Hew Phelype iijs iiijd paid xxd and owes xxd

---

[169] the sum is xijs ixd, see above fol 73

Item Sir Hew Gee vs

Item Robert Draper xxd

Item Robert Tomson vs

Item M John Johnson vs paid xxd and owes iijd iiijd

Item M John Russell vjs viijd paid iijs iiijd and owes iijs iiijd

Item M George Kyrham vjs viijd the qwech was payd to Robert Martyndall and so
  he ys qwytte

Item Thomas Foldyngton vjs viijd

Item Fr John Eyake warden of the Gray frerres vjs viijd paid iijs iiijd and owes iijs
  iiijd [Robert Martyndall *in margin*] [*note*: paid to Robert Martyndall]

Item Mathew Wetton wyffe xxd which paid and she is quit

The new Bredern and systers thes yer

fferst Elyzabeth Wastlen and for the sowles of Rychard Wastelyn and Harre hyr
  son vjs viijd the qwech ys payd and so sche ys qwytte et quieta est

Item Thomas Nettylham and Katherine hys wyffe and schall pay vjs viijd

Item William Nettylham and Joan hys wyff and schall pay vjs viijd

M Thomas Webster and scall pay vjs viijd

ffor Waxshotte

fferst William Radclyff

M Christopher Brown

Marre Phelype

Dna Aungnes Lech

Sir John Byrdon

Sir Thomas Foster

Aungnes Skynner

John Cobbe

Joan Tyard

Thomas Couper

Robert Beamont

John a Lee

Aungnes Wade

William Inkkersall

Joan Stodarte

Ellyn Day

William Grenfeld

Thomas Jakson

M Watler [sic] Fayrday

James Thestylwhayte

Morres Johnson
John Thomas
Robert Parsons
Robert Sandwaytt
Rawlyn Lokkey
William Rychardson
Robert Clerk
Fr William Henson
Sir Thomas Rychardson
John Thornney
Ellyn Odby
Edward Store
Richard Hoggeson
Fr Richard Thorpe
John Adew
John Warde
Fr John Kyrton
Davy Roberts
Thomas Hannford
John Lerefaxe
John Boston
Richard Wryght
John Bassham
Richard Harde
Sir Thomas Fokleyn
Thomas Maydwell
John Parische
Roger Gowght
Joan Trygge
M Robert Barnard
Edward Brown glover

fol 75
Thomas Wyllyams
Robert Haddon
Alexander Gebson
The ankeres at the Nunes
Sir William Fescher
Thomas Langer wyffe
Sir Robert Scheppey

Robert Martyndall
John Walles
Robert Sted
William Rankell
Roger Belle
Fr John Tennell
Harre Ley
George Robynson
Thomas Stannard
William Wryght
M Davy Cessyll
Robert Stevenson
Robert Cobbe
Thomas Crosse
William Muston
Sir Thomas Worthyngton of Fodrynghay
Harre Parsons
Sir Hew Gee
Robert Thomson
John Nettylham
Thomas Watters
M Doctour Roston
M pryore of Newsted
M John Johnson
William Graunte
Jeane Spenser
Robert Draper
Mathew Wetton
The pryore of Spaldyng
The abbott of Crowland
M Harre Nettylham
Robert Hundesley
Augnes Claypoll
John Welles of Uffyngton
Thomas Welles of Eston
Thomas Tampeon
M Harre Bownde
Robert Morraunt
William Frend
M John Russell

M George Kyrham
Thomas Foldyngton
Fr John Ayke

The stoke money
fferst John Thurlbe owth xs plege Christopher Brow[n]e
Item Mawde Deneyll oweth xxijd plege John Yetson
John Fescher oweth iijs iiijd
Item John Selbe oweth xls plege Robert Martyndall and John Schelton
Item in the aldermans hands xls

The Eleccion of offecers for thys yer
fferst the alderman William Radclyff ; steward of the lands Robert Martyndall;
Stewards of the fest Thomas Crosse and Robert Sandwaytte; bedell Robert Sted

Md that thys ys the accompte of Edward Brown glover steward of the fest as ytt
aperes by a bell therof made the qwech cummes to the sum of xxjs ixd the
qwech ys payd and so he ys qwytte et quietus est

Md that thes ys the accompt of Robert Martyndall steward of the lands: ferst he ys
charged with xvijd of the last accompt. Alsso with xs that he hayth ressaved of
my lady ankeres. Alsso he ys charged with xviijs viijd of the lande that longs to
the geld. The sum of the holl charge ys xxxs jd; wherof he axes to be alowed as
ytt aperres by a bell therof made xxxiijs vijd And so the sayd Robert Martyndall
ys owyng [iijs vjd *obscure*] the qwech ys payd and so he ys qwytte et quietus est

Md that all thyngs rekynned and accompted ther remannes at thys day xvs jd the
whech ys delyvered to Robert Martyndall steward of the landes

fol 75d

**The Acts of the Geld of sent Kateryn the yer of owre lord a m^l v^c and xviij
and the x yer of kyng harre the viijth**

fferst for Entres money
fferst Alexander Gebson iijs iiijd
Item John Morton iijs iiijd
Item Roger Belle xxd
Item William Wryght xxd
Item Sir William Fescher xxd

Fr Robert Staunford vjs viijd
Item John Nettylham iijs iiijd
The pryour of Spaldyng vjs viijd
Thomas Tampon vjs viijd
William Frend vjs viijd
M Doctour Roston vs
The pryore of Newsted vs paid xxd and owes iijs iiijd
M Hew Phelype xxd which paid and is quit
Robert Draper xxd which paid and is quit
Robert Tomson vs
M John Johnson iijs iiijd paid xxd and owes xxd
M John Russell iijs iiijd which paid and is quit
Thomas Foldyngton vjs viijd paid xxd and owes vs
Fr John a Eayke iijs iiijd which paid and is quit
Thomas Netylham vjs viijd paid xxd owes vs
William Nettylham vjs viijd   paid xxd and owes vs, payd to Robert Martyndall
   xxd
M Thomas Webster vjs viijd paid xxd and owes vs

The new Bredern thys yer
fferst Richard Clerke kervour and Joan hys wyffe and schall pay vjs viijd
Item Robert Graunte of Taylyngton and Alice hys wyffe and pay vjs viijd

ffor Waxshotte thys yer
fferst William Radclyff
M Christopher Brown
Mare Phelepe
Dna Augnes Lech
Sir John Byrdon
Sir Thomas Foster
Augnes Skynner
John Cobbe
Joan Tyard
Thomas Couper
Robert Beaumont
John Lee
Augnes Wade
William Inkkersall
Joan Stodarte
Ellyn Day

William Grenfeld
Thomas Jakson
M Watter Fayrday
James Thystylwhayte
M Morres John [sic]
John Thomas
Robert Parsons
Robert Sandwayte
Rallyn Lokkey
William Rychardson
Robert Clerk
Fr William Henson
Sir Thomas Rychardson
John Thorney
Ellyn Odby
Edward Store
Richard Hoggeson
Fr Richard Thorpe
John Adew
John Warde
Fr John Kyrton
Davy Roberts
Thomas Hannford
Alyce Lerefaxe
John Boston
Richard Wryght
John Bassam
Richard Harde
Sir Thomas Fokleyn
Thomas Maydwell
John Parische
Roger Gowght
Joan Trygge
M Robert Barnard
Edward Brown glover
Thomas Wyllams
Robert Haddon
Alexander Gebson
The ankeres at the Nunes
Sir William Fescher

Thomas Langer wyffe
Sir Robert Martyndall
John Walles
Robert Sted
William Rankell
Roger Belle
Fr John Tennell
Harre Ley
George Robynson
Thomas Stannard

fol 76
William Wrght
M Davy Cessyll
Robert Stevenson
Robert Cobbe
M Thomas Crosse
William Muston
Sir Thomas Worthyngton of Fodrynghay
Harre Parsons
Sir Hewe Gee
Robert Thomson
John Nettylham
Thomas Watters
M Doctour (Uffyngton *del)* Roston
M pryore of Newsted
M John Johnson
William Graunt
Jeane Spenser
Robert Draper
Mathew Wetton
The pryore of Spaldyng
The abbott of Crollande
M Harre Nettylham
Robert Hundesley
Augnes Claypoll
John Welles of Uffyngton
Thomas Welles of Eston
Thomas Tampon
M Harre Bounde

Robert Morraunt
William Frend
M John Russell
M George Kyrkham
Thomas Foldyngton
Fr John Eayke
Thomas Nettylham
William Nettylham
M Thomas Webster

The stoke money
fferst John Thurleby owes xs plege Christopher Brow[n]e
Mawde Deneyll owes xxijd plege John Yetson
Item John Fescher owes iijs iiijd
Item John Selbe owes xls plege Robert Martyndall and John Schelton
Item in the aldermans hands xls wherof payd to the prest xixs iiijd and so I have
   yett in my hands xxs viijd

The Election of offecers thys yer
fferst William Radclyff   Alderman; steward of the lands Robert Martyndall;
   Stewards of the fest Robert Sandwaytte and Richard Wryght; bedell Robert
   Stede

Md that thys ys the accompte of Robert Martyndall steward of the lands: Ferst he
   ys charged with xvs jd of the last accompte. Also he ys charged with xviijs viijd
   of the lande that longs to the gelde. The sum of the holle charge ys, with iijs iiijd
   that he hade of the warden of the Gray freres, Sum xxxvijs jd; wherof he axes to
   be alowed as ytt aperres by a bell therof made, Sum xxxiiijs xd. And so he owes
   yett ijs iiijd

Md that thys ys the accompte of Thomas Crosse steward of the fest as ytt aperes
   by a bell therof made the qwech drawes to the sum of xxijs ixd the qwech ys
   payd and so he ys qwytte

Md that all thyngs rekynned and accompted ther remannes at thys day xs viijd the
   qwech ys delyvered to Robert Martyndall steward of the landes

fol 76d

The Acts of the geld of sent Kateryn the yer of owre lord a m^l v^c and (xviij *del*) xix and xj yer of kyng harre the viijth

fferst for Entres money
fferst Alexander Gebson iijs iiijd
Item John Morton iijs iiijd
Item Roger Belle xxd
Item William Wryght xxd
Item Sir William Fescher xxd
Item John Nettylham iijs iiijd
Item the pryour of Spaldyng vjs viijd
Fr Robert Staunford vjs viijd
Thomas Tampeon vjs viijd
Item William Frend vjs viijd paid iijs iiijd and owes iijs iiijd
M Doctour Roston' vs
Item the pryore of Newsted iijs iiijd paid xxd and owes xxd
Robert Tomson vs
M John Johnson xxd which paid and he is quit
Thomas Foldyngton vs paid xxd and owes iijs iiijd
Thomas Nettylham vs paid xxd owes iijs iiijd
William Nettylham vs paid xxd and owes iijs iiijd
M Thomas Webster vs paid xxd and owes iijs iiijd
Richard Clerke kervour vjs viijd he paid xxd and owes vs
Robert Graunte of Talyngton vjs viijd
M Hew Phelep xxd
Sir Hewe Gee vs paid xxd and owes iijs iiijd

The new [sic]
fferst Dam Elyzabeth the countes of Oxynford and schall pay vjs viijd the qwech
   ys payd and so sche ys qwytte
Thomas Stoddalffe and hys wyffe and schall pay vjs viijd paid xxd and owes vs
Thomas Watson and Elyzabeth hys wyffe vjs viijd
Fr John Lumeley and schall pay vjs viijd
Alexander Johnson ys admytted and schall pay vjs viijd
Andrew Ganno and Joan hys wyffe and schall pay vjs viijd
Sir William Stokkes prest and schall pay vjs viijd
Roger Knotte and Joan hys wyffe and schall pay vjs viijd

John Walker and Alice hys wyffe and schall pay vjs viijd

ffor Waxshotte thys yer
fferst William Radclyff
Dna Augnes Lech
Sir John Byrdon
Sir Thomas Foster
Augnes Skynner
John Cobbe
Joan Tyard
Thomas Couper
Robert Beaumont
John a Lee
William Ynkersall
Joan Stodarte
Ellyn Day
William Grenfeld
Thomas Jakson
M Walter Fayrday
James Thystylwhayte
M Morres Johnson
M John Thomas
Robert Parsons
Robert Sandwaytte
Rawllyn Lokkey
William Rychardson
Robert Clerke
Fr William Henson
Sir Thomas Rychardson
John Thornney
Ellyn Odby
Edward Store
Richard Hoggeson
Fr Richard Thorpe
John Adew
John Warde
Fr John Kyrton
Davy Roberts
Thomas Hannford
Robert Hundesley

John Boston
Richard Wryght
John Bassam
The wife of Richard Harde
Sir Thomas Foklyn

fol 77
Thomas Maydwell
The wife of John Parische
Roger Gowght
Joan Trygge
M Robert Barnard
Edward Broune
Thomas Wyllams
Robert Haddon
Alexander Gebson
The ankeres of the Nunes
Sir William Fescher
Thomas Langer wyffe
Robert Martyndall
John Walles
Robert Sted
M William Rankell
Roger Belle
Harre Lee
George Robynson
Thomas Stannard
William Wryght
M Davy Cessyll
Emma Stevenson
Robert Cobbe
M Thomas Crosse
William Muston
Sir Thomas Worthyngton of Fodrynghay
Harre Parsons
Sir Hew Gee
Robert Thomson
John Nettylham
Thomas Watters
M Doctour Roston

M pryour of Newsted
M John Johnson
William Graunte
Jeane Spenser
Robert Draper
Mathew Wetton
My lord of Spaldyng
My lord of Crowland
M Harre Nettylham
Robert Hundesley
Augnes Claypoll
John Welles of Uffyngton
Thomas Welles of Eston
Thomas Tampeon
M Harre Bownde
Robert Morraunt
William Frend
M John Russell
M George Kyrkham
Thomas Foldyngton
Fr John Eayke
Thomas Nettylham
William Nettylham
M Thomas Webster
Richard Clerke kervour
Robert (Cler *del*) Graunte of Talyngton

The Elecion of offecers thys yer
fferst the alderman William Radclyff
steward of the lands Morres Johnson
steward of the fest Richard Wryght and John Warde
bedell Robert Stede

Md that thys ys the accompt of Robert Sandwayte steward of the fest as ytt aperes by a bell therof made the Somes to the sume of xxjs vjd ob the qwech ys payd and so he ys qwytte and quietus est

M that thys ys the accompte of Robert Martyndall steward of the lands for serteyn reparacions done by hym as ytt a perres by a bell therof made the qwech ys xvjs vd wherof he hayffe in hys hands sens the last accompt as ytt aperes by the boke xiiijs vijd and so ys owyng to hym xxijd the qwech ys payd and so he ys qwytte

Item payd to the Skalter[170] and hys man for iij days warke ijs vjd. Item halffe a sem lym and naylles vjd

The stoke money thys yer
fferst John Thurlby owes xs pleg Christopher Brown
John Fescher owes iijs iiijd
John Selby owes xls pleg Robert Martyndall and John Schelton
Item in the aldermanes hands xls wherof payd to the preste xixs iiijd and so I have yett in my hands xxs viijd

Md that all thyngs rekynned and accompted ther remaines at thys day xs iiijd the qwech ys delyvered to Morres Johnson steward of the lands to the next accompt. Item iijs iiijd delyvered by M parson of Mychell and so the holle summe ys xiijs viijd

fol 77d

The Acts of the geld of Sent Kateryn the yer of owre lord anno m^l v^c and xx, the xij yer of kyng harre the viijth

Waxshotte thys yer
fferst William Radclyff
Dna Augnes Lech
Sir John Berdon
Sir Thomas Foster
Augnes Skynner
M John Cobbe
Joan Tyard
Thomas Couper
Robert Beamont
John a Lee
William Ynkkersall
Joan Stodarte
Ellyn Day
William Grenfeld
Thomas Jakson

---

[170] i.e. sclater (slater)

M Walter Fayrday
James Thestylwhayte
M Morres Johnson
M John Thomas
Robert Parsons
Robert Sandwaytte
Rawlyn Lokkay
William Rychardson
Robert Clerk
Sir Thomas Rychardson
John Thorney
Ellyn Odby
Edward Store
Richard Hoggeson
Fr Richard Thorpe
John Adew
John Warde
Fr John Kyrton
Davy Roberts
Thomas Hannford
Robert Hundesley
John Boston
Robert Morraunt
Richard Wryght
John Bassam
The wife of Richard Harde
Sir Thomas Foklyn
Thomas Madwell
The wife of John Parische
Roger Gowght
Joan Trygge
(Robert *del*) (Edward *ins*) Browne
Thomas Wyllams
Robert Haddon
Alexander Gebson
The ankeres of the Nunes
Sir William Fescher
The wyff of Thomas Langer
John Walles
Robert Sted

M William Rankell
Roger Bell
Harre Lee
George Robynson
Thomas Stannard
William Wyrght
M Davy Cessyll
Emma Stevenson
Robert Cobbe
M Thomas Crosse
William Muston
Sir Thomas Worthyngton of Fodrynghay
Harre Parsons
Sir Hew Gee
Robert Thomson
Thomas Watters
M Doctour Roston
M pryour of Newsted
M John Johnson
William Graunte
Jane Spenser
Robert Draper
Mathew Wetton
My lord of Spaldyng
My lord of Croland
M Harre Nettylham
Robert Hundesley
Augnes Claypoll
Thomas Welles of Eston
Thomas Tampeon
M Harre Bownde
Robert Morraunt
William Frend
M John Russell
M Jeorge Kyrkham
Thomas Foldyngton
Fr John Ayeke
Thomas Nettylham
William Nettylham
M Thomas Webster

Richard Clerke kervour
Robert Graunt of Talyngton
Dna Elyzabeth countes of Oxford
M Thomas Stoddalffe
Thomas Watson
Fr John Lumley
Alexander Johnson
Andrew Ganno
Sir William Stokkes perst [priest]
Roger Knott
John Wakker [sic]

The new breder thys [sic]
fferst John Hadon and Elyzabeth hys wyff and schall pay vjs viijd
John Nessam and Alice hys wyffe and schall pay vjs viijd
M John Tomson parson of Grayngham and schall pay vjs viijd
Robert Johnson of Gretford and Alice hys wyffe vjs viijd
John Fenton and Augnes hys wyff vjs viijd

The Eleccion of offecers thys yer
ferst the alderman William Radclyff; steward of the lands Mores Johnson; steward
of the fest John Warde and Richard Clerk; bedell Robert Stede

fol 78

ffor entres money
fferst Alexander Gebson iijs iiijd
Item Roger Belle xxd
Item William Wryght xxd
Item Sir William Fescher xxd
Fr Robert Staunford vjs viijd
Item John Nettylham iijs iiijd
My lord of Spaldyng vjs viijd
Item Thomas Tampeon vjs viijd
Item William Frend iijs iiijd paid xxd and owes xxd
M Doctour Roston' vs
The pryore of Newsted xxd which he paid and is quit
Item Robert Tomson vs
Item Thomas Foldyngton iijs iiijd
Item Thomas Nettylham iijs iiijd paid xxd and owes xxd

Item William Nettylham iijs iiijd paid xxd and owes xxd
M Thomas Webster iijs iiijd paid xxd and owes xxd
Item Richard Clerke vs he paid xxd and owes iijs iiijd
Item Robert Graunte of Talyngton vjs viijd
Item Sir Hew Gee iijs iiijd
M Thomas Stodalffe vs
Item Thomas Watson vjs viijd paid xxd and owes vs
Item Alexander Johnson vjs viijd
Item Andrew Ganno vjs viijd
Sir William Stokkes vjs viijd paid iijs iiijd and owes iijs iiijd
Item Roger Knott vjs viijd paid xxd and owes vs
Item (Walker *del*) John Walker vjs viijd paid xxd and owes vs

Md that thys ys the accompte of Richard Wryght steward of the fest as ytt aperes by a bell therof made the qwech ys xxiijs the qwech ys payd and so he ys qwytte and quietus est

Md that thys [sic] the accompte of Mores Johnson steward of the lands: fferst he ys charged with xiijs viijd of the last accompt. Also he ys charged with the rents thys yer xviijs viijd. Item ij stone of led xijd. Item xxs payd by the Alderman. Sum of hys holle ressaytts thys yer liijs iiijd wherof he axes to be alowed for reparacions of the capell and oder thyngs as ytt aperes by a bell therof the qwech ys iij li xijs vjd wherof he hayffe ressaved liijs iiijd and yet ys owyng to hym xxs iiijd wherof he hayth ressaved that lefft of the (laste *ins*) accompt ixs and xs of Robert Sandwaytte for John Selbe and viijd for Stevenson wyff and so ys owyng to hym yett vijd. Item payd to the prest thys yer by the Aldermans hands xxvjs wherof I hade in my hands sens the laste accompte xxs viijd and so ys owyng to me yett vs iiijd and xxs that I delyvered to the steward and so ys owyng to me yet xxvs iiijd. Item payd for iiij obbetts xxd. Item for the generall obbett vd. Item payd to the bedell ijs iiijd

The stok money thys yer
fferst John Thurlbe xs plege Christopher Brown
Item John Fescher owes iijs iiijd
Item John Selbe owes xls plege Robert Martyndall and John Schelton wherof Robert Sandwaytte haythe payd thys yer xs and so remaines yett xxxs

fol 78d

226

The yer of owre lord a m^l v^c xxj for the geld of sent kateryn and the xiij yer of kyng harre the viijth

for Entres money
fferst Alexander Gebson iijs iiijd
Item Roger Belle xxd
Item William Wryght xxd which paid and quietus est
Sir William Fescher xxd
Fr Robert Staunford vjs viijd
John Nettylham iijs iiijd
My lord of Spaldyng vjs viijd
Thomas Tampeon vjs viijd
William Frend xxd
M Doctour Roston' vs
Robert Tomson vs
Thomas Foldyngton iijs iiijd paid xxd and owes xxd
Thomas Nettylham xxd which paid and is quit
William Nettylham xxd
M Thomas Webster xxd which paid and is quit
Richard Clerke iijs iiijd paid xxd and owes xxd
Robert Graunt of Talyngton vjs viijd
Sir Hew Gee iijs iiijd which paid and is quit
M Thomas Stodalffe vs
Thomas Watson vs paid xxd and owes iijs iiijd
Alexander Johnson vjs viijd
Andrew Ganno vjs viijd
Sir William Stokes iijs iiijd which paid and is quit
Roger Knott vs paid xxd and owes iijs iiijd
John Walker vs paid xxd and owes iijs iiijd
John Haddon vjs viijd paid xxd and owes vs
John Nessam vjs viijd paid xxd and owes vs
M John Tomson vjs viijd
Robert Johnson vjs viijd paid xxd and owes vs
John Fenton vjs viijd paid xxd and owes vs

The new Breder thys yer
fferst John Hardgrave and Jeane hys wyffe and schall pay vjs viijd
Harre Lacy and Kateryn (hys *ins*) wyffe owes vjs viijd
Item Sir Robert Holte vjs viijd
John Bradschawe and Augnes vjs viijd

Thomas Carby and Augnes vjs viijd

Robert Day and Alice vjs viijd

John Webster and Alice vjs viijd

The Eleccion of offecers thys yer

fferst William Radclyff Alderman; steward of the lands Morres Johnson; stewards
of the fest (Richard W *del*) Richard Clerk and Edward Store; bedell Robert Stede

The stoke money

fferst John Thurlbe owes xs by pledge of Christopher Browne

John Fescher owes iijs iiijd

John Selby owes xls by pledge of Robert Martyndall and John Schelton wherof
Robert Sandwaytte hayth payd xs and so remaines yett xxxs

fol 79

Md that thys ys the accompte of Jhon Ward steward of the fest as ytt aperes by a
bell theroff made to the sume of xxs vijd the qwech ys payd etc so he ys qwytte
and quietus est

Md that thys ys the accompte of Morres Johnson steward of the lands: ferst he ys
charged with the rent thys yer xviijs wherof ys in dekay thys [sic] vjs and so ys
dew to the geld yet xijs; wherof he axes to be alowed for wax and reparacions
and oder thyngs as ytt aperes by a bell therof made xvjs ob and vijd of the laste
yer accompt, the qwech ys payd and quietus est. Item payd to the prest thys yer
by the Alderman xxvjs wherof ressaved at thys day xijs jd and so ys owyng to me
yett of thys xiijs xjd and of the last yer xxvs iiijd And so ys owyng to me clerly at
thys accompte xxxixs iijd wherof ressaved of Sir William Stokkes iijs iiijd for hys
entres money and of Thomas Watters for waxschott iiijd. And so ys owyng to
me clerly all thyngs rekynned xxxvs vijd

ffor Waxshott thys yer

fferst William Radclyff

Dna Augnes Lech

Sir Thomas Foster

Augnes Skynner

John Cobbe

Joan Tyard

Thomas Couper

John a Lee

William Ynkkersall

Joan Stodart
Ellyn Day
William Grenfeld
Thomas Jakson
Watter Fayrday
James Thestylwhaytte
Morres Johnson
John Thomas
Robert Parsons
Robert Sandwaytte
Rawlyn Lokkey
William Rychardson
Robert Clerk
Edward Store
Richard Hoggeson
Fr Richard Thorpe
John Adew
John Warde
Fr John Kyrton
Davy Roberts
Thomas Hannford
John Boston
Richard Wryght
John Bassame
The wife of Richard Harde
Sir Thomas Foklyn
Thomas Maydwell
The wife of John Pasche
Roger Gowght
Joan Trygge
Edward Browne
Thomas Wyllams
Robert Haddon
Alexander Gebson
The ankeres of the Nunes
Sir William Fescher
The wyff of Thomas Langer
The wife of John Walles
Robert Sted
William Rankkell

Roger Bell
Harre Lee
George Robynson
Thomas Stannard
William Wryght
Davy Cessyll
Robert Cobbe
Thomas Crosse
William Muston
Sir Thomas Worthyngton of Fodrynghay
Harre Parsons
Sir Hew Gee
Robert Thomson
Thomas Watters
M Doctour Roston
M pryour of Newsted
M John Johnson
Robert Graunte
Jeane Spenser
Robert Draper
Mathew Wetton
My lord of Spaldyng
My lord of Crowland
M Harre Nettylham
Augnes Claypoll
Thomas Welles of Eston
Thomas Tampeon
M Harre Bownde
William Frend
M John Russell
M George Kyrkham

fol 79d
Thomas Foldyngton
Fr John Ayke
Thomas Nettylham
William Nettylham
M Thomas Webster
Richard Clerke
Robert Graunt of Talyngton

Dna Elyzabeth countes of Oxford
Thomas Stodalffe
Thomas Watson
Fr John Lumley
Alexander Johnson
Andrew Ganno
Sir William Stokkes prest
Roger Knott
John Walker
John Haddon
John Nessam paynter
M John Thomson parson of Graynham
Robert Johnson of Gretford
John Fenton

The yer of owre lord a m¹ vᶜ and xxij for the geld of sent Kateryne and the xiiij yer of kyng harre the viijth

for waxschott thys yer
fferst William Radclyff
Dna Augnes Lech
Sir Thomas Foster
Augnes Skynner
John Cobbe
Joan Tyard
Thomas Couper
John a Lee
William Ynkkersall
Joan Stodart
Ellyn Day
William Grenfeld
Thomas Jakson
Walter Fayrday
Morres Johnson
James Thestylwhaytte
John Thomas
Robert Parsons
Robert Sandwaytte
Raulyn Lokkey
William Rychardson

Robert Clerk
Edward Store
Richard Hoggeson
Fr Richard Thorpe
John Adew
John Warde
Fr John Kyrton
Davy Roberts
Thomas Hannford
John Boston
Richard Wryght
John Bassam
The wife of Richard Harde
Sir Thomas Foklyn
Thomas Maydwell
The wife of John Pasche
Roger Gowght
Joan Trygge
Edward Brown
Thomas Wyllyams
Robert Haddon
Alexander Gebson
The ankeres of the Nunes
Sir William Fescher
The wyff of Thomas Langer
Margett Walles
Robert Sted
William Rankell
Roger Bell
Harre Lee
George Robynson
Thomas Stannard
William Wryght
M Davy Cessyll
Robert Cobbe
Thomas Crosse
William Muston
Sir Thomas Worthyngton of Fodrynghay
Harre Parsons
Sir Hew Gee

Robert Thomson
Thomas Watters
M Doctour Roston
M pryore of Newstyd
M John Johnson
Robert Graunte
Jeane Spenser
Robert Draper
Mathew Wetton
My lord of Spaldyng
My lord of Crowland
M Harre Nettylham
Augnes Claypoll
Thomas Walles of Eston
Thomas Tampeon
M Harre Bounde
William Frend
M John Russell
M George Kyrkham
Thomas Foldyngton
Fr John Ayke
Thomas Nettylham
William Nettylham
M Thomas Webster
Richard Clerk
Robert Graunt of Talyngton
Dna Elyzabeth countes of Oxford
Thomas Stodalffe
Thomas Watson
Fr John Lumley
Alexander Johnson
Andrew Ganno
Sir William Stokkes
Roger Knott
John Walker
John Haddon
John Nessam
M John Tomson
Robert Johnson
John Fenton

The new bredern thys yer
[blank]
fol 80

The entres money thys yer
fferst Alexander Gebson iijs iiijd
Roger Belle xxd
Sir William Fescher xxd
Fr Robert Staunford vjs viijd
John Nettylham iijs iiijd
My lord of Spaldyng vjs viijd
Thomas Tampeon vjs viijd
William Frend xxd
Doctour Roston' vs
Robert Tomson vs
Thomas Foldyngton xxd
William Nettylham xxd
Richard Clerke xxd which he paid and is quit
Robert Graunt vjs viijd
Sir Hew Gee iijs iiijd
M Thomas Stodalffe vs
Thomas Watson iijs iiijd of which paid xxd and owes xxd
Alexander Johnson vjs viijd
Andrew Ganno vjs viijd
Roger Knott iijs iiijd of which paid xxd and owes xxd
John Walker iijs iiijd of which paid xxd and owes xxd
John Haddon vs of which paid xxd and owes iijs iiijd
M John Tomson vjs viijd
Robert Johnson vs
John Fenton vs of which paid xxd and owes iijs iiijd
M John Hardgrawe vjs viijd of which paid xxd and owes vs
M Harre Lacy vjs viijd of which paid xxd and owes vs
Sir Robert Holte vj viijd of which paid xxd and owes vs
John Bradschawe vjs viijd of which paid xxd and owes vs
Thomas Carby vjs viijd of which paid xxd and owes vs
Robert Day vjs viijd
John Webster vjs viijd of which paid xxd and owes vs
John Nessam vjs viijd of which paid xxd and owes vs

The Eleccion of offecers

The Alderman William Radclyff; steward of the lands Morres Johnson; steward of the fest Edward Store and Thomas Watson; the bedell Robert Sted

Md that thys ys the accompt of Richard Clerk steward of the fest as ytt aperres by a bell ther of made xvijs iijd ob the qwech ys payd and so he ys qwytte and is quit

Md that thys ys the accompt of Morres Johnson steward of the lands: ferst he ys charged with the rent thys yer xviijs wher of he axes for dekayes thys yer xijs And so ys owyng to the geld vjs wherof he axed to be alowed for obbetts and waxe makyng iijs xd and so ys owyng to the geld yett ijs ijd. Item payd to the prest thys yer xxvjs and to the bedell ijs iiijd. And so remannes to the geld thys yer ijs ijd. Md ther ys owyng to the Alderman of the laste yer all thyngs rekynned xxxvs vijd

The stoke money

fferst John Thurleby owes xs plege Christopher Browne

John Fescher owes iijs iiijd

John Selbe owes xls pleg Robert Martyndall and John Schelton wher of Robert Sandwaytte hayth payde xs and so remannes xxxs

fol 80d

The yer of owre lord a m^l v^c xxiij for the geld of sent Kateryn and xv yer of kyng Harre the viijth

ferst for Waxschott

fferst William Radclyff

Dna Augnes Leche

Sir Thomas Foster

Augnes Skynner

John Cobbe

Joan Tyard

Thomas Couper

John A Lee

William Ynkkersall

Joan Stodart

Elyn Day

William Grenfeld

Thomas Jakson

Watter Fayrday
Morres Johnson
James Thestylwhaytte
John Tomas
Robert Parsons
Robert Sanwhaytte
Raulyn Lokkey
William Rychardson
Robert Clerk
Edward Store
Richard Hoggeson
Fr Richard Thorpe
John Adew
John Warde
Fr John Kyrton
Davy Roberts
Thomas Hannford
John Boston
Richard Wryght
John Bassam
Wife of [Uxor] Richard Harde
Sir Thomas Foklyn
Thomas Maydwell
Wife of John Parische
Roger Gowght
Joan Trygge
Edward Browne
Thomas Wyllams
Robert Haddon
Alexander Gebson
The ankeres of the Nounnes
Sir William Fescher
Wife of Thomas Langer
Margett Walles
Robert Stede
William Rankell
Roger Bell
Harre Lee
George Robynson
Thomas Stannard

William Wryght
Davy Cessyll
Robert Cobbe
Thomas Crosse
William Muston
Sir Thomas Worthyngton of Fodrynghay
Harre Parsons
Sir Hew Gee
Robert Tomson
Thomas Watters
M Doctour Roston
Sir Stevyn Sherpe
M John Johnson
Robert Graunte
Jane Spenser
Robert Draper
Mathew Wetton
My lord of Spaldyng
My lord of Crowland
M Harre Nettylam
Augnes Clapoll
Thomas Welles of Eston
Thomas Tampeon
M Harre Bownde
William Frend
M John Russell
M George Kyrham
Thomas Foldyngton
Fr John Ayke
Thomas Nettylham
William Nettylham
M Thomas Webster
Richard Clerke
Dna Elyzabeth countes of Oxford
M Thomas Stodalffe
Thomas Watson
Fr John Lumley
Alexander Johnson
Andrew Ganno
Sir William Stokkes

Roger Knott
John Walker
John Haddon
John Nessam
M John Tomson
Robert Johnson
John Fenton
John Hardgrawe
Harre Lacy
Sir Robert Holt
John Bardshawe
Thomas Carby
Robert Day
John Webster

fol (80 *del*) 81

ffor Entres money thys yer
fferst Alexander Gybson iijs iiijd
Roger Bell xxd
Sir William Fescher xxd
Fr Robert Staunford vjs viijd
John Nettylham iijs iiijd
My lord of Spaldyng vjs viijd
Thomas Tampeon vjs viijd
William Frend xxd
Doctour Roston vs
Robert Thomson vs
Thomas Foldyngton xxd
William Nettylham xxd
Robert Graunte vjs viijd
Sir Hew Gee iijs iiijd
M Thomas Stodalffe vs
Thomas Watson xxd
Alexander Johnson vjs viijd
Andrew Ganno vjs viijd
Roger Knotte xxd
John Haddon iijs iiijd paid xxd and owes xxd
M John Tomson vjs viijd

Robert Johnson vs paid xxd and owes iijs iiijd
John Fenton iijs iiijd
M John Hardgrawe vs
M Harre Lacy vs paid xxd and owes iijs iiijd
Sir Robert Holte vs paid iijs iiijd and owes xxd
John Bradshawe vs
Thomas Carby vs paid xxd and owes iijs iiijd
Robert Day vjs viijd
John Webster vs
John Nessam vs

The new Breder thys yer
fferst Sir William Wardell parson of Langton and schall pay vjs viijd
M Roger Baynthorpe parson of Gretford and schall pay vjs viijd
Esabell Store and schall pay iijs iiijd
Margett Sted and schall pay iijs iiijd

The Eleccion of offecers thys yer
fferst the Alderman William Radclyff; steward of the lands Morres Johnson; steward of the fest Thomas Watson and William Jakson; the bedell Robert Sted

Md that thys ys the accompt of Morres Johnson steward of the lands: ferst he ys charged with ijs ijd that left at the laste accompt. Also with the rent thys yer xviijs. Sum xxs ijd. Wher of he axes to be alowed for dekayes and oder thys [sic] as ytt aperes by a bell therof made xxxijs ijd and so ys owyng to hym now at thys accompt xijs

Md that thys ys the accompt [of] Edward Store steward of the fest as ytt peres by a bell ther of made to the sum of xvij[s] iiijd the qwech ys payd and so he ys qwytte and is quit

Item payd to the bedell thys yer ijs iiijd; payd for the generall obbett vijd. And so remannes xxjd. Item ressaved of Edward Store wyffe of stuffe that lefte at the dener [dinner] ijs. Item ress[aved] of Robert John and John Haddon for Entres money and Waxshott iiijs. Item ress[aved] of Sir William Stokkes for Entres money iijs iiijd. Sum total xjs id

Memd that the Alderman hayth payd to the prest thys yer xxvjs wher of ressaved at thys accompt xjs jd. And so ys owyng of thys yer for the prest xiiijs xjd. And of the laste yer xxxvs vijd. Sum total ls vjd

239

fol 81d

The stoke money thys yer
fferst John Thurleby owes xs pleg Christopher Browne. John Fescher owes iijs
iiijd. John Selbe owes xls pleg Robert Martyndall and John Schelton wherof
Robert Sandwaytte hayth payd xs and so ys owyng yett xxxs. Wher of Joan
Martyndall hayth payd iijs iiijd. And so ys owyng yett of that money xxvjs viijd.

**The yer of owre lord A⁰ mˡ vᶜ xxiiij for the geld of sent Kateryn and xvj yer
of kyng Harre the viijth**

fferst for Waxschott
fferst William Radclyff
Dna Augnes Leche
Sir Thomas Foster
Augnes Skynner
Augnes Cobbe
Joan Tyard
John A Lee
Wife of Thomas Couper
Wife of William Yngkerssall
Joan Stodart
William Grenfeld
Thomas Jakson
Watter Fayrday
Morresse Johnson
James Thesselwaytte
John Thomas
Robert Parsons
Robert Sandwaytt
Rawlyn Lokkey
William Rychardson
Robert Clerk
Edward Store
Richard Hoggeson
Fr Richard Thorpe

John Adew
John Warde
Fr John Kyrton
Davy Roberts
Thomas Hannford
John Boston
Richard Wryght
John Bassam
Sir Thomas Foklyne
Thomas Maydwell
Wife of John Parische
Roger Gowght
Joan Trygge
Edward Browne
Thomas Wyllams
Robert Haddon
Alexander Gebson
The ankeres of the Nonnes
Sir William Fescher
Wife of Thomas Langer
Margett Walles
Robert Sted
William Rankell
Roger Belle
Harre Lee
George Robynson
Thomas Stannard
William Wryght
Davy Cessyll
Robert Cobbe
Thomas Crosse
William Muston
Sir Thomas Worthyngton of Fodrynghay
Harre Parsons
Sir Hew Gee
Robert Thomson
Thomas Watters
M Doctour Roston
Sir Stevyn Sherpe
M John Johnson

Robert Graunte
Jane Spenser
Robert Draper
Mathew Wetton
My lord of Spaldyng
My lord of Crolland
M Harre Nettylam
Augnes Clapoll
Thomas Tampeon
M Harre Bownde
M John Russell
M George Kyrham
Thomas Foldyngton
Fr John Ayke
Thomas Nettylham
William Nettylham
M Thomas Webster
Richard Clerke
Dna Elyzabethe countes of Oxford
M Thomas Stodalffe
Thomas Watson
Fr John Lumley
Alexander Johnson
M Andrew Ganno
Sir William Stokes
Roger Knotte
John Walker
John Haddon
John Nessam
M John Tomson
Robert Johnson
John Fenton
John Hardgrawe
Harre Lacy
Sir Robert Holte
John Bradshawe
Thomas Careby
Robert Day
John Webster
Sir William Wardell parson of Langton

M Roger Baynthorpe

fol 82

ffor Entres (money ins) thys yer
fferst Alexander Gebson iijs iiijd
Roger Bell xxd
Sir William Fescher xxd
Fr Robert Staunford vjs viijd
John Nettylham iijs iiijd
My lord of Spaldyng vjs viijd
Thomas (S *del*) Tampeon vjs viijd
William Frend xxd
M Doctour Boston vs
Robert Thomson vs
Thomas Foldyngton xxd
William Nettylham xxd
Robert Graunte vjs viijd
Sir Hew Gee iijs iiijd
M Thomas Stodalffe vs
Thomas Watson xxd
Alexander Johnson vjs viijd
M Andrew Ganno vjs viijd
Roger Knotte xxd
John Haddon xxd which paid xxd and is quit
M John Tomson vjs viijd
Robert Johnson iijs iiijd
John Fenton iijs iiijd paid xxd and owes xxd
M John Hardgrawe vs
Harre Lacy iijs iiijd paid xxd and owes xxd
Sir Robert Holte iijs iiijd
John Bradshawe vs
Thomas Carby iijs iiijd
Robert Day vjs viijd
John Webster vs
John Nessam vs *of which he paid xxd and owes iijs iiijd*[171]

---

[171] different hand

Sir William Wardell parson of Langton vjs viijd

M Roger Baynthorpe vs

Elyzabeth Store iijs iiijd paid xd and owes ijs vjd

Margett Sted iijs iiijd paid xd and owes ijs vjd

The new Breder thys yer

fferst John Hawe of Badyngton and hys wyffe and schall pay vjs viijd vjs viijd

The Eleccion of offecers thys yer

fferst the William Radclyff Alderman; steward of the lands Morres Johnson; steward of the fest William Jakson and John Fenton; bedell Robert Sted

Md that thys ys the accompt of Morres Johnson steward of the lands: ferst he ys charged with the rent thys yer xixs, wher of he axes to be alowed for dekayse thys yer vjs vjd and so he owes xjs vjd; wher of he axes to be alowed for wax and oder thyngs as ytt aperres by a bell ther of made vjs ijd and so he owes yett vs iiijd; wherfor he ys owyng of the last yer xijs[172] wher of payd at thys day vs iiijd and so ys owing to hym yett all thyngs rekynned vjs viijd.

Md that thys ys the accompt of Thomas Watson steward of the fest as ytt aperres by a bell ther of made to the sum of xiijs xjd the qwech ys payd and so he ys qwytte and quietus est.

Item payd to the bedell thys yer ijs iiijd; (to the *del*) Item to the generall obbett vjd. Item payd to the prest thys yer xxvjs wher of ress[aved] at thys day vjs viijd. And so ys owyng to me for thys yer xixs iiijd and for the laste accompte afor thys ls vjd. And so ys owyng me now clerly all thyngs rekynned iij li ixs xd

fol 82d

The yer of owre lord anno m¹ vᶜ xxv and the xvij yer of the reign of king Henry VIII for sent Kateryns geld

fferst for the Waxschott

fferst William Radclyff

Dna Augnes Leche

Sir Thomas Foster

Augnes Cobbe

John Tyard

---

172 the earlier figure was xijs ijd

John A Lee
Wife of William Ynkersall
Joan Stodart
William Grenfeld
Thomas Jakson
Watter Fayrday
Morres Johnson
James Thestylwhaytte
John Thomas
Robert Parsons
Robert Sandwaytte
Rawlyn Lokkey
William Rychardson
Edward Store
Richard Hoggeson
Fr Richard Thorpe
John Adew
John Ward
Fr John Kyrton
Davy Roberts
Thomas Hannford
John Boston
Richard Wryght
John Bassam
Sir Thomas Foklyne
Thomas Maydwell
Wife of John Parische
Roger Gowght
Joan Trygge
Edward Browne
Thomas Wyllams
Robert Haddon
Alexander Gebson
The ankeres of the Nonnes
Sir William Fescher
Margett Walles
Robert Sted
William Rankell
Roger Belle
Harre Ley

Georges Robynson
Thomas Stannard
William Wryght
Davy Cessyll
Robert Cobbe
Thomas Crosse
William Muston
Sir Thomas Worthyngton of Fodrynghay
Harre Parsons
Sir Hew Gee
Robert Thomson
Wife of Thomas Watters
Sir Stewyn Scherpe
John Johnson
Robert Graunte
Janne Spenser
Robert Draper
Mathew Wetton
My lord of Spaldyng
My lord of Crowland
M Harre Nettelam
Augnes Claypoll
Thomas Tampeon
M Harre Bownde
M John Russell
M George Kyrham
Thomas Foldyngton
Fr John Ayke
Thomas Nettylham
William Nettylham
M Thomas Webster
Richard Clerke
Dna Elyzabeth countes of Oxford
M Thomas Stodalffe
Thomas Watson
Fr John Lumley
Alexander Johnson
Andrew Ganno
Sir William Stokkes
Roger Knott

John Walker
John Nessam
John Haddon
M John Thomson
Robert Johnson
John Fenton
John Hardgrawe
Harre Lacy
Sir Robert Holte
John Bradshawe
Thomas Cayrby
John Webster
Robert Day
Sir William Wardalle parson of Langton
M Roger Baynthorpe

The new breder thys yere
Fr Robert Hampton gray frerre and schall pay vjs viijd
Dna [sic] Christopher Wellye pryour of sent leonards and schall pay vjs viijd
paid iijs iiijd and owes iijs iiijd
William Haylyday and Alice hys wyffe and schall pay vjs viijd
John Harres and Margett hys wyff and schall pay vjs viijd

fol 83

ffor Entres money thys yer
fferst Alexander Gebson iijs iiijd
Roger Bell xxd
Sir William Fescher xxd
Fr Robert Staunford vjs viijd
John Nettylham iijs iiijd
My lord of Spaldyng vjs viijd
My lord of Crowland vjs viijd
Thomas Tampeon vjs viijd
William Frend xxd
Robert Thomson vs
Thomas Foldyngton xxd
William Nettylham xxd
Robert Graunte vjs viijd
Sir Hew Gee iijs iiijd

M Thomas Stodalffe vs
Thomas Watson xxd
Alexander Johnson vjs viijd
Andrew Ganno vjs viijd
Roger Knotte xxd
M John Thomson vjs viijd
Robert Johnson iijs iiijd
John Fenton xxd which he paid and is quit
John Hardgrawe vs
Harre Lacy xxd
Sir Robert Holte iijs iiijd
John Bradshawe vs
Thomas Carby iijs iiijd
Robert Day vjs viijd
John Webster vs
John Nessam vs
Sir William Wardyll parson of Langton vjs viijd
Roger Baynthorpe vs
Elyzabeth Store ijs vjd she paid xd and owes xxd
Margett Sted ijs vjd she paid xd and owes xxd
John Hawe of Baynton vjs viijd

The Eleccion of offecers thys yer
fferst the Alderman William Radclyff; steward of the lands Morres Johnson;
steward of the fest John Fenton and William Jakson; bedell Robert Sted

Md that thys ys the accompt of Morres Johnson steward of the lands: ferst he ys
charged with the rent thys yer xviijs wherof in dekay for sent Kateryns Howse
ijs; for the oder Howse vjs; Sum viijs and so ys owyng to the geld xs; wher of
he axes to be alowed for obbetts waxe cheffe rents and oder thyngs as ytt
aperres by a bell ther of ijs vijd and so he owes to the geld vijs vd; wherof payd
to hym for the last yer vjs viijd and so he owes yett ixd the qwech ys payd and so
he ys qwytte

Md that thys ys the accompt of John Fenton steward of the fest as ytt aperres by
a bell ther of made to the sum of ixs xjd the qwech ys payd and so he ys qwytte
and quietus est.

Also payd to the bedell thys yer ijs iiijd; remannes all thyngs rekynned and payd
vs ixd

fol 83d

The yer of owre lord A m^l v^c xxvj and the xviij yer of kyng harre the viijth for sent Kateryn geld

fferst for Waxschott
fferst William Radclyff
Dna Augnes Leche
Sir Thomas Foster
Augnes Cobbe
Joan Tyard
John A Lee
Wife of William Ynkersall
Joan Stodart
William Grenfeld
Thomas Jakson
Walter Fayrday
Morres Johnson
James Thestylwhaytte
John Thomas
Robert Parsons
Robert Sandwaytte
Rawlyne Lokkey
William Rychardson
Edward Store
Richard Hoggeson
Fr Richard Thorpe
John Adew
John Warde
Fr John Kyrton
Davy Roberts
Thomas Hannford
John Boston
Richard Wryght
John Bassam
Sir Thomas Fokleyn

Thomas Maydwell
Wife of John Parische
Roger Gowght
Joan Trygge
Edward Browne
Thomas Wyllams
Robert Haddon
Alexander Gebson
The ankres of the Nonnes
Sir William Fescher
Margett Walles
Robert Sted
William Rankell
Roger Beylle
Harre Ley
George Robynson
Thomas Stannard
William Wryght
M Davy Cessyll
Robert Cobbe
Thomas Crosse
William Muston
Sir Thomas Worthyngton off Fodrynghay
Harre Persons
Sir Hew Gee
Robert Thomson
Wife of Thomas Watters
Sir Steven Scherpe
M John Johnson
Robert Graunte
Jeanne Spenser
Robert Draper
Mathew Wetton
My lord of Spaldyng
My lord of Crowlande
M Harre Nettylham
Augnes Claypolle
Thomas Tampeon
M Harre Bownde
M John Russell

M George Kyrkham
Thomas Foldyngton
Fr John Ayke
Thomas Nettylhan
William Nettylham
M Thomas Webster
Richard Clerk
Dna Elyzabethe countes of Oxford
M Thomas Stodalffe
Thomas Watson
Fr John Lumley
Alexander Johnson
Andrew Ganno
Sir William Stokkes
Roger Knotte
John Walker
John Nessam
John Haddon
M John Thomson
Robert Johnson
John Fenton
John Hargrawe
Harre Lacy
Sir Robert Holte
John Bardshawe
Thomas Carby
John Webster
Robert Day
Sir William Wardalle
M Roger Baynthorpe
Elyzabeth Store
John Hawe
Fr Robert Hampton Gray frere
Dna [sic] Christopher Welley pryor of sent lenard
William Haylyday
John Harrysse

The new Bredder thys yer
fferst Robert Ellys and schall pay vjs viijd
Robert Hawe and Augnes hys wyffe vjs viijd

Elyzabeth Warde and pay iijs iiijd she paid xd and owes ijs vjd
M John Browne Rector of Chesterton and schall pay vjs viijd
Dna Margett Loftes pryoresse of Rowell vjs viijd
Sir William Freesby Rector of Desboro vjs viijd
fol 84

ffor Entres money thys yer
fferst Alexander Gebson iijs iiijd
Roger Belle xxd
Sir William Fescher xxd
Fr Robert Staunford vjs viijd
John Nettylham iijs iiijd
My lord of Spaldyng vjs viijd
Thomas Tampeon vjs viijd
William Frend xxd
Doctour Boston vs
Robert Thomson vs
Thomas Foldyngton xxd
William Nettylham xxd
Robert Graunte vjs viijd
Sir Hew Gee iijs iiijd
M Thomas Stodalffe vs
Thomas Watson xxd
Alexander Johnson vjs viijd
Andrew Ganno vjs viijd
Roger Knott xxd
M John Tomson vjs viijd
Robert Johnson iijs iiijd
John Hardgrawe vs
Harre Lacy xxd
Sir Robert Holte iijs iiijd
John Bradshawe vs
Thomas Carby iijs iiijd
Robert Day vjs viijd
John Webster vs
John Nessam vs
Sir William Wardall parson of Langton vjs viijd
M Roger Baynthorpe vs
Elyzabeth Store xxd
Margett Sted xxd she paid xd and owes xd

John Hawe vjs viijd

Fr Robert Hampton Gray frere vjs viijd

Dna [sic] Christopher Welley pryour of sent lenards iijs iiijd which he paid and is quit

William Haylyday   vjs viijd

John Harrysse vjs viijd

The Election of offecers thys yer

fferst William Radclyff Alderman;   steward of the lands Morres Johnson; Stewards of the fest John Fenton, William Grenfeld; bedell Robert Stede

Md that thys ys the accompte of William Jakson steward of the fest as yt aperes by a bell ther of made to the Summ of xs ijd the qwech ys payd and so he ys qwytte; alsso payd to the bedell thys yer ijs iiijd and remannes at thys day xijs iijd and of the laste yer (x *del*) vs ixd. Sum total xviijs wher of payd to the prest for thys yer xiijs and so remannes vs.

Md that thys ys the accompt of Morres Johnson steward of the lands: ferst he ys charged with the rent thys yer xviijs wherof in dekay viijs as yt aperes by a bell ther of made; and alsso he axes to be alowed for reparacions, obbetts and waxe as yt aperes by a bell therof vjs ijd. Sum total xiiijs ijd, and so he owes yett iijs xd which he paid and is quit

The stoke money

fferst John Thurlbe xs pleg Christopher Browne

John Selbe xxvjs viijd wherof payd by Robert Sanwayte wyffe iijs iiijd and so remannes xxiijs iiijd

fol 84d

The yer of owre lord a m^l v^c and xxvij and the xixth yer of kyng harre the viijth for sent kateryn geld

fferst for (entres money del) Waxschott[173]

-fferst William Radclyff

Dna Augnes Leche

Sir Thomas Foster

Augnes Cobbe

---

[173] two sets of marks are put against these names – o and - ; it is not clear what these mean

-Joan Tyard
-John A lee
-(Wife of *del*) William Yngkersall
-Joan Stodard
-William Grenfeld
-Thomas Jakson
oWalter Fayrday
-Morres Johnson
oJames Thestylwayte
-John Thomas
-Robert Parsons
-Robert Sandwayte
M Rawlyn Lokkey
M William Rychardson
-Edward Store
oRichard Hoggeson
-Fr Richard Thorpe
oJohn Adewe
-John Warde
Fr John Kyrton
Wife of Davy Roberts
Thomas Hanford
oJohn Boston
oRichard Wryght
oJohn Bassam
-Sir Thomas Foklyne
-Thomas Maydwell
oWife of John Parische
Roger Gowght
-Joan Trygge
-Edward Browne
-Thomas Wyllams
-Robert Haddon
-Alexander Gebson
oThe ankers of the Nonnes
oSir William Fescher
-Margett Walles
oRobert Sted
-William Rankell
oRoger Beylle

-Harre Ley
-George Robynson
oThomas Stannerd
oDavy Cessyll
oRobert Cobbe
oThomas Crosse
oWilliam Muston
-Sir Thomas Worthynton of Fodrynghay
oHarre Parsons
oSir Hew Gee
oRobert Thomson
-Wife of Thomas Watters
oSir Stephen Scherpe
oJohn Johnson
oRobert Graunte
Jeane Spenser
-Robert Draper
-Mathew Wetton
My lord of Spaldyng
oMy lord of Crowland
M Harre Nettylham
oThomas Tampeon
M Harre Bonde
oM John Russell
-M George Kyrham
(Thomas Ayke *del*)
-Thomas Foldyngton
oFr John Ayke
-Thomas Nettylhan
oWilliam Nettylham
-M Thomas Webster
oRichard Clerke
Dna Elyzabeth countes of Oxford
M Thomas Stodalffe
-Thomas Watson
-Fr John Lumley
oAlexander Johnson
oAndrew Ganno
oSir William Stokks
oRoger Knott

oJohn Walker
oJohn Nessam
oJohn Haddon
oM John Thomson
oRobert Johnson
-John Fenton
oJohn Hardgrawe
-Harre Lacy
oSir Robert Holte
oJohn Bradschawe
oWife of Thomas Carby
oJohn Webster
oRobert Day
oSir William Wardall
oM Roger Baynthorpe
-Elyzabeth Store
oJohn Hawe
Fr Robert Hampton gray frerre
Dna [sic] Christopher Welle pryor of sent lenards
-William Haylyday
-John Harrys

The stoke money
fferst John Thurlbe owes xs pleg Christopher Browne
John Selbe owes xxvjs viijd wherof payd iijs iiijd by Robert Sandwayte wyffe and
so he owed yett xxiijs iiijd

The Eleccion of offecers ther yer
fferst William Radclyff Alderman; steward of the lands Morres John[son];
Stewards of the feste William Grenfeld and Robert Hawe; bedell Robert Sted.

fol 85

For Entres money thys yer
fferst Alexander Gebson iijs iiijd
Roger Beylle xxd
Sir William Fescher xxd
Fr Robert Staunford vjs viijd
John Nettylham iijs iiijd
Thomas Tampeon vjs viijd

William Frend xxd
Robert Thomson vs
Thomas Foldyngton xxd
William Nettylham xxd
Robert Graunte vjs viijd
Sir Hew Gee iijs iiijd
M Thomas Stodalffe vs
Thomas Watson xxd which paid and is quit
Alexander Johnson vjs viijd
Andrew Ganno vjs viijd
Roger Knotte xxd
M John Tomson vjs viijd
Robert Johnson iijs iiijd paid xxd and owes xxd
John Hardgrawe vs
Harre Lacy xxd which paid and is quit
Sir Robert Holte iijs iiijd
John Bradshawe vs
Thomas Carby iijs iiijd
Robert Day vjs viijd
John Webster vs
John Wessam vs
Sir William Wardall parson of Langton vjs viijd
M Roger (Bynt *del*) Baynthorpe vs
Elyzabath Store xxd paid xd and owes xd
Margett Sted xd which paid and is quit
John Hawe vjs viijd
Fr Robert Hampton vjs viijd
William Haylyday   vjs viijd
John Harres vjs viijd paid xxd and owes vs
Fr Robert Ellys vjs viijd   paid xxd and owes vs
Robert Hawe vjs viijd paid xxd and owes vs
Elyzabeth Ward ijs vjd paid xd and owes xxd
M John Brow[n]e parson of Chesterton vjs viijd paid xxd and owes vs
Dna Margaret Loftes pryores of Rowell vjs viijd paid xxd and owes vs
Sir William Fresby vecare of Desborow vjs viijd paid xxd and owes vs

Md that thys ys the accompte of John Fenton steward of the fest as ytt aperes by a bell therof made xiiijs ixd the qwech ys payd so he ys qwyte. Item payd to the bedell ijs iiijd. Item to the prest xiijs thys yer. Summa totall thys yer xxxs jd.

Md that thys ys the acompte of Morres Johnson steward of the lands: ferst he ys charged with the rent of the lands thys yer xviijs; wher of he axes to be alowed for dekays for thys yer viijs, and for obbetts and Cheffe rent and oder thyngs as ytt aperres by a bell therof made ijs xjd. Summa xs xjd and so he owes yett xijs vd[174]

fol 85d blank

fol 86 [small inscription: *An accompt made with Mr Bars on Sept 20 1614*]

fols 86d, 87, 87d, 88, 88d, 89 blank

fol 89d

[175]**Staunford: Acts of the Gild of St Katherine virgin held in the common hall there Sunday after the feast of St Andrew Apostle [3 December] anno domini 1531 and the 23rd year of the reign of king Henry VIII.**

New Brethren
John Thomas by himself (*per se*) is admitted and will give vjs viijd
Reginald Cob admitted and wife and owe vjs viijd
William Holmes and Elizabeth admitted and will give vjs viijd
William Hude and Elena admitted and will give vjs viijd
Thomas Freschwater and Margeria admitted and owe vjs viijd
Elizabeth Clerke widow admitted and will give vjs viijd
Dom John Thorneton admitted [blank]

For entry
Alexander Gibson owes iijs iiijd
Roger Balle [sic] owes xxd
Dom William Fyscher owes xxd
John Nettlame owes iijs iiijd
Thomas Tampion owes vjs viijd
Robert Thomson vs
Thomas Foldyngton owes xxd
William Nettlame owes xxd
Robert Graunte owes vjs viijd

---

[174] these figures do not add up
[175] A new start: formal Latin and elaborate handwriting, heavy ruling.

Dom Hugh Gee owes iijs iiijd
Thomas Stodallff owes vs
Alexander Johnson owes vjs viijd
Andrew Ganno owes vjs viijd
John Thomson owes vjs viijd
Robert Johnson owes xxd
John Hardgrave owes vs
Dom Robert Holt owes iijs iiijd
John Bradshaw owes vs
Thomas Careby owes iijs iiijd
Robert Dey owes vjs viijd
John Webster owes vs
John Nysame owes vs
Dom William Wardall Rector of Langton owes vjs viijd
Dom Roger Banthorp Rector of Grettfford owes vs
Elizabeth Storie owes xd
John Hawe owes vjs viijd
William Halyday owes vjs viijd which he paid xxd and owes vs
John Harres iijs iiijd paid xijd and owes ijs iiijd

fol 90
Fr Robert Elis vs
Robert Hawe owes xxd which he paid and quit
John Browne Rector of Chesterton owes xxd
Margaret prioress of Rowell owes xxd
Dom William Fresby Rector of Desburgh owes xxd
[176]Robert Frend and Margery his wife owe vjs viijd
John Hall and Elena his wife owe vjs viijd of which paid xxd and owe vs
Alice wife of Mathew Wytton owes iijs iiijd of which she paid xxd and owes xxd
Dom Ralph [blank] chaplain of Byrton owes vjs viijd of which paid xxd and
owes vs

Stock (De Stipite)
John Thurleby by pledge of Christopher Browne owes xs
John Selby owes xxiijs iiijd
Memor' that William Dubdyke owyth xxs pleg John Hardegrave
Memor' that John Harres owes for his Rents up to this day vs he owes in the
feast of St Michael last past

---

[176] the following four entries were admitted during the missing years of this book.

Waxshotte
[177]Dna Agnes Lech annocarita
Agnes Cobbe
Joan Tyard
John Ley
John Stodard
William Grenefeld
Thomas Jakson
Maurice Johnson
Robert Thomas
Robert Sandwayte
Edward Storie
Richard Hodgeson
Fr Richard Thorpe
John Adew
John Warde
Fr John Kyrton
Thomas Handford
John Boston
Roger Gohe
Joan Trigge
Edward Browne
Thomas Williams
Robert Stede
William Rankell
Roger Beale
M David Cecell
Robert Cobbe
Thomas Crosse
William Muston
Henry Persons
Robert Thomson
M John Johnson
Robert Graunte
Joan Spencer
Robert Draper
Mathew Wytton

---

[177] set out in two and a half columns

My lord Crowlande
Henry Wetylhame [sic]
Thomas Tampion
M John Russell
Fr John Ayke
William Nettlame
M Thomas Webster
Thomas Watson
Alexander Johnson
Andrew Ganno
Dom William Stoxe
Roger Knott
John Walker
John Nessame
John Hadon
M John Thomson
Robert Johnson
John Fenton
John Hardgrave
Henry Lacy
Thomas Carby
John Webster
Robert Dey
Dom William Wardall
Dom Roger Banthorpe
Edward Storie
John Hawe
Fr Robert Thamton [sic]
William Halyday
John Harres

fol 90d

Election of officers
Henry Lacy was elected Alderman for the coming year
Robert Sandwath steward of lands for the coming year
William Halyday elected as bedell
Robert Sandwath and William Halyday stewards of the entertainment

Waxshott vijs viijd, dyner sylver iiijs vjd, entrynge money ixs iiijd, Herres hath payd his Rents xvs. Summa Rec xxxvjs vjd

Expenses for breakfast (*jantaculo*) xvs viijd; paid to the friar (*fratri*) for ij years xvijs iiijd. In regards bedelle vjd. In regards the obits (*In regards pro exequiis?*) and funerals? (*pussaciones*[178]) vijd. And delivered to John Ley ijs vd to be accounted for elsewhere.

Staunford: Acts of the gild of St Katherine virgin held in the common hall there Sunday after the feast of St Andrew the Apostle millimo ccccc^mo xxxij° and xxiiij year of the reign of Henry VIII

New brethren
Rev father Dom William Astalonenses[179] bishop, friar minor admitted and will give vjs viijd
M Thomas Byrd presentor of Fodryngay vjs viijd
Frauncis Browne and Beatrix his wife vjs viijd of which paid xxd and owes vs
Geoffrey Vyllers and Anna his wife vjs viijd of which paid xxd and owes vs
Fr John Depynge vjs viijd of which paid xxd and owes vs
John Edengrove vjs viijd
Robert Wallett and Elizabeth his wife vjs viijd of which paid xxd and owe vs
Dom William Hygdon vicar of All Saints vjs viijd
Fr Thomas Sheppey of the order of Carmelites viijd
Fr Dom Staford prior of friars preachers vjs viijd

fol 91

Entry fines
John Thomas by himself admitted and he will give vjs viijd
Reginald Cobb admitted with his wife and owes vjs viijd of which paid xxd and owes vs
William Holmes and Elizabeth owe vjs viijd paid xxd and owe vs
William Hude and Elena owe vjs viijd paid xxd and owe vs
Thomas Freschewater and Margery owe vjs viijd paid xxd and owe vs
Elizabeth Clerke widow owes iijs iiijd paid xd and owes ijs vjd
Dom John Thornton admitted
Dom Ralph chaplain of Byrton owes vs paid xxd and owes iijs iiijd

---

[178] I think this means the general obit and individual funerals
[179] I have been unable to trace this bishopric (*in partibus?*)

Alexander Gybson owes iijs iiijd

Dom William Fyscher owes xxd

John Nettlame owes iijs iiijd

Thomas Tampyon owes vjs viijd

Robert Thomson owes vs

Thomas Foldyngton owes xxd

William Nettlame owes xxd

Robert Graunte owes xxd

Dom Hugh Gee owes iijs iiijd

Thomas Stodalff owes vs

Alexander Johnson owes vjs viijd

Andrew Ganno owes vjs viijd

John Johnson[180] owes vjs viijd

John Hardegrave owes vs

Dom Robert Holte owes iijs iiijd

John Bradshaw owes vs

Robert Dey owes vjs viijd

John Webster owes vs

John Nysame owes vs

Dom William Wardall Rector of Langton owes vjs viijd

Roger Banthorp Rector of Grettfford owes vs

Elizabeth Storie owes xd

John Haw owes vs paid xxd and owes iijs iiijd

Alice wife of Mathew Wytton owes xxd

William Halyday owes vs

John Harres owes ijs iiijd

Fr Robert Elis owes vs

John Browne Rector of Chesterton owes xxd

Margaret prioress of Rowell owes xxd

Dom William Fresby rector of Desburugh owes xxd

Robert Frend and Margery owe vjs viijd

John Hall and Elena owe vs

fol 91d

Stock

John Thurleby by pledge of Christopher Browne owes xs

---

[180] It is likely the clerk conflated two entries here, one for John Thomson and one for Robert Johnson.

John Selby owes xxiijs iiijd

Memo that William Dubdyke owyth xxs plege of John Hardgrave

Memo that John Harres owes for his Rent up to this day vs paid

And also John Harres paid for his rent for this day what had been owed at Michaelmas last past xs

Waxshott[181]

Dom Agnes Leche annocarita

Agnes Cobb

Joan Tyard

John Ley

Joan Stodard

William Grenfeld

Thomas Jakson

Maurice Johnson

John Thomas

Robert Sandwath

Edward Storie

Richard Hodgeson

Fr Richard Thorpe

John Adew

John Warde

Fr John Kyrton

Thomas Handford

John Boston

Roger Goghe

Joan Trigge

Edward Browne

Thomas Williams

Robert Stede

William Rankell

Roger Beall

David Cecell

Robert Cobbe

Thomas Crosse

William Muston

Henry Persons

Robert Thomson

---

[181] names listed in three columns with line drawn between columns one and two.

M John Johnson
Robert Graunte
Joan Spencer
Robert Draper
Mathew Wytton
My lord of Croyland
Henry Northame
Thomas Tampion
M John Russell
Fr John Ayke
William Nettlame
M Thomas Webster
Thomas Wattson
Alexander Johnson
Andrew Ganno
Dom William Stox
Roger Knott
John Walker
John Nesame
John Hadon
(M John Jonson *del*)
Robert Thomson
John Fenton
John Hardgrave
Henry Lacy
Thomas Carby
John Webster
Robert Dey
Dom William Wardall
Dom Roger Bainthorpe
Edward Storie
John Haw
Fr Robert Hamton
William Halyday
John Hares
Reginald Cob[182]
William Holmes
William Hude

---

[182] The names that follow are gild members who have been admitted during the 'gap years'.

Thomas Freschwater
Elizabeth Clerke
Robert Wallett
M Thomas Byrd presentour of Fodryngay
Francis Browne
Geoffrey Vyllers
Fr John Depynge
John Edengrove
Dom William Hygdon
Fr Thomas Sheppey
Fr Dom Stafford prior of the Austens
Reverend pater Dom William Astalonens Eps Frs Minor

fol 92

Election of officers
Henry Lacy is elected Alderman for the coming year
Robert Sandwath steward of lands for the coming year
William Dubdyke is elected bedell
William Haliday and John Halle stewards of entertainment

The accompte off Roberd Sandwath stuerd off the feest [sic]: Fyrst the Rent off John Harres xs and off Rent off the last yeer vs. Item the Rent off whippe howse this half yeer iijs. Item the dyner iiijs ijd. Item waxshott vjs. The new bretherne admittaunce xvs xd. Summa xliiijs.
And deducte theroff for the coosts off the fest as apperithe by the byll therof made xvs vd ob. Item for quyte Rente vjd. Item iij li of Wax xviijd. Item iij obetts xvd. Item the generall obbetts vijd. Summa xixs iijd ob. Whiche is payd and so Quyte with hym Quietus

Item payd to Maurice Johnson this day for reparaciones vjs. Item paid to the Frear viijs viijd. Item to the bedell vjd. Item to the clerk for makyng the boke ixd ob. And so Remeynyth [no total]

Remanz   viijs ixd which is delivered to Robert Sandwath to account for next year.

Staunford: Acts of the gild of St Katherine virgin held in the common hall there Sunday feast of St Andrew [30 November] anno domini millimo ccccc^{mo} xxxiij° and xxv year of reign of king Henry VIII

New brethren

John Turnour and [blank] his wife admitted and will give vjs viijd of which paid xxd and owe vs

William Dove and Elizabeth his wife were admitted and will give vjs viijd of which paid xxd and owe vs

[No heading: Entry fines]

John Thomas owes vjs viijd

Reginald Cob and his wife owes vs paid xxd and owe iijs iiijd

William Holmes and [blank] his wife owe vs paid xxd and owe iijs iiijd

William Hude and Elena his wife owe vs paid xxd and owe iijs iiijd

Thomas Freschewater and Margery his wife owe vs paid xxd and owe iijs iiijd

Elizabeth Clerke owes ijs vjd paid xijd and owes xviijd

Dom John Thorneton was admitted and owes iijs iiijd paid xd and owes ijs vjd

Dom Ralph chaplain of Byrton owes iijs iiijd

Alexander Gybson owes iijs iiijd

Dom William Fysher owes xxd

fol 92d

Entry fines

John Nettlame owes iijs iiijd

Thomas Tampion vjs viijd

Robert Thomson vs

Thomas Foldyngton xxd

William Nettlame xxd

Robert Graunte xxd

Dom Hugh Gee iijs iiijd

Thomas Stodalff vs

Alexander Jonson vjs viijd

Andrew Ganno vjs viijd

John Thomson vjs viijd

Robert Dey vjs viijd

Dom William Wardale Rector of Langto[n] vjs viijd

Robert Frende and Margery his wife vjs viijd

Reverend Father Dom William Astalonensis epo vjs viijd

M Thomas Byrde presentour of the college of Foderyngay vjs viijd

Robert Jonson xxd
John Hardgrave vs
Robert Holte iijs iiijd
John Bradshaw vs
John Webster vs
John Nysame vs
Dom Roger Baymthorp vs
Elizabeth Storie xd
John Hall iijs iiijd of which he paid xx[d] and owes xxd
William Halyday vs of which he paid xxd and owes iijs iiijd
Dom William Hygden iijs iiijd of which he paid xd and owes ijs vjd
Alice wife of Mathew Wytton xxd
John Haw iijs iiijd
John Harres ijs iiijd of which he paid viijd and owes xxd [sic]
Fr Robert Elys vs
John Broune rector of Casterton vs
Fr John Depynge vs
Margar' prioress of the monastery of Rowell xxd
Dom William Fresby rector of Desburgh xxd
Frauncis Broune armiger vjs viijd of which he paid xxd and owes vs

fol 93
Geoffrey Vytler and Anna his wife owes vs of which paid xxd and owe iijs iiijd
John Wyngrove owes vjs viijd of which he paid xxd – owes vs
Robert Wallett owes vs of which he paid xxd and he owes iijs iiijd
Fr Stafford prior of the Friars Preachers vjs viijd
Fr Thomas Sheppey owes ijs vjd

Stock
John Thurleby by pledge of Christopher Broune owes xs
John Selby owes xxiijs iiijd
Md that William Dubdyke owyth xxs plege John Hardgrave

Waxshott
Dna Agnes Leche annocarita
Agnes Cob
Joan Tyard
John Ley
Joan Stodard
William Grenfeld

Thomas Jakson
Maurice Jonson
John Thomas
Robert Sandwath
Edward Storie
Richard Hodgeson
John Adew
John Ward
Fr John Kyrton
Thomas Handford
John Boston
Roger Gogh
Edward Broune
William Rankell
Roger Bedale
David Cecill
William Muston
Henry Parsons
Robert Thomson
M John Johnson
Robert Graunt
Mathew Wytton
Robert Draper
My lord off Croylande
Mathew Wytton
Henry Nettlame
M John Russell
Fr John Ayke
William Nettlame
M Thomas Webster
Thomas Watson
Alexander Jonson
Andrew Ganno
John Walker
Roger Knott
John Nesame
John Hadon
Robert Thomson
John Fenton
John Hardgrave

Henry Lacy
John Webster
Robert Dey
Edward Storie
William Halyday
John Harres
Reginald Cob
William Hud
Thomas Freschewater
Elizabeth Clerke
Robert Wallett
M Thomas Byrd
Francis Broune
Fr John Depynge
Geoffrey Vyllers
John Edyngrove
Fr Thomas Sheppey
Dom William Hygden
Fr Stafford prior off the Austyns
Rev father Dom William Astalonens' bishop of the friars minor

fol 93d

Election of officers
Henry Lacy gent elected Alderman for the coming year
steward of the lands Robert Sandwath
Stewards off the feeste John Hall, William Hude
bedell William Dobdyke

The accompte off Robert Sandwath steward off the lands: ffyrst the Rent off John Harres xs. Item recevyed for (*ins* ij) Cresses and for slate xvjd. Item for wood xviijd. Item receyved for one hundrith slate vjd. Item recevyd off Sharpe for slate ijs. Item the dynner ijs vjs. Item waxshote iijs iiijd. The new bred annuataye[183] xxiiijs ijd.
Summa xlvs iiijd
And deducte theroff for the cost off the dynner as apperith by a byll theroff made xvs vijd. Item for quyte Rent vjd. Item for iiij obetts xvjd. Item for ij

---

[183] the hardship of these years is well known; it is not clear where this sum came from.

pounde Wax xiiijd. Item for reparacyons thys yeer made off the gylde halle and wyppes howse xxxjs. Item the generall obett vijd. Whych is paid and so quytte
Item payd the prestes wages viijs viijd
Item payd to the bedell iiijd

Staunford: Acts of the gild of St Katherine virgin held in the common hall there on Sunday before the feast of St Andrew the apostle [29 November] in the year 1534 and the 26th year of the reign of King Henry VIII.

New brethren
Fr John Newthorpe friar minor was admitted and will give [blank]
Fr Richard Pye friar minor
Fr Alexander Rattffor of the order of [friars] minor
Fr Mathew Braffeld of the order of [friars] minor
William Miles and [blank] his wife
Stephan Ley and [blank] his wife
Robert Parker Fremason

fol 94

Entry fines
John Thomas owes for himself vjs viijd
Reginald Cok and Alice iijs iiijd
William Holmes and Elizabeth iijs iiijd paid xxd and owe xxd
William Howe and Elena iijs iiijd
Thomas Fresschewater and Margaret iijs iiijd paid xxd and owe xxd
Elizabeth Clerk xviijd paid ixd and owes ixd
Dom John Thorneton ijs vjd paid xd and owes xxd
Dom Ralph chaplain of Byrton iijs iiijd paid xxd and owes xxd
Alexander Gybson owes iijs iiijd
Dom William Fysssher xxd
John Nettlame iijs iiijd
Thomas Tampyon vjs viijd
Robert Thomson vs
Thomas Foldyngton xxd
William Nettlame xxd
Robert Graunte xxd
Dom Hugh Gee iijs iiijd
Thomas Stodalff vs
Alexander Jonson vjs viijd
Andrew Ganno vjs viijd

John Thomson vjs viijd
Robert Johnson xxd
John Hardgrave vs
Robert Holte iijs iiijd
John Bradshawe vs
Robert Dey vjs viijd
John West vs
John Nysame vs
Dom William Wardale rector of Langton vjs viijd
Dom Roger Baynthorpe rector of Grettford vs
Robert Frende and Margery vjs viijd
Elizabeth Storie xd
John Hall xxd paid ixd and owes xjd
Alice wife of Mathew Wytton xxd
Dom William Hygdon ijs vjd paid xd and owes xxd
John Russell Master of the college of Fodrynghay gave gratuity xxd
John Hawe iijs iiijd

fol 94d
John Harres owes xxd paid and quit
Fr Robert Elis owes vs
John Broune rector of Casterton owes xxd paid and quit
Margaret prioress of nuns of Rowell owes xxd
Dom William Fresby owes xxd
Reverend father Dom William Astalonens bishop of friars minor owes vjs viijd
Dom Thomas Byrd presentor of Fodryngay owes vjs viijd
Francis Browne owes vs paid xxd and owes iijs iiijd
Geoffrey Vyllers owes iijs iiijd paid xxd and owes xxd
Fr John Depynge owes vs
John Wyngrove owes vs
Robert Wallett owes iijs iiijd paid xxd and owes xxd
Fr William Stafford prior of friars preachers owes vjs viijd
Fr Thomas Sheppey owes ijs vjd paid xijd and owes xxd [sic]
John Turnour armiger owes vs
William Dove and Elizabeth owe vs paid xxd and owe iijs iiijd

Stock
John Thurleby by pledge of Christopher Browne xs
John Selby owes xxiijs iiijd
Md William Dobdyke owyth xxs pleg M John Hargrave

Waxshott

xDna Agnes Leche annocarita
-Agnes Cobbe
-Joan Tyard
xJoan Stodard
-William Grenefeld
-Thomas Jakson
-Maurice Johnson
-John Thomas
-Robert Sandwath
-Edward Storie
xJohn Adew
John Ward
-Fr John Kyrkton
xThomas Handford
xRoger Goghe
-John Boston
-William Rankell
-Edward Broune
xDavid Cecell
-Roger Beale
-Henry Lacy
xWilliam Muston
-Henry Parsones
Robert Thomson
xM John Jonson
xRobert Graunte
xMathew Wytton
-Robert Draper
xMy lord off Croyland
-M John Russell
-Fr John Ayke
xM Thomas Webster
xAlexander Johnson
xJohn Walker
-Andrew Ganno
xRoger Knott
-John Nysame
-John Haddon

-John Fenton
-John Hardgrave
xJohn Webster
xRobert Dey
-William Halyday
-John Harres
-Reginald Cobbe
-Thomas Freschewater
Elizabeth Clerke
-Robert Wallett
xM Thomas Byrd
-Francis Browne
xFr John Depynge
-Geoffrey Vyllers
xJohn Edyngrove
xFr Thomas Sheppey
-Dom William Hygden
xDom William Fresby
-Dom William Stafford
-John Turnour
-William Dove
John Hall

fol 95

Election of officers
Henry Lacy gent elected Alderman for the coming year
Stuerd of the lands Robert Sandwayth
Stuerds of the ffest Thomas Freschewater and William Holmes
bedell William Dubdyke

The accompte of Robert Sandwath Stuerd off the lands: ffyrst receyved off John
Harres ffor his Rente xs. Item the rente off John Bolland vjs. Sum xvjs
Sum of receipts xvjs. Of which paid for the obits of Fr Thorpe, Fr Depynge,
John Ley, Joan Trigge, wife of Edward Broune, William Nettlame, wife of
Robert Wallett and Thomas Wyllams for each of them iiijd. Sum iijs [sic]
For wages of Fr Richard Thorpe for half a year iiijs iiijd; for wages of Fr Richard
Sheppey for another half year iiijs iiijd; for rents resolute vjd. Item for wax
xiiijd. Also for making wax and for the clerk in the vigil of St Katherine iiijd.

Total payments xiijs viijd and thus owed ijs viijd [sic] which are paid in exchequer and he is quit

The accompte off John Hall the Stuerd off the Feast. In primis waxshott vs ijd. Item the dynner sylver iijs. Item the entrye money xixs xd. Item receyved off Roberd Sandwath off the Rest off the Rente off the Gylde ijs viijd [Total] xxxs viijd
Sum xxxs viijd
Deducte off this summe For the expens off dynner as doth appeyr by his byll whych amountith to the sume off xiiijs ijd. Item for the generall obbett vijd. And remains for this day clearly xvs xd [sic].

Clear sum xvs xd which was delivered to Robert Sandwathe steward of the lands for which he will render account elsewhere.

Ordinance[184] of the brothers and sisters such that quarterly one of the brothers of the gild shall celebrate the quarterly for the confreres, the finish of shall begin and thus for each.

fol 95d

Very small note at bottom of page

Ext et post Blomefield[185]

---

[184] the wording is odd but the sense is more or less clear.
[185] Francis Blomefield the historian was a member of CaiusCollege in the 18th century.

INDEX

There may be more than one entry on any page. The letter n after a page number indicates the word occurs in one or more footnote on that page.

Baynthorp, Bainthrope, Banthorpe, Baynthorpe Roger 239, 242-3, 247-8, 251-2, 256-7, 259, 261, 263, 265, 268, 272

Baynton, Badyngton 244, 248

Beale, Beall, *see* Bedale, Bell(e)

Beamo(u)nde, Beamont Emma 13, 140; Robert 8, 13, 111, 113, 116, 118, 122, 124, 127, 129 , 136, 140, 142, 147, 152, 158, 163, 168, 174, 179, 184, 189, 194, 197, 202, 206, 210, 214, 219, 222

Beaufort Lady Margaret countess Richmond and Derby 1, 5, 7-9, 12-13, 18, 36n, 134-5, 139, 143-4, 148, 154, 159, 164, 170; servant of 8n, 149, 176 - *see* Cotmount; Walter

Bedale Roger 269; *see* Bell(e)

Bedwyn Elizabeth 142, 147, 153; Isabella 103; Richard 20, 103-4, 106-7, 111, 113, 116, 118, 123-4, 126, 129, 132, 137-8

Beele, Beell, *see* Bell(e)

Been(e), Bene Joan 42; John 38, 40, 42-8, 50-3, 55-6, 58-9, 61-3, 65-7, 69, 71, 73-5, 77-80, 82, 84-6, 89, 91, 93, 94-5, 97-8, 100, 102-3, 107, 111, 117, 122, 131

Bekenfelde, *see* Bokenfeld

Belesby *see* Billesby

Bell, *see* Balle

Bell(e), Beale, Beell, Bele, Joan 150, 156, 161, 166; Roger 150, 156, 160-1, 165, 170, 172, 176-7, 181, 183, 186, 197, 207, 212-3, 216, 218, 220, 223, 225, 227, 229, 232, 234, 236, 238, 241, 243, 245, 247, 252, 260, 264, 273 ; *see* Bedale , Beylie

Bellesbe, *see* Billesby

Belton Margery 139, 144, 154

Ber(e)cok Thomezona 140, 145, 149-50, 154, 156, 160-1, 164, 166, 172, 176-7

Berdon John 222; *see* Burton

Berkeley Sir William 100n

Beverston, Glos 100n

Bewshir Alice 131, 135, 138; William 131

Beylie, Beyll Roger 187, 191-2, 195, 199, 201, 203, 205, 209, 250, 254, 256

Billesby John 36, 38, 41, 43, 45, 47, 49, 51, 53, 55, 59, 64, 67, 71, 75, 79, 83, 88, 93, 97, 102, 106, 113, 118, 124, 129, 136, 142, 147, 152, 158, 163, 169, 174, 180, 185, 189, 194

Billesden Katherine 73, 82, 87, 91; Nicholas 73, 76, 78, 80, 82-3, 87, 91-2, 95-6, 101, 105, 112, 117, 123, 128, 137, 141, 146, 152, 157

bishop, *see* Astalonens

Blogwyn Richard 35

Blomefield Francis 275

Bocher David 143, 148, 153; Robert 143, 148, 153

Bokenfeld, Bekenfeld, Bokynffelde Katherine 78; W 148; William 78, 82, 84, 87, 89, 91, 93, 95, 97, 102, 106, 114-5, 119-21, 125-6, 130, 137, 143, 153, 159

Bolland John 274

Bonde, *see* Bownd

Boston 35n

Collyweston 1, 8, 36n, 79, 83, 88, 93, 134

Co(u)per Thomas 19, 72, 75-6, 78, 80, 82-3, 86, 88, 90, 92, 94-5, 97-8, 101, 106, 113, 118, 124, 129, 136, 142, 147, 151-2, 158, 163, 167-8, 173-4, 178-9, 184, 189, 194, 197, 202, 206, 210, 214, 219, 222, 228, 231, 235, 240

Corland, *see* Crowland

Cotmount Richard 8n, 21, 135, 140, 148, 143, 145, 154, 159, 164,

Coton Agnes 58; Humfrey 63-4, 67

Couper, *see* Co(u)per

Coventry 6

Crane Agnes 92; Elizabeth 92; Robert 92, 96, 100-1, 104-5, 112, 117, 123, 128, 136, 141, 146, 152, 168

Crolland, *see* Crowland

Cromwell lord 36n

Crosse Agnes 160, 167; Thomas 160, 167, 171-2, 176, 178, 182, 186, 191, 196, 199, 203, 208, 212-3, 216-7, 220, 224, 230, 232, 237, 241, 246, 250, 255, 260, 264

Crowland, Corland, Crolland 8-9, 15, 171, 182, 187, 192, 196-7, 200, 204, 208, 212, 216, 221, 224, 230, 233, 237, 242, 246-7, 250, 255, 260, 265, 269, 273; abbot of, *see* Bardeney Richard; Welles John

Croxton Thomas 36, 38

Dacke, Dak, Dakke John 34, 37, 39, 43, 47, 51-2, 55-6, 60-1, 64-5, 68, 73, 77, 80, 84-5, 89, 94, 98, 102-3, 107, 111, 117, 122, 131; William 34

Dalton Alice 149, 155, 161, 166 ; John 149, 155, 160-1, 165-6, 170, 172, 176, 181, 186, 191, 195, 199, 203

Daneyll, Danyell *see* Denyell

Darley, Derley Alice 139, 145; William 139, 145, 149-50, 154, 156, 160-1, 164, 170, 176, 181, 186, 191, 195, 199, 203

Day(e), Dey Alice 227; Elena, Ellyn 99, 202, 206, 210, 214, 219, 222, 228, 231, 235; John 261; Richard 98-9, 100, 102, 104, 106, 111, 114, 116, 118, 120, 124, 136, 142, 147, 153. 158, 163, 169, 174, 180, 185, 189, 194, 198; Robert 227, 234, 238-9, 242-3, 247-8, 251-2, 256-7, 259, 263, 265, 267, 270, 272-3

de la Pole, *see* Grey, Pole de la

Denyell, Denell, Danyell, Dynyell Matilda/Mawde 80, 89, 93-4, 98, 102-3, 107, 111, 117, 122, 131, 146, 151, 156, 162, 167, 173, 179, 183, 196, 201, 205, 209, 213, 217; Thomas 36, 38, 40-2, 44-6, 48-9, 50, 52-4, 56-7, 59, 61-3, 65, 67, 69, 71, 73, 75, 77, 80, 84-5, 89

Depynge John 25, 262, 266, 268, 270, 272, 274

Derley, *see* Darley

Desborough, Desboro(w), Desburgh 251, 257, 259, 263, 268

Dey, *see* Day

Dobdyke, *see* Dubdyke

Dodyngton 36

Dove Elizabeth 267, 272; William 267, 272, 274

Dowce Richard 37, 39, 41

Draper Robert 204-5, 208, 210, 212, 214, 216, 221, 224, 230, 233, 237, 241, 246, 250, 255, 260, 265, 269, 273

Dubdyke, Dobdyke William 20, 259, 264, 266, 268, 270, 272, 274

Dyc(c)ons Alice (*see* Cecil) 15; Elizabeth 103-4, 106, 111, 116, 121, 127, 132; John 15, 103

Dynyell, *see* Denyell

Easton, Eston 177, 182, 187, 193, 196, 200, 204, 208, 212, 216, 221, 224, 230, 233, 237

Eayke, *see* Ayke

Edengrove, Edyngrove John 262, 266, 270, 274

Edward(e) Thomas 7, 14, 92, 96, 100-1, 104-5, 110, 112, 117, 123, 128, 136, 141, 146, 152

Elis, Ellys Robert 251, 257, 259, 263, 268, 272

Elmes Elizabeth 10, 135, 154, 159, 170; John 10; William 9, 10, 13, 134-5, 143, 148, 154, 159, 164, 176

Erpingham Ellen 10

Eyake, *see* Ayke

Faireday, *see* Fayreday

Faux, Fawkes William 20, 34, 37, 39, 43, 47-8, 51-2, 55-7, 59, 60-1, 64, 67-71, 73, 75, 79, 84, 89, 93, 97, 102

Fayreday, Faireday, Feyreday Walter, Watter 87, 91, 93, 96-7, 100-1, 104-5, 113, 119, 121, 123-4, 126, 130-1, 137, 142, 153, 158, 163, 169, 175, 180, 185, 190, 194, 198, 202, 206, 210, 215, 219, 222, 229, 231, 236, 240, 245, 249, 254

Fenton Agnes 225; John 20, 225, 227, 231, 233-4, 238-9, 242-4, 247-8, 251, 253, 256-7, 261, 265, 269, 273

Feyr(e)day, *see* Fayreday

Fis(s)her, Fescher, Fyscher, Fyssher John 13, 27, 36, 38, 41-2, 45-6, 49-50, 53-4, 57-9, 61-3, 65-7, 69, 71, 73, 75, 77, 79-80, 83, 85, 88-9, 93-4, 97-8, 102-3, 106-7, 111, 113, 117-8, 122, 124, 129, 131, 136, 142, 147, 151-2, 156, 158, 162-3, 167, 169, 173, 177, 179, 181, 183, 186-7, 191-2, 196-7, 199, 201, 203, 205, 207, 209, 211, 213, 215, 217-8, 220, 222-3, 225-6, 227-9, 234-6, 238, 240-1, 243, 245, 247, 250, 252, 254, 256; Richard 144, 146; W 154; William 144-5, 149-50, 156, 159, 161, 164, 166, 170, 172, 176, 195, 232, 258, 262, 267, 271

Foldyngton Alice 206; Thomas 206, 210, 213-4, 217-8, 221, 224-5, 227, 230, 233-4, 237-8, 242-3, 246-7, 250, 252, 255-6, 258, 263, 267, 271

Folkelyn, Fok(e)leyn Thomas 131, 135, 138-9, 143, 145, 148, 150, 154, 159, 164, 169, 175, 181, 186, 190, 195, 198, 203, 207, 211, 215, 220, 223, 229, 232, 236, 241, 245, 249, 254

Forster, Foster Elena, Ellyn 175, 180, 185, 190; John 13, 155, 165, 171, 175, 180, 190, 194, 198, 202; Margaret 35, 97; Richard (MP) 7, 35; Richard ropemaker 35n; Richard 38, 41, 45, 49, 51, 55, 60, 64, 68, 72, 76, 79, 83, 88, 92, 194; Thomas 109, 111, 113, 116, 118, 141, 147, 152, 158, 163, 168, 174, 179, 184, 189, 194, 197, 202, 206, 210, 214, 219, 222, 228, 231, 235, 240, 244, 249, 253

Fotheringhay, Foderynghay, college, chaunter, master, precentor 8-10, 139, 143, 145, 154, 159, 164, 166-7, 172, 176, 178, 182, 187, 191, 196, 199, 203, 206, 208, 212, 216, 220, 224, 230, 232, 237, 241, 246, 250, 255, 262, 266, 267, 272 ; *see* Barnard Robert, Byrde Thomas, Cal(de)cott Christopher, Hud(e), Russell John, Wordington Thomas

Fre(e)man Alice 103-4, 111, 116, 119, 121, 127, 132; Isabell 69; William 69, 71-2, 74, 76, 78, 80, 82, 84-6, 88-9, 90, 93-4, 97-8, 102-4, 106-7, 111, 114, 116-7, 121-2, 127, 131-2, 138, 145

Freesby, *see* Fresby

Frend(e) Margery 259, 263, 267, 272; Robert 259, 263, 267, 272; William 197, 200-1, 204-5, 208-9, 212, 214, 217-8, 221, 224-5, 227, 230, 233-4, 237-8, 243, 247, 252, 256

Fresby William 251, 259, 263, 268, 272, 274

Freschewater Margery, Margaret 258, 262, 267, 271; Thomas 19, 258, 262, 265, 267, 270-1, 274

Fyscher, *see* Fis(s)her

Ganno Andrew 218, 225-7, 231, 233-4, 237-8, 242-3, 246-7, 251-2, 255, 257, 259, 261, 263, 265, 267, 269, 271, 273; Joan 218

Garald, *see* Jeralde

Gebon John 42, 45, 47, 49, 51, 53, 55, 58, 60, 62, 64, 66; Margaret 42

Gebson, *see* Gibson

Gee Hugh/Hew 204-5, 208, 210, 212, 216, 218, 220, 224, 226-7, 230, 232, 234, 237-8, 241, 243, 246-7, 250, 252, 255, 257-8, 263, 267, 271

Gennefeld William 185, 194; *see* Gren(e)feld

Geralde, *see* Jeralde

Gibson, Gebson Alexander 23n, 144, 149-50, 154-5, 159, 161, 164, 166, 170-1, 176-7, 181-2, 186-7, 191-2, 195, 197, 199, 201, 203, 205, 207, 209, 211, 213, 215, 218, 220, 223, 225, 227, 229, 232, 234, 236, 238, 241, 243, 245, 247, 250, 252, 254, 256, 258, 262, 267, 271; Alice 144, 155, 159, 161, 166; John 23n, 151, 157

Gild, *see* St Katherine

Godeale, *see* Goodale

Godfrey, Godf(f)ray(e) William 34, 37, 39, 40, 43-4, 46-8, 51-2, 54, 56, 59-61, 63, 65, 67-9, 73, 77, 80, 84, 88, 93, 97, 102

Gogh(e), *see* Gough

Goldesworth Richard 35

Goldsmyth Margaret 42; Robert 42, 45, 47, 51, 55, 60

Gonville and Caius College, Cambridge 1

Goodale, Godeale Agnes 135, 150, 155, 161, 166, 171; Thomas 135, 139, 144-5, 149, 154

Gough, Gogh(e) Gowgh(t) Margaret 131; Roger 131, 135, 138, 140, 143-4, 148, 150, 154, 159, 164, 170, 175, 181, 186, 191, 195, 199, 203, 207, 211, 215, 220, 223, 229, 232, 236, 241, 245, 249, 254 260, 264, 269, 273

Goylen, Goylyn John 15, 20, 76, 78, 80-3, 87-8, 91-2, 97, 101, 105, 113, 118, 123, 129, 133, 136; Margaret 76, 78, 80, 147, 152,

Grace Thomas 155, *see* Grave

Hawe Agnes 251; Alice 131; Antony 131, 135, 138, 148, 154; John 244, 248, 251-2, 256-7, 259, 261, 263, 265, 268, 272; Robert 251, 256-7, 259; *see* Howe

Hawkes, Haux, Elena, Helena 106, 114, 119; William 34, 37, 39, 42-3, 46-7, 50-2, 54, 56, 59-61, 63, 65, 67-8, 71, 73, 75, 77, 79-80, 84-5, 88-9, 93-4, 98, 102-3, 107, 111, 117, 122, 131

Haylyday, *see* Halliday

Hebbes William 35, 37, 39, 43, 48, 51-2, 55-6, 59-61, 64-5, 68-9, 73

Help(i)ston 166, 172, 177

Hen(n)son John 185; W 130; William 117, 128, 140, 185, 190, 194, 198, 202, 206, 211, 215, 219

Herde, *see* Harde

Hernes Thomas 140

Herryson, *see* Haryson

Hert(e), *see* Harte

Hi(c)kson Henry 116, 119, 121, 124, 127, 130, 132, 137, 142, 147, 153, 158, 163, 169; John 19, 37, 39-41, 43-4, 56, 105, 117, 120, 122, 131, 146, 151, 156; Margery 118, 120, 124, 129, 136, 147, 152, 158, 163, 169; *see* Yetson

Hikeham, Hickham, Hyckham, Hykeham, Ikeham Thomas 42, 45, 47, 49, 51, 53, 55, 58, 60, 64, 68, 72, 75, 79, 83, 88, 92, 96, 101, 105, 112, 117, 123, 128, 136, 141, 146, 152; William 34, 43, 47, 51, 55, 59

Hill John 35

Hinklay, *see* Hyn(c)keley

Hobson Margaret 89, 93, 98, 102, 106, 114, 119, 125, 130, 137, 143, 148, 153, 159, 164, 169, 175, 180

Hode, Hud [no first name] 139, 143, 145, 148, 154; *see* Fotheringhay, Hude

Hodg(e)son, Hoggeson Joan 150, 156, 161, 166; Richard 150, 156, 161, 166, 185, 188, 190, 193-4, 198, 200, 202, 207, 211, 215, 219, 223, 229, 232, 236, 240, 245, 249, 254, 260, 264, 269

Holmes Elizabeth 258, 262, 271; William 258, 262, 265, 267, 271, 274

Holt(e) Robert 227, 234, 238-9, 242-3, 247-8, 251-2, 256-7, 259, 263, 268, 271

Holywell 82, 83, 86, 88, 91, 92, 95, 99, 123, 129

Honne John 36, 38, 40-2, 44-6, 48-50, 52, 54, 56, 59, 61, 63, 65, 69, 73, 77

Hoton, Hooton, Horton, Houghton, Howghton, Howton, Hughton Edward 42, 45, 47, 49, 51, 53, 55, 58, 60, 62, 64, 66, 68, 71-2, 74-5, 78-9, 82-3, 86, 91, 95, 97, 100-1, 105, 113, 118

Howe Antony 143; Elena 271; William 271; *see* Hawe

Hud(e) Elena 258, 262, 267 ; William 19, 258, 262, 265, 267,270; *see* Hode

Hunde(r)sley Robert 177, 182-3, 187-8, 192, 196, 200, 204, 208, 212, 216, 219, 221, 223-4

Hussey Sir John 7-8, 18; *see* Stamford, steward of manor

Hychson, Hyckson, *see* Hickson

Hyckham, *see* Hikeham

Hygden William 262, 266, 268, 270, 272, 274

Hykeham, *see* Hikeham

Lac(e)y Agnes 155, 161, 167, 187, 192, 196, 199; Henry/Harre 6-9, 18, 227, 234, 238-9, 242-3, 247-8, 251-2, 256-7, 261, 265-6, 270, 273-4; Kateryn 227; Thomas 7, 155, 161, 165, 167, 170, 172, 175, 177, 180

Langar Emma 135, 139, 145; Thomas 135, 139, 143, 145, 148-9, 154, 160, 165, 170, 176, 181, 186, 191, 195, 199, 203, 207, 211, 216, 220, 223, 229, 232, 236, 241

Langton 239, 242-3, 247-8, 252, 257, 259, 263, 267, 272

Lay Alice 18, 150, 155, 161, 166; Henry 18, 150, 155, 160-1, 165-6, 170-1, 176; *see* Lee

Lech(e), Lecche Agnes 11-12, 103-4, 106, 174, 179, 184, 189, 194, 197, 201, 206, 210, 214, 219, 222, 228, 231, 235, 240, 244, 249, 253, 259, 264, 268, 272; John 11-12; *see* Le(e)ke

Ledgate, *see* Legat(e)

Lee Harre 181, 186, 191, 195, 199, 203, 207, 212, 216, 220, 224, 229, 232, 236, 241, 245, 250, 254; Joan 34; John (a) 8, 19, 25, 103-4, 106, 111, 113, 116, 118, 121, 124, 127, 129, 132, 136, 142, 147, 152, 158, 163, 168, 174, 179, 183-5, 188-9, 193-4, 198, 200, 202, 204-6, 209-10, 214, 219, 222, 228, 231, 235, 240, 244, 249, 253, 260, 262, 264, 268, 274; Stephan 271; *see* Lay

Le(e)ke Richard 87, 91, 93, 95-6, 100-1, 104-5, 112, 118

Legat(e) Robert 131, 135, 143, 148, 154, 156, 159, 164, 169, 175, 181, 186, 190, 195

Leicester, Leycester New College, Newark in 8, 144-5, 149, 154, 159, 164, 176, 181, 186, 191, 195

Lerefax, *see* Loryfax

Ley, *see* Lay, Lee

Li(t)ster Isabelle 85, 87; John 87, 88, 91-2, 95, 97, 100-1, 104-5, 110, 113, 118, 124, 129, 136, 141, 147, 152, 158, 168; Margaret 85

Loftes Margaret 251, 257

Lokkey, Lok, Lokhey Isabella 87; Joan 160, 167, 172, 176, 178, 182, 193; Ralph 150; Rawlin, Raulins 106, 114, 119, 125, 130, 137, 143, 148, 153, 156, 159-60, 164, 167, 169, 175, 180, 185, 190, 194, 198, 202, 206, 211, 215, 219, 223, 229, 231, 236, 240, 245, 249, 254; Reginald 87, 91, 93, 96-7, 100, 102, 104, 110, 115, 121, 127, 132

Loryfax, Lerefax. Lyryffax Alice 126, 215; John 126, 128, 130, 133, 138, 140, 143, 148, 153, 159, 164, 169, 175, 181, 185, 190, 195, 198, 200, 202, 204, 207-8, 211

Loryng Elizabeth 69; John 69, 71-2, 74, 76-7, 79, 82-3, 88, 92, 97, 102, 106, 113, 118, 124, 129, 136, 142; Robert 35

Lum(e)ley John 218, 225, 231, 233, 237, 242, 246, 251, 255

Lyndesey John 34

Lyryffax, *see* Loryfax

Lytster, *see* Li(t)ster

Maidewell Agnes 131; Thomas 131, 135, 138, 140, 143, 145, 148, 154, 159, 164, 169, 175, 181, 186, 190, 195, 198, 203, 207, 211, 215, 220, 229, 232, 236, 241, 245, 249, 254

Malpas, Malpace David 7, 14, 16, 36, 38, 41-2, 45-6, 49-50, 53-4, 58-9, 62-3, 66-7, 70-1, 74-5, 78, 82-3, 86-7, 91-2, 95-6, 99, 101, 104, 110, 115

Maltby William 171

Manby John 78, 82, 87, 91-2, 96

Marberry Robert 144-5, 149, 154, 159, 164, 170

Marchaunt William 33; *see* Artikel

Margaret prioress, *see* Rowell

Markeby Elizabeth 99; John 99, 100, 102, 104, 106, 110, 114, 116, 119, 125, 130, 137, 143, 148, 153

Market Overton 36, 39, 41, 43, 47, 51, 55, 59, 64, 67, 72, 75, 79, 83

Martyndall Joan 149, 155, 161, 166, 240; Robert 19, 149, 155, 160-1, 165-7, 170, 172-3, 176, 179, 181, 184, 186, 191, 195-6, 199, 201, 203, 205, 207-10, 212-3, 216-7, 220-2, 226, 228, 235, 240

Maydwell, *see* Maidewell

Meerys, Meyres Elizabeth 104; Joan 135; W 147; William 104-6, 111, 113, 116, 118, 121, 124, 127, 129, 133, 135-6, 142, 152, 156, 158, 161, 163, 166, 168, 172

Melles Mathew 177; *see* Milling

Miles William 271

Milling alias Millys Mathew 149, 156, 160-1, 165-6, 170-1, 176

Molle William 91

Moore William 1

Morande, Morraunt Alice/Allis 188; Robert 188, 193, 196-7, 200-1, 204-5, 208-9, 212, 217, 221, 223-4

Mores, *see* Moreys

Moreton, *see* Morton

Moreys Elizabeth 42; John 42, 45, 47, 49, 51-3, 55-6, 58, 60, 62, 64, 66

Morraunt, *see* Morande

Morton Elizabeth 135; John 135, 140, 144-5, 149-50, 154, 156, 159, 161, 166, 170, 172, 177, 183, 187, 192, 197, 201, 205, 209, 213, 218; Thomas 15, 20, 34, 146

Murdok John 35

Muston Agnes 109; John 34; W 153; William 109, 111, 113, 116, 119, 122, 125, 127, 130, 137, 142, 147, 158, 169, 176, 178, 182-3, 187, 189, 191, 196, 199, 203, 208, 212, 216, 220, 224, 230, 232, 237, 241, 246, 250, 255, 260, 264, 269, 273

Mylton Laurence 34

Ne(e)le Agnes 46, 84; John 6, 46, 50-1, 53, 55, 58, 60, 62, 64, 68, 72, 76, 79, 84

Nesame, Nessam, Nysame (Wessam) Alice 225; John 225, 227, 231, 233-4, 238-9, 242-3, 246, 248, 251-2, 255, 257, 259, 261, 263, 265, 268-9, 272-3

Netlam, Nettelham, Nettylham Elizabeth 166; Harre/Henry 171, 178, 182-3, 187-8, 192, 196-7, 200-1, 204-5, 208, 212, 216, 221, 224, 230, 233, 237, 242, 250, 255, 269; Joan 210; John 87, 91, 93, 96-7, 100-1, 104-5, 166, 172, 177-8, 182-3, 187-8, 191-2, 196-7, 199, 201, 204-5, 208-9, 212, 214, 216, 218, 220, 225, 227, 234, 238, 243, 246-7, 252, 256, 258, 260, 263, 267, 271; Katherine 210; Thomas 210, 214, 217-8, 221, 224-5, 227, 230, 233, 237, 242, 246, 250, 255; William 25, 210, 214, 217-8, 221, 224-5, 227, 230, 233-4, 237-8, 242-3, 246-7, 251-2, 255-6, 258, 261, 265, 267, 269, 271, 274

Newstead 9, 204-5, 208-9, 212, 214, 216, 218, 220, 224-5, 230, 233

Newthorpe John 271

Nor(th)burgh 9, 166, 172, 177

Stamford

Alderman (borough) 4, 6-7, 14-15, 18, 36, 61, 107, 123, 128, 135

All Saints in the Market church and parish 8, 10, 12, 262

Broad Street, 23; *see* Claymount

Browne's Hospital, 8, 17

Claymount, Cleymont, 23, 33

coin hoard of St George's 17

Corpus Christi gild 3, 7, 18

councillors (of borough) 36n

friars 8, 10, 262, 266; Augustinian 15, 20, 87, 91, 95-6, 103-4, 116, 123, 129, 133, 136, 141, 266, 270; Black/preachers, 117, 122, 125, 133, 137, 140, 143, 148, 153, 155, 159, 175, 180, 262, 268; Carmelite/White 80, 117, 122, 125, 131, 133, 135, 137-8, 140, 143, 148, 153, 155, 159, 175, 180, 185, 262; Grey 197, 200-1, 204, 206, 210, 217, 247, 251-2, 256

grammar school18

Holy Trinity parish104

Nunnery of St Michael 11; *see* anchoress

Parliament, members of for 7, 14

plays of Stamford 3

recorder of Stamford 134

St George church and parish 8, 13, 17, 33n, 83, 88, 155; churchyard 17

St Leonard's priory 5, 8, 16, 78, 82-4, 87, 91, 117, 122, 125, 128, 130, 133, 171, 178, 182, 187, 251-2, 256

St Martin church and parish 79, 83, 88

St Mary church and parish 3, 8, 107, 121, 123, 128, 136, 141, 146, 152, 158, 163, 174; gild 3; churchwarden 11

St Michael the Greater church and parish 8, 109, 122-3, 127, 129, 136, 222

St Paul's, Poules church and parish 1, 3, 5, 7-12, 23-4, 27, 29, 32-3, 84, 91, 96, 104, 110, 115, 121, 123, 125, 127-8, 130, 132-3, 138-9, 145, 149-50, 156, 166, 168, 177; church porch 4, 29

St Peter church and parish 79, 83, 88, 92, 96, 104

St Thomas Hospital 11

Star Lane 23, 33, 204

steward of the manor 7, 8, 18

taxer (of borough) 36

town councillors 6-7

Stannard Margaret 150, 156, 161, 166; Thomas 150, 156, 160-1, 165-6, 170, 172, 176, 181, 186, 191, 195, 199, 203. 207, 212, 216, 220, 224, 230, 232, 236, 241, 245, 250, 254

Staunford, Stainford John 76, 80; Robert 155, 165, 167, 171-2, 175, 178, 180, 183, 185, 188, 190, 192, 194, 197, 201, 205, 209, 214, 218, 225, 227, 234, 238, 243, 247, 252, 256; Thomas 161

Sted(e) Anabel 42; John 15, 42, 45, 47, 50, 53, 55, 57-8, 60, 62, 64-6, 68-9, 72-3, 76-7, 79, 83, 85, 88-9, 92, 94, 96, 98, 101, 103, 105, 107, 110, 112, 117, 123, 128, 136, 141; Margett 149, 156, 161, 167, 239, 243, 248, 252, 257; Robert 20, 149, 151, 156-7, 160-2, 165, 167, 170, 172-3, 176, 178-9, 181, 183-4, 186, 188, 191, 193, 195, 199, 200, 203-4, 207-8, 212-3, 216-7, 220-1, 223, 225, 229, 232, 235-6, 241, 244-5, 248, 250, 253-4, 256, 260, 264

Stevenson 226; Emma 139, 145, 155, 160, 220, 224; Robert 139, 145, 150, 161, 165, 167, 170, 173, 176, 178, 181, 186, 191, 196, 199, 203, 208, 212, 216

St Katherine's gild

Alderman 3-9, 12, 14, 18-22, 24, 26-7, 30-2, 37, 41, 49, 54, 57, 59, 61-3, 66-71, 74-5, 77, 79, 81, 82-3, 86-7, 90, 95-6, 99, 101, 103, 105, 107, 110, 112, 114-5, 117, 120-1, 126, 132, 141, 144, 146, 151, 156, 162, 173-4, 178-9, 183-4, 188-9, 193, 196-7, 200-1, 204-5, 208-9, 211, 213, 215, 217, 220-2, 225-6, 228, 234-5, 239, 244, 248, 253, 256, 261, 266, 270, 274; oath 30; stand-in 20, 22; *see* Trygge

almsbox 17

bedell (bailiff/beadle) 15, 20, 21, 24, 26-7, 38, 41, 53, 57, 60, 65, 68, 70, 73, 82, 85-6, 90, 94-5, 98-9, 103, 109, 115, 121, 123, 127, 132, 140, 145, 146, 151, 156-7, 160, 162, 167, 173, 178, 183, 184n, 188, 193, 200, 204, 208, 213, 217, 221, 225, 226, 228, 234-5, 239, 244, 248, 253, 256-7, 261-2, 266, 270, 274

bell 31, 193

bellman 5, 32

bread annuity 270

chapel of gild (in St Paul's church) 4-5, 15-6, 20-2, 24, 29, 30-1, 116, 120

chaplain of gild 20-2, 24-6, 37, 60-1, 70, 77, 120, 132, 138, 143, 145, 148, 157, 173, 253, 257, 270

clergy and gild 6, 8, 10

clerk of gild 24, 32, 81, 146, 156, 162, 167, 266

cook 20-1, 24, 85-6, 90, 94-5, 98-9, 103, 109, 115, 121, 123, 126, 132, 156, 200

entertainment, *see* feast

feast of gild, dyner, entertainment (steward of/ providers of/provisioners) 5, 18-24, 27, 31-2, 38, 43-4, 48, 52-3, 57, 59-62, 66, 70, 74, 77, 81-2, 85-6, 90, 92n, 94, 98-9, 103, 109-10, 114-5, 120-1, 123, 126, 131, 138, 146, 151, 156-7, 162, 167, 173, 178, 183-4, 188-9, 193, 200, 204-5, 208, 213, 217, 221, 225-6, 228, 234-5, 239, 244, 248, 253, 256-7, 261, 266, 270, 274

gild/geldhall, gyldehall, Saint Kateryns hall 5, 20-24, 30-1, 139, 149, 155, 160, 162, 165, 168, 171, 173, 177, 179, 182, 184, 187, 189, 193, 200, 204, 209, 248, 258, 262, 266, 270-1

hearse of gild 9n, 100

image of saint Katherine 15, 24, 197, 197n, 200

mazer 11, 33

membership of gild 5-6

oath of officers of gild 30

occupations of gild members 7; *see* occupations

property of gild/cottage/hows/tenement   23, 33, 43, 86, 90, 94-5, 114, 120, 123, 151, 157, 162, 168, 173, 179, 184, 189, 193, 200, 204, 248, 266, 270; *see* gildhall, Whipp

provisioners, *see* feast, steward of

St Katherine cult of 3; image of 15, 24, 197, 200

statutes of the gild 4, 29

steward (of gild, of lands) 4, 11, 15, 18-22, 26-7, 32, 37, 41, 44-5, 48-9, 52-3, 56-7, 59, 61-62, 66, 68, 70, 74, 77, 81, 86, 90, 94-5, 98-9, 103, 109-10, 114-5, 120-1, 123, 126, 132, 138, 140, 144, 146, 151-2, 156-7, 162, 167-8, 173, 178-9, 183-4, 188-9, 193, 200, 204-5, 208-9, 213, 217, 221-2, 225-6, 228, 234-5, 239, 244, 248, 253, 256-7, 261, 266, 270, 275

steward of the feast, *see* feast

stock/store 5, 21-2, 25-7, 32, 37n, 39, 40, 43-4, 48, 52, 56, 61-2, 65, 68-9, 70, 73, 77, 80, 85, 89, 91, 94, 98, 110-1, 117, 122, 205, 213, 217, 221, 226, 228, 235, 240, 253, 256, 268

underbayly 112, 114, 116, 119, 122, 124

women and gild 1, 6, 10

Stodalffe, Stodaff Thomas 218, 225-7, 230, 233-4, 237-8, 242-3, 246-7, 251-2, 255, 257-8, 263, 267, 271

Stodard, Stottard Andrew 14, 19-20, 54-5, 57, 81, 83, 85, 88-9, 93-4, 97-8, 101, 103, 106-7, 110, 113, 118, 121, 123-4, 126, 129, 131-2, 136, 138, 142, 145-6, 151-2, 156-8, 162-3, 168, 173-4, 178, 180-1; Joan 50, 58, 60, 63-4, 66, 68-9, 70, 72-4, 76-7, 79, 140, 147, 162, 167, 178, 185-6, 189, 191, 194-5, 198-9, 202-3, 206, 210, 214, 219, 222, 228, 231, 235, 240, 244, 249, 253, 264, 268, 273; John 135, 139, 143, 145, 149, 260

Stok(k)es, Stox William 218, 225-8, 231, 233, 237, 239, 242, 246, 251, 255, 261, 265

Store(y), Storie, Story Edward 139, 145, 149-50, 154-5, 161, 165, 170, 176, 181, 185, 190, 194, 198, 202, 207, 211, 215, 219, 223, 229, 235-6, 239-40, 245, 249, 254, 260-1, 264-5, 269-70, 273; Elyzabath/Esabell 139, 145, 239, 243, 248, 251-2, 256-7, 259, 263, 268, 272

Storeton William 34, 100n

Straker Robert 35

Stretton (in le Strete) 8, 125, 128, 130, 133, 137, 139, 143, 148, 153, 159, 164, 169, 175

Sutton Hugh 72, 76, 78, 80, 82, 84, 88, 93, 95, 97-9, 102, 106-7, 113, 118, 124; *see* Smyth Hugh; William 16, 36, 38, 41, 43, 45, 47, 49, 51, 55, 60, 64, 67, 72, 75, 79, 83, 88, 93, 98, 102

Sycell, *see* Cecil

Sylton Isabell 69; John 69, 72, 76, 80; *see* Shylton

Taillour alias Thistulthwayte Alice 99; James 99; Taylour James 124, 130, 137, 142, 147, 153, 158, 163, 169, *see* Thistilthwayte; Robert 50, 54-5, 58, 60, 63-4, 66, 68, 71-2, 74, 76, 79, 83, 88, 92, 96, 101, 105, 112, 118

Tales, Talys (a), Taylles, Tayllys , At(t)alles Agnes 112; Robert 112, 116, 119, 122, 124, 128, 130, 133, 137, 142, 147, 153, 158, 163, 169, 174, 180, 185, 190, 194, 198, 202

Tallington, Taylyngton 8-9, 193, 217-8, 221, 224, 226-7, 230, 233

Tamp(e)on, Tampyon Thomas 177, 182-3, 187-8, 192-3, 196-7, 200-1, 204-5, 208-9, 212, 214, 216, 218, 221, 224-5, 227, 230, 233-4, 237-8, 242-3, 246-7, 250, 252, 255-6, 258, 260, 263, 265, 267, 271

Taverners Thomas 209

Taylour, *see* Taillour

Templar, Templer Joan 126, 128, 133, 140; W 153; William 19-20, 26, 34, 37-9, 41-4, 46-8, 50, 52-4, 56-7, 59, 61, 63, 65, 67-8, 70-1, 73, 75, 77, 79, 81-2, 84-6, 89-90, 93-5, 97-9, 102-3, 106, 109, 114-5, 119-21, 123, 125-8, 130, 132-3, 137, 140, 142, 148, 158

Tennell John 178, 183, 199, 203, 207, 212, 216

Thamton, *see* Hampton

Therlbe, *see* Thurlby

Thew Henry 171, 178

Thistilthwayte, Thesselwaytt, Thystlethwayte James 100, 102, 104, 106, 110, 114, 116, 119, 175, 180, 185, 190, 194, 198, 202, 206, 210, 215, 219, 222, 229, 231, 236, 240, 245, 249, 254; *see* Taillour

Thomas, Thomasse, Tomas Katherine 99, 169; John 13, 99-100, 102, 104, 106, 110, 114, 116, 119, 125, 130, 137, 142, 148, 153, 158, 163, 175, 180, 185, 190, 194, 198, 202, 206, 211, 215, 219, 223, 229, 231, 236, 240, 245, 249, 254, 258, 262, 264, 267, 269, 271, 273; Robert 260

Thomson, Tomson John 225, 227, 231, 233-4, 238, 242-3, 246, 248, 251-2, 255, 257, 259, 261, 267, 271; Margett 204; Robert 204, 206, 208, 210, 212, 214, 216, 218, 220, 224-5, 227, 230, 232, 234, 237-8, 241, 243, 246-7, 250, 252, 255-6, 258, 260, 263-5, 267, 269, 271, 273

Thorneff, Thornyffe John 155, 161, 165, 167, 171-2, 175, 177, 180, 185, 190, 194, 198, 202; Katerina 155, 161, 167

Thorneton John 258, 262, 267, 271

Thorney, Throney Henry 36, 39, 40; John 206, 211, 215, 219, 223

Thornhawe 109

Thorp(e) Richard 25, 155, 161, 165, 167, 171-2, 175, 178, 180, 183, 185, 188, 190, 192, 195, 198, 202, 207, 211, 215, 219, 223, 229, 232, 236, 240, 245, 249, 254, 260, 264, 274

Thurlby, Therlbe, Thurby, Thurlbe Elizabeth 69; John 7, 27, 69, 71-2, 74, 76-7, 80-3, 85, 88-9, 92, 94, 97-8, 101, 103, 105, 107, 112-3, 117-8, 122, 124, 129, 131, 136, 142, 146-7, 151-2, 156, 158, 162-3, 167-8, 173-4, 179, 183-4, 189, 196, 201, 205, 209, 213, 217, 222, 226, 228, 235, 240, 253, 256, 259, 264, 268, 272

Thystelthwayte, *see* Thistilthwayte

Tissington, Tussyngton, Tyssyngton Elizabeth 6, 36, 39, 40

Tolthorpe 6, 10, 36n

Tomas, *see* Thomas

Tomson, *see* Thomson

Tong Emma 11

Trolop George 138, 142; Joan 137, 142

Trygge, Trigge Joan 25, 135, 139, 142, 186, 191, 195, 199, 203, 207, 215, 220, 223, 229, 232, 236, 241, 245, 249, 254, 260, 264, 274; N 196, 201, 205, 209; Nicholas 18, 20, 22n, 134-5, 139, 143, 145-6, 148, 150, 154-7, 159, 162, 164, 167, 170, 173-5, 179, 181, 184, 189

Tubman Emma 135, 139, 145; William 135, 139, 145, 149, 150, 154-5, 159, 164, 170, 176, 181, 186, 191

Turnour John 267, 272, 274

Tussington *see* Tissington

Tyard(e) Joan 109, 197, 202, 206, 210, 214, 219, 222, 228, 231, 235, 240, 249, 253, 260, 264, 268, 273; John 109, 111, 113, 116, 118, 122, 124, 127, 129, 136, 142, 147, 152, 158, 163, 168, 174, 179, 184, 189, 194, 197, 244

Tynnell John 166, 169, 172, 177, 186, 188, 191, 195

Tyssyngton, *see* TissIngton

Uffington 9, 177, 182, 187, 193, 196, 200, 204, 208, 212, 216, 221

Vicars, Vicary Nicholas 36, 38, 41, 43, 45, 47, 49, 51, 53, 55, 58-9, 62, 64, 66-7, 70, 72, 74-5, 78-9, 82, 84, 86, 91, 96, 98, 100

Vyllers Anna 262, 268; Geoffrey 262, 266, 268, 270, 272, 274

Wade, Wady Agnes 99, 158, 168, 174, 180, 185, 189, 194, 198, 202, 206, 214, 210; Hugh 99, 100, 102, 104, 106, 110, 113, 116, 118, 124, 129, 136, 142, 147, 152, 163

Walker (Wakker) Alice 219; John 219, 225-7, 231, 233-4, 238, 242, 246, 251, 255, 261, 265, 269, 273

Walles, Wallys John 149, 155, 160-1, 165-6, 170-1, 176, 181, 186, 191, 195, 199, 203, 207, 212, 216, 220, 223, 229; Margaret 149, 155, 161, 166, 232, 236, 241, 245, 250, 254; Thomas 233

Wallett Elizabeth 262; Robert 25, 262, 265, 268, 270, 272, 274

Walter (servant) 144, 149, 154, 159, 164, 176

Ward(e) Elizabeth 251, 257; Joan 160, 167; John 160, 167, 171-2, 175, 178, 180, 185, 190, 195, 198, 202, 207, 211, 215, 219, 221, 223, 225, 228-9, 232, 236, 245, 249, 254, 260, 264, 269, 273

Wardale, Wardell William 239, 242-3, 247-8, 251-2, 256-7, 259, 261, 263, 265, 267, 272

Waren, Wareyn, Waryn lady 123, 128, 135, 141, 146, 152, 163, 174; Agnes 157; Alyzabeth 179; William, 36, 38, 41, 43, 45, 47, 49, 51, 55, 59, 64, 67, 72, 75, 93, 96, 101, 105, 112

Warmington 12

Warmouth, *see* Wermouth

Warner Geoffrey 35

Washingburgh Alice 54; John 54, 58, 63, 67, 71, 76-7, 81-2, 84-5, 88, 93, 97, 102, 106, 114, 119, 131, 138, 149

Wastelyn, Wastlen Elizabeth 13, 210; Harre 13, 210; Richard 13, 210

Wat(t)ers Agnes 166; Thomas 166, 172, 177-8, 182-3, 187-8, 191-2, 196, 199, 204, 208, 212, 216, 220, 224, 230, 233, 237, 241, 246, 250, 255

Wat(t)son Elizabeth 218; Thomas 218, 225-7, 230-1, 233-5, 237-9, 242-4, 246-7, 251-2, 255, 257, 261, 265, 269

watermark in account book 2

Watt(e)s John 8, 112, 116, 119, 122, 124, 128, 130, 133, 137, 142, 147, 153, 158, 169; Margaret 112

Webster Alice 227; John 227, 234, 238-9, 242-3, 247-8, 251-2, 256-7, 259, 261, 263, 265, 268, 270, 273; Thomas 210, 214, 217-8, 221, 224-5, 227, 230, 233, 237, 242, 246, 251, 255, 261, 265, 269, 273

Welle, Welley, Wellye Christopher 247, 251-2, 256

Welles Cecily lady de 5, 9, 144, 149, 154, 159, 164

Welles John 15, 177, 182-3, 187-8, 192-3, 196-7, 200, 204, 208, 212, 216, 221, *see* Crowland; Thomas 177, 182-3, 187-8, 192-3, 196, 200, 204, 208, 212, 216, 221, 224, 230, 237

Wermouth Richard 13, 36, 38, 41, 43, 45-6, 49, 51, 55, 59, 63, 67, 71, 75, 79, 83, 88, 92, 96, 101, 105, 112

Wessam, *see* Nessam

West Joan 92, 124, 129, 136; John 272; William 92-3, 96-7, 100-1, 104-5, 113, 118

Wetton, Whetton, Witton Alice 188, 193, 259, 263, 272; Joan 171; Mathew 171, 178, 182-3, 187-8, 192-3, 196, 199, 204, 208, 210, 212, 216, 221, 224, 230, 233, 237, 241, 246, 250, 255, 259, 260, 263, 265, 268-9, 272-3

Wettylbere, *see* Wittelberry

Wetylhame, *see* Netlam

Wheteley Thomas 36, 39, 40

Whetton, *see* Wetton

Whip(p)(e), Whypp John 23, 50, 54-5, 58, 60, 63-4, 66, 68, 72, 76, 79, 83, 89, 93, 97, 102, 106, 114, 119, 125, 130, 137, 143, 151, 162, 173, 266, 270; Matilda 50

White Margaret 12, 144-5, 170; *see* anchoress

Wiks, *see* Wykes

Williams, Willyams, Wylliams Agnes 144; Thomas 25, 144, 149-50, 154, 156, 159, 161, 164, 166, 170, 176, 181, 186, 191, 195, 199, 203, 207, 211, 215, 220, 223, 229, 232, 236, 241, 245, 250, 254, 260, 264, 274

Wittelbery Anna 166, 172, 177-8, 182-3, 187-8, 192

Witton, *see* Wetton

Wo(o)de Joan 109; Randalff (a) 109, 113, 116, 118, 121, 127, 133

Worcester, archdeacon of, *see* Burton Richard

Wordington, Worthyngton Thomas 166-7, 172, 176, 178, 182, 187, 191, 196, 199, 203, 208, 212, 216, 220, 224, 230, 237, 241, 246, 250, 255

Wright, Wryght Joan 193; Margaret 150, 156, 161, 166; Rauffe 193; Richard 177, 182-3, 187-8, 190, 195, 198, 203, 207, 211, 215, 217, 220-1, 223, 225-6, 229, 232, 236, 241, 245, 249, 254; William 150, 156, 160-1, 165-6, 170, 172, 176-7, 181, 183, 186-7, 191-2, 196-7, 199, 201, 203, 205, 207, 209, 212-3, 216, 218, 220, 224, 227, 230, 232, 237, 241, 245, 250

Lightning Source UK Ltd.
Milton Keynes UK
UKOW031630091111

181764UK00001B/7/P